University of Reading European and International Studies

Published in association with the Graduate School of European and International Studies, University of Reading

General Editor: **Richard Bellamy**

This series includes books which discuss some of the major contemporary European and international issues from a comparative perspective. National experiences with a relevance for broader European and international issues are also covered by this series. The collection is interdisciplinary in nature with the aim of bringing together studies that emphasise the role of political, economic, historical and cultural factors in shaping the course of international cooperation and international conflicts, particularly from the point of view of Europe and its relations with the rest of the world. The influence of the processes of European integration (economic, political, cultural) on both Europe and the rest of the world, as well as the impact on Europe of global integration processes and non-European integration schemes, are some of the themes that run through the volumes included in the series.

Titles include:

Christoph Bluth
GERMANY AND THE FUTURE OF EUROPEAN SECURITY

K. R. Dark with A. L. Harris
THE NEW WORLD AND THE NEW WORLD ORDER

Barry Holden (*editor*)
THE ETHICAL DIMENSIONS OF GLOBAL CHANGE

Yelena Kalyuzhnova
THE KAZAKSTANI ECONOMY

Athena Leoussi
NATIONALISM AND CLASSICISM

Robert D. Pearce
THE INTERNATIONALIZATION OF RESEARCH AND DEVELOPMENT BY MULTINATIONAL ENTERPRISES

Stelios Stavridis, Theodore Couloumbis, Thanos Veremis and Neville Waites (*editors*)
THE FOREIGN POLICIES OF THE EUROPEAN UNION'S MEDITERRANEAN STATES AND APPLICANT COUNTRIES IN THE 1990s

University of Reading European and International Studies
Series Standing Order ISBN 0–333–71510–1
(*outside North America only*)

You can receive future titles in this series as they are published by placing a standing order. Please contact your bookseller or, in case of difficulty, write to us at the address below with your name and address, the title of the series and the ISBN quoted above.

Customer Services Department, Macmillan Distribution Ltd, Houndmills, Basingstoke, Hampshire RG21 6XS, England

Germany and the Future of European Security

Christoph Bluth
Professor of International Studies
University of Leeds

in association with
GRADUATE SCHOOL OF EUROPEAN AND
INTERNATIONAL STUDIES
UNIVERSITY OF READING

First published in Great Britain 2000 by
MACMILLAN PRESS LTD
Houndmills, Basingstoke, Hampshire RG21 6XS and London
Companies and representatives throughout the world

A catalogue record for this book is available from the British Library.

ISBN 0–333–65070–0

First published in the United States of America 2000 by
ST. MARTIN'S PRESS, LLC,
Scholarly and Reference Division,
175 Fifth Avenue, New York, N.Y. 10010

ISBN 0–312–23558–5

Library of Congress Cataloging-in-Publication Data
Bluth, Christoph.
    Germany and the future of European security / Christoph Bluth ; in association
    with Graduate School of European and International Studies, University of
    Reading.
        p.   cm.
    Includes bibliographical references and index.
    ISBN 0–312–23558–5
    1. Germany—Foreign relations—Europe, Western. 2. Europe, Western–
    –Foreign relations—Germany. 3. Europe, Western—Defenses. 4. Germany–
    –Defenses. 5. National security—Germany. 6. Security, International. I.
    University of Reading. Graduate School of European and International
    Studies. II. Title.

    D1065. G3 B58 2000
    327.4304—dc21

                                                        00–033330

This book is printed on paper suitable for recycling and made from fully managed and sustained
forest sources.

10   9   8   7   6   5   4   3   2   1
09   08   07   06   05   04   03   02   01   00

Printed and bound in Great Britain by
Antony Rowe Ltd, Chippenham, Wiltshire

For Alison

Contents

Acknowledgements

This book is the result of a two-year research programme funded by the Leverhulme Trust. I wish to thank the Trust for its generous support and the University of Reading for hosting the programme. Barbara L. Wells was Research Associate on the programme and without her tireless efforts, which included putting together a unique collection of documentation on German foreign and security policy this book could not have been written. Her extensive expertise on the Adenauer era was invaluable for the preparation of the historical section.

Michael Clarke, Director of the Centre for Defence Studies, University of London and Willie Paterson, Director of the Institute for German Studies at the University of Birmingham, provided crucial support when the project was initiated. I am grateful for their generous support and advice.

Many other people generously shared their expertise with me while I was engaged in the research. Among them are Timothy Garten Ash, Simon Duke, Heather Grabbe, Beatrice Heuser, Catherine Kelleher, Juliet Lodge, David Marsh, Gale Mattox, Hanns Maull, Ernest May, John Mearsheimer, Franz-Josef Meiers, Steven Miller, Karl Kaiser, Ingo Peters, Robert Rinne, John Roper, Reinhardt Rummel, Alex Sauder, Peter Schmidt, Siegmar Schmidt, Susanne Schmidt, Hans-Henning Schröder, Jane Sharp, James Sperling, Heinrich Vogel, Angelika Volle, Celeste Wallander and Michael Williams.

I am grateful to my colleagues at the University of Reading who provided an intellectually stimulating environment for the research, and Margaret Guntrip for secretarial assistance.

My thanks also to Alison Williams for her continuing love and support.

List of Abbreviations

CAP	Common Agricultural Policy
CIS	Commonwealth of Independent States
CDP	Common Defence Policy
CDU	Christlich Demokratische Union
CEE	Central and Eastern Europe
CEEC	Central and East European Countries
CFSP	Common Foreign and Security Policy
CJTF	Combined Joint Task Force
CFE	Conventional Forces in Europe
CPC	Conflict Prevention Centre
CPSU	Communist Party of the Soviet Union
CSCE	Conference on Security and Cooperation in Europe
CSO	Committee of Senior Officials
CSU	Christlich-Soziale Union
EC	European Community
ECB	European Central Bank
EMU	Economic and Monetary Union
EPC	European Political Cooperation
FDP	Freidemokratische Partei
FRG	Federal Republic of Germany
GDP	Gross Domestic Product
GDR	German Democratic Republic
IFOR	Implementation Force
IR	International Relations
JNA	Yugoslav National Army
FSU	Former Soviet Union
ICBM	Intercontinental Ballistic Missile
INF	Intermediate Nuclear Forces
LRTNF	Long Range Theatre Nuclear Forces
KFOR	Kosovo Force
NATO	North Atlantic Treaty Organization
NVA	Nationale Volksarmee
ODIHR	Office for Democratic Institutions and Human Rights
OSCE	Organization for Security and Cooperation in Europe
PDS	Partei des demokratischen Sozialismus
PfP	Partnership for Peace

PTBT	Partial Test Ban Treaty
SEA	Single European Act
SFOR	Stabilization Force
SACEUR	Supreme Allied Commander Europe
SALT	Strategic Arms Limitation Treaty
SED	Sozialistische Einheitspartei Deutschlands
SNF	Short Range Nuclear Forces
SPD	Sozialdemoktratische Partei Deutschlands
TEU	Treaty on European Union
UN	United Nations
UNITAF	United Taskforce
UNPROFOR	United Nations Protection Force
US	United States
WEU	Western European Union
WTO	Warsaw Treaty Organization

1
Germany in the International System

No Western European country was more deeply affected by the end of the East–West confrontation in Europe than the Federal Republic of Germany (FRG). The changes in the European security landscape, the dissolution of the Warsaw Pact (WTO), German unification and the withdrawal of Soviet forces from Eastern Europe constituted a substantial shift in the balance of power in Europe, with the united Germany the main beneficiary. Germany has essentially regained those elements of its sovereignty which were lost in the Second World War. Unification – a principal objective of West German declaratory foreign policy for the last forty years – has been achieved. Germany has become less dependent on the Western Alliance for its security, and because of its geographic location and its economic potential Germany has become a major West and East European power.

The collapse of Soviet power in Europe has been widely understood as signifying a fundamental shift from military power to economic strength as the key factor defining the role of states in the international system, at least as far as Europe is concerned. Germany has therefore become the most important actor in Europe, because of its geographic location and its economic performance. While some fears about the growth of German power and influence have been expressed, there has also been the expectation that Germany should now assume greater responsibilities concomitant with its new position. Germany has become the central focus of integration in Western Europe and is expected to be one of the principal architects of a new security order.

If the changing international environment had profound implications for Germany itself, it raised once again the German question for its neighbours. After the trauma of the Second World War, the containment of Germany had been a high priority not only for the Soviet Union, but also for the Western powers. While West Germany achieved its rehabilitation into international society and became a loyal member of the Western Alliance, the divided Germany remained the central axis of the cold war in Europe. While European status quo created by the cold war remained a continuing source of international tension, at the same time it provided stability that was comforting and that the major Western states were not so keen to give up. The dissolution of the Warsaw Pact and the Soviet Union and the disappearance of the massive military threat in Central Europe resulted in considerable uncertainty about the shape of the newly emerging security environment, the relative weight of the regional powers and the requirements for national security in the future. The role and foreign policy of a future Germany was one element of this uncertainty. Would the firm commitment to the Western Alliance and European integration continue after unification, or would there be a renationalization of Germany foreign and security policy? Would Germany become more assertive, given its weight as a regional power, to the detriment of alliance commitments and the interests of other states?

The purpose of this study is to provide an analysis of the development of German foreign and security policy since unification. It will consider the development of Germany's understanding of the European security environment, Germany's national interests, its role in Europe and the world, and the policy instruments at its disposal. This provides a context for testing various views about the future of European security more generally.

Power and politics: theoretical conceptions about German foreign and security policy

After the agreements for German unification had been concluded and the East–West conflict faded into history a remarkable consensus developed among scholars and politicians that a seismic shift in power had occurred, of which the united Germany was one of the principal beneficiaries. This gave rise to the expectation that, with the shackles of the postwar settlements having been removed, Germany would now develop a foreign and security policy in keeping with its position in the international system. It would overcome its *Machtvergessenheit*, in the words of Hans-Peter Schwarz, and assert its national interests directly. As the largest economy in Europe, with substantial military forces, and with more influence in Central and Eastern Europe than other European states by virtue of its geography and its economic support for the region, it would assume a leadership role in Europe.

Such views arise from thinking that has been knowingly or unknowingly informed by neorealism. Realism and neorealism have dominated the analysis of international relations, especially in the United States. The basic principles of neorealism can be stated as follows: the international system is fundamentally characterized by anarchy. States are the principal actors and unit of analysis. In the competition for power, no state can guarantee its own survival and security. A state's international behaviour is shaped by its power relative to other states. In view of the absence of an international authority, states have to defend their interests in competition with other states. International co-operation is rare, because states will as a rule avoid a strategy that will permit another state to achieve gains at their cost, even if a co-operative strategy would mean greater gains for both.[1] In terms of security, this leads to what is known as the 'security dilemma'. The security dilemma arises from the behaviour of states who seek to maximize their security by the procurement of arms and the development of military technology. Their success in this endeavour, however, creates a perceived threat to other states, thereby leading to competitive arms races. Military alliances are formed to gain time, so that states can pursue their own interests and balance the power position of competing or threatening states. The problem of international security is best resolved by the formation of stable balances of power, whereas the search for absolute security by a state is a source of instability and threat in the international system.

One particular form of realist thinking is called 'hegemonic stability theory', based on the notion that a stable international order comes into existence by the action of a strong state who imposes it because it sees it to be in its interest. The bipolar system of the cold war is the obvious example, where the United States and the Soviet Union created regimes and structures which consolidated their position and from which the allies benefited in terms of security. If the hegemon became weak and unable to maintain its influence over its allies, interstate conflict would be more likely. This is the reason why neorealists like John Mearsheimer have predicted conflicts in Central and Eastern Europe and proposed the creation of new balances of power to stabilize the European system of states after the collapse of Soviet power.

There is a perception that the degree of international co-operation that actually exists runs counter to the predictions of neorealism and that international institutions result in co-operation despite the anarchy of the international system. This is explained on the basis that membership of international institutions alter the perceptions that states have of their interests, and that states consider it to be advantageous to remain in the institutions because of the perceived disadvantages of exclusion. To use an analogy from game theory, in the so-called prisoner's dilemma the prisoner will choose to forego the gains of co-operation due to lack of information about the intention of the other side. Institutions enable a close exchange of information and therefore encourage a different outcome, maximizing co-operation. This view is usually described as *institutionalism*.

Institutions impose constraints on the foreign policies of states. There are mainly three kinds of constraints – conventions, such as in international law, regimes which prescribe norms and principles in particular areas and international organizations.

The main problem with both neorealist and institutionalist approaches was that they failed to explain the phenomenon of advancement of international norms and international law as a major basis for international co-operation that seemed to be effective in mitigating the effects of international anarchy. A more recent approach, called *constructivism*, is based on the notion that while the international system is inherently anarchic, states can transcend the anarchy by advancing international norms and common interests. It is not inevitable that states will choose to play zero-sum games. Constructivism has three basic elements: first is the view that shared norms and values guide state behaviour. As a consequence the international system is, even in the absence of an overarching authority, no longer purely anarchic. Second, the structure of conventions, norms and values affect the self-perception of the actors (states) in the international system. There is a process of socialization which results in the construction of a shared identity among states. Third, structures and agents in the international system determine each other and although structures determine the identity of actors, the actors can also change structures. In contrast to neorealism, the order in the international system derives not merely from the hierarchy of power, but also from shared norms and international law.[2]

All of the theoretical approaches outlined so far are based on the assumption that states are rational actors. This means that their international behaviour is designed to achieve certain specific objectives and, therefore, foreign policy is aimed at producing certain outcomes. There are other approaches that deny the rational actor assumption. The bureaucratic politics model developed by Graham Allison is based on the view that policies are shaped by the structure of the bureaucracy and the domestic political objectives of political actors. The external environment then acts as a constraint used to legitimate policies devised for other reasons. The important contribution of the bureaucratic politics model is that it highlights the interaction between domestic and foreign policy which is obscured or denied by other approaches.

The study of the foreign and security policy of the Federal Republic of Germany is interesting from the point of view of the theoretical debates because it was based on explicit denial of the assumptions neorealism and the embrace of an institutionalist approach although from a contemporary of perspective it could be interpreted as a form of constructivism. In order to understand how the intellectual and normative framework of contemporary German security policy has come about, it is necessary to provide a brief historical resumé of the foreign and security policy of the Bonn republic.

West German security policy

It was self-evident that the structure of global power would be permanently changed as a result of the Second World War; what was not so clear was the nature of this change. The central determinative factors of the balance of power in the postwar world, namely the strategic role of nuclear weapons and the resultant bipolarity of world power relations centring around the two superpowers and the new alignment of world economic relations, did not emerge for some time after the war.[3] The containment of Germany was a principal element of the policies of the Allies after the war, but it was the emerging East–West confrontation – the cold war – which meant that Germany would be divided.

For West Germany, the principal goal of its foreign policy, once it had regained some degree of national sovereignty, was its rehabilitation as a member of international society in general and the step-by-step removal of external constraints imposed by the Western powers and the Soviet Union.[4] In view of the legacy of the Second

World War, this was only acceptable if West Germany were to be firmly integrated within a Western Alliance which would serve both to contain West Germany and harness its strength to the benefit of the common security of the West. The foreign policy objectives for West Germany which derived from this situation can be summarized as follows:

1 the preservation of West German security against the Soviet threat.
2 acceptance of the Federal Republic as an equal member of the Alliance with the optimal freedom of action in foreign policy.
3 the reunification of Germany.[5]

There was an integral relationship between all three objectives. The perception of the Soviet threat prevalent in the Federal Government led by Chancellor Konrad Adenauer was based on a view of the Soviet Union as being poised on the verge of expansion towards the West. It was therefore of overriding importance to check Soviet aggression. This image of outwardly directed expansionism was complemented by one of inner weakness and domestic social and economic problems which, in the long term, the Soviet Union would be unable to solve. *Politik der Stärke* ('policy on the basis of strength') implied the resistance of all Soviet attempts at political and military expansionism until the situation became untenable for the Soviet Union and it would be prepared to reach an accommodation with the West.[6]

The view of Soviet foreign policy objectives prevalent in the Adenauer administration was evidently strongly influenced by the experiences of the early postwar years, in particular Soviet behaviour in Eastern Europe and the events giving rise to the division of Germany. The notion that the Soviet Union was planning to expand its sphere of influence even beyond that which it had established for itself in the aftermath of the Yalta Agreement, possibly by the use of military force, received much credence in the West, including in the Federal Republic of Germany, as a consequence of the Korean War in 1950. Thus Adenauer expressed his conviction that Stalin had plans, along similar lines as the Korean War, for West Germany.[7] The fact that both South Korea and West Germany were on the frontline of the East–West conflict was seen to be of particular significance. West Germany was in a dangerously exposed geographic position.

In the view of the Adenauer administration, the Soviet Union was an expansionist, imperialist power in pursuit of world domination. The threat which derived from this comprised two elements:

the military threat arising from the enormous military potential of the Soviet armed forces, and the ideological threat of propaganda and subversion. In order to be in a position to pursue a decisive conflict with the United States, it was necessary for the Soviet Union to bring Western Europe under its domination and thereby gain a solid economic and military basis. West Germany occupied a key position for the Soviet Union: if West Germany could be brought into the Soviet sphere of influence, its economic resources – provided they were not destroyed in a major war – and human potential would be added to that already under Soviet domination and the remaining West European states would find it hard to resist the Soviet advance.[8]

If the requirements of West German security constituted motivation for closer integration within the Alliance, the need to regain an equal status in the Western community of states also constituted an important force in West German foreign policy which pointed in the same direction.

There was an inner tension between this approach to security policy and the goal of German reunification. It was clear that the path to reunification inevitably had to lead through Moscow. There were several Soviet approaches which suggested that reunification might be possible if Germany were to accept restrictions on her foreign policy. This implied withdrawal from the Western Alliance and complete neutrality. Rejecting these approaches out of hand, Adenauer based his views on a different concept of how reunification was to be achieved. This was the concept of 'reunification from a position of strength' – *Politik der Stärke*.[9]

It was a basic premise of *Politik der Stärke* that *Westintegration* was not an obstacle to the achievement of German reunification, but rather a prerequisite. Adenauer recognized that reunification required not only the consent of the Soviet Union, but also that of the Western Allied powers. German unification was only a realistic option if the Soviet Union came to recognize that its expansionist objectives could not be realized, even in the long term, and would redirect its energies to the resolution of the its own internal problems. This would allow the creation of a framework of global detente in which a stable *modus vivendi*, including the unification of Germany, could be negotiated. He understood that German unification would not be possible with the establishment of a new order for the whole of Eastern Europe. Only the combined strength of the Western Alliance would be capable of achieving this objective.

It has to be recognized that in this context the concept of detente as it came to be pursued by other Western powers, most notably the United Kingdom but also the United States, came to be perceived to be in conflict with West German foreign policy objectives. The German concept of *Entspannung* (relaxation of tension) assumes that there are sources of *Spannung* (tension), which in Adenauer's view existed in the Soviet Union which posed both a military and ideological/political threat to Western Europe and wrongfully controlled part of German territory. This engendered very deep scepticism with regard to the feasibility of any meaningful detente with the Soviet Union. Furthermore, detente within the existing framework of the European security environment and Soviet foreign policy was considered undesirable, insofar as it was based on an acceptance of the status quo while one of the central objectives of West German foreign policy, namely German reunification, constituted a fundamental challenge to the status quo. Arms control was problematic for other reasons. A principal feature of Adenauer's *Deutschlandpolitik* was the Hallstein Doctrine, according to which the Federal Republic assumed the right of sole representation of all Germans. Its implementation consisted principally in a policy designed to diplomatically isolate the German Democratic Republic. The Soviet Union, for whom the ratification of the existing status quo in Europe was a central objective in arms control negotiations, sought to involve the GDR at the same level as the Western Allies involved the FRG. The implementation of any arms control agreement, such as the various disengagement schemes, or the nuclear test ban, posed a threat to this fundamental principle of West German foreign policy. Western efforts at disarmament and detente in Adenauer's view posed a great risk of damaging West German interests.[10]

At the same time there was deep concern about the security implications of various arms control measures which were being discussed with the Soviet Union. Schemes for nuclear-free zones (such as the Rapacki plan), for example, were interpreted as having been designed for the introduction of nuclear weapons into the Bundeswehr. West German Ministry of Defence documents distinguish between 'allgemeine kontrollierte Abrüstung' (general controlled disarmament) which would substantially change the security environment and 'regionale Abrüstung' (regional disarmament), which would primarily affect the Federal Republic and was therefore perceived as fundamentally inimical to West German security interests.[11] However, a rigid adherence to Adenauer's approach of supporting only general detente and disarmament and taking a very negative stance toward the various British and American proposals, was perceived by many in the Federal Republic as unrealistic and detrimental to the goal of reunification. This was precisely the thrust of the rejection of Adenauer's security policy on the part of the SPD opposition which saw a collective security system in Europe in which the security interests of the Soviet Union would be duly recognized as the way forward.[12]

Only in such a context would the Soviet Union agree to German unification. Furthermore the reliance on the Allies for its security meant that the Federal Republic could not sustain a completely negative position without detrimental consequences in the long run. The result was that by 1957/58 some flexibility was induced into the position of the Adenauer administration and the Chancellor was willing to engage more positively in the discussions about partial measures of disarmament in Central Europe. This was accompanied by greater stress on the *Junktim* (linkage) between disarmament, security and reunification, which was affirmed in the Berlin Declaration of 27 July 1957 by France, Great Britain, the United States and the FRG.

The security policy of the Federal government led by Adenauer was very controversial. The reliance on military power to deter the Soviet Union, while accepted within an Alliance context generated an emphasis on German rearmament which was perceived as critical by the Alliance partners to render the defence of Central Europe feasible and for Adenauer constituted an important element of Germany's regaining of national sovereignty. In the German population as a whole anti-military sentiment however was still strong and while rearmament was accepted in principle it met with a degree of reluctance which rendered the emphasis on, and the scale of rearmament planned by the Adenauer administration, controversial.

The main opposition party, the SPD, advanced a quite different solution to the German security dilemma. It recognized the existence of a growing military threat from the Soviet Union which required an effective German contribution to the defence of Europe.[13] Nevertheless, the principal task of a West German security policy must be to reduce the tension in the world and preserve the peace. The path for the preservation of peace and German reunification as outlined by the SPD was not through the Western Alliance, but rather through a European system of collective security. The SPD leadership took great care to distinguish the rejection of

Westintegration as pursued by Adenauer from 'neutralism'. It was clearly acknowledged that Germany had chosen a political system such as only existed in the West. At the same time, Germany should not represent an instrument of American policy in the cold war. Germany should not appear to pose a threat to the Soviet Union.

The 'middle path' between East and West as envisaged in various forms by leading SPD representatives would result in a collective security system in Europe, with a united Germany at the centre which would not be neutral, but 'bündnislos' – it would not count in the balance of forces for either side. Such a solution would address the problem of reunification and security simultaneously. The collective security system would act as the guarantor for the security of a united Germany, while the whole process would involve disarmament measures and political confidence building which would substantially reduce the threat to German security.[14] This way of thinking made itself felt in three principal ways in the arena of practical politics: (1) criticism of *Westintegration* and rearmament; (2) support for a more active policy towards reunification; and (3) support for diplomatic moves towards detente and disarmament.

The vision of the SPD was by no means shared by the majority of the West German electorate. It was too close to 'neutralism' to find sufficient support. While in the end the Adenauer line predominated in West German foreign policy until 1963, nevertheless elements of the policy of the opposition found an echo in the population and restrained Adenauer's freedom of action. Thus the issue of reunification was kept high on the agenda by the opposition and Adenauer remained under pressure to adopt a more flexible attitude to disarmament proposals.

The impasse of Deutschlandpolitik *under Adenauer*

The fundamental dilemma of the security policy advocated by the SPD remained in its incompatibility with the geopolitical realities that were taking shape in the second half of the 1950s. The United States and the Soviet Union had reached a strategic compromise consisting an uneasy recognition of each others spheres of influence. The development of strategic nuclear arsenals meant that a direct military conflict between the superpowers had to be avoided at all costs. In this strategic context measures of disarmament and arms control could have no other function than to regulate the military competition on the basis of the existing territorial status quo. If the leading figures of the SPD advocated disarmament measures and detente as instruments of promoting German reunification, they were seriously out of tune with the perceptions which guided Soviet, American and British policies.

The Berlin crisis which was launched by Khrushchev in November 1958 and resulted in the erection of the Berlin Wall in August 1961 became the ultimate test of all *Deutschlandpolitik*. Both Adenauer's *Politik der Stärke* and the SPD version of a policy of reunification through detente fell victim to the political realities which became manifest in this strategic confrontation.[15]

Politik der Stärke had always been based on unrealistic assumptions of Western commitments to a resolution of the German question. The evident unwillingness of the Kennedy administration to take substantial risks in the defence of Western rights with regard to the whole of Berlin, and what amounted to more or less Western acquiescence in the building of the wall as a measure which would stabilize the SED regime in the GDR and thereby the postwar order in Europe, finally demonstrated the untenability of Bonn's *Deutschlandpolitik*. Nevertheless, the German question touched so deeply basic political convictions associated with the very identity of the Federal Republic, that it took until the end of the decade for the required shifts in West German foreign policy to find a sufficiently broad base of political support. The process of adaptation to political reality within the CDU/CSU coalition has to be understood in the context of two distinct approaches that had developed towards German foreign policy and which became more significant in the first half of the 1960s: on the one hand there were the 'Atlanticists', led by Ludwig Erhard (who succeeded Adenauer as chancellor), Gerhard Schröder (the foreign minister in Adenauer's government after the 1961 elections and under Erhard) and the Kai-Uwe von Hassel (who succeeded Strauß as defence minister after the Spiegel affair in 1962); on the other those described as 'Gaullists' (particularly the leading politicians of the CSU, Strauß and Guttenberg, but also Adenauer himself). The latter favoured a more European-based approach and closer Franco-German co-operation (although they were not 'Gaullists' in the true sense of the word).[16]

Adenauer did not see relations with France as a substitute for transatlantic relations, nor did he believe that France could provide an adequate security guarantee for the Federal Republic. But a close relationship with France was a central political concern for Adenauer. De Gaulle's vision for the future of Europe was fundamentally different from that pursued by the United States or other members of the

Western Alliance. The essence of it was that de Gaulle wanted to restrain the process of integration on a European and transatlantic level and return to an emphasis on national sovereignty. He did not propose the end of the Atlantic Alliance, but suggested changes in its structure and military organization which would have transformed it into a looser association along the lines of more traditional alliances. He was particularly concerned about American dominance in the Alliance, as manifested by the fact that the supreme command of NATO forces in Europe was in American hands and that the American president retained a veto over the use of all American nuclear weapons stationed in Europe. One attempt to restore a special leadership position for France was de Gaulle's proposal in 1958 for a triumvirate of the nuclear powers in the Alliance (the United States, France and the United Kingdom) to coordinate foreign and defence polices. He also advocated the formation of a European group in the Alliance with the implication that France should lead it. Adenauer's reaction to de Gaulle's vision was marked by an ambivalence that had important consequences for British–German and German–American relations. On the one hand he was deeply convinced that the only path that could satisfy the requirements of West German security was that of closer integration in the Atlantic Alliance. From that point of view, he was deeply opposed to de Gaulle's vision and considered it to be downright dangerous. If forced to choose between the United States and France, there was no question in Adenauer's mind that the Federal Republic would have to choose to maintain its relationship with the United States. In other areas, however, Adenauer was more open to compromise. As far as closer integration within the EEC was concerned, Adenauer was willing, for domestic political reasons, to support de Gaulle in his endeavours to slow down the process. The relationship with France was important insofar as it represented at least the option of an alternative framework for West German security policy which would prevent German isolation if the United States moved towards disengagement from Europe and could serve, at least in Adenauer's view, as a means of promoting West German security interests in the face of increasing Soviet–American convergence on the German question.

The conduct of the Adenauer administration in the final phases of the Berlin crisis, its perceived weakness and the implications for its *Deutschlandpolitik* contributed to its poor showing in the 1961 federal elections. Adenauer had to enter a coalition with the FDP and the Atlanticist wing of his party gained influence. In the final years of Adenauer's chancellorship this manifested itself primarily in the determination by Foreign Minister Schröder to eschew any form of criticism of American initiatives at promoting detente and disarmament.[17] In the meantime Adenauer engaged in an endeavour to open up a discrete dialogue with Moscow to explore the options for any advances in the German issue. The resolute refusal by the Soviet leadership to compromise meant that this approach was condemned to failure. Western unwillingness to exert economic pressure on the Soviet Union for this purpose and the conclusion of the Partial Test Ban agreement (PTBT) marked the end of *Politik der Stärke*. The Federal Government had had deep reservations about the implications of the PTBT, which was precisely the kind of limited arms control measure which Adenauer had generally opposed. In particular, the Bonn government was concerned about the treaty clause which allowed 'all states' to become signatories, which implied that East Germany might acquire some sort of diplomatic recognition simply by virtue of signing the PTBT. Eventually the United States and Britain managed to reassure the Federal Government and in August 1963 the West German cabinet decided unanimously that the FRG should become a signatory to the treaty.[18]

The Atlanticist foreign policy pursued by Gerhard Schröder, first within the constraints of a government led by Adenauer, then after October 1963, with the support of Chancellor Erhard, did not yet signal a complete departure from the policy of nonrecognition of the GDR and the Hallstein doctrine. But Schröder was convinced that an opening to Eastern Europe, that is closer relations with other Eastern European countries was essential to a more dynamic foreign policy that could move Germany's *Ostpolitik* out of its impasse. In this he faced severe opposition from the conservative and Gaullist elements, particularly von Brentano, Krone and Strauß. He was supported by the FDP (led by Erich Mende) and to some extent by the opposition party (the SPD). It turned out however, that Schröder was not prepared to go far enough. A policy predicated on loosening up Eastern Europe, while at the same time seeking to ostracize the GDR and opposing any extension of Soviet–American relations, proved to be rather fruitless and increased West Germany's isolation, particularly since it also ran counter to de Gaulle's policy of loosening transatlantic ties and seeking improved relations with Eastern Europe and the Soviet Union in a framework which deliberately excluded the United States. The 'peace note' of 25 March

1966 which suggested various arms control measures with regard to nuclear weapons in Europe and offered the exchange of a formal declaration of the renunciation of force suffered from the fundamental limitations of Schröder's *Ostpolitik* and generated only a very mute response from Eastern Europe.[19] The general impasse of German foreign policy was a contributing factor to the failure of the Erhard government and the creation of the Grand Coalition with the SPD in 1966.

The origin of Ostpolitik

The final attempt to promote the concepts of *Entspannung* based on the security political framework of the SPD in the 1950s was the *Deutschlandplan* put forward in March 1959 which was based on the principle of a linkage between collective security in Europe and German reunification. German political and economic union was to be reestablished by means of a series of steps of detente and arms control in Central Europe along the lines of the Rapacki plan.[20] The plan was published immediately after a visit by Erler and Schmid to Moscow, the result of which was less than encouraging for the central notions contained in it. In the shadow of Khrushchev's Berlin ultimatum and the emerging realities of a world order defined by superpower bipolarity, the *Deutschlandplan* appeared to most of the leading members of the SPD, including, in particular, Willy Brandt, the governing mayor of Berlin, too far removed from reality to represent a basis for a future SPD *Deutschlandpolitik*. Within the SPD, a fundamental shift was taking place designed to make the party fit to take over the reigns of power. This involved a much greater emphasis on the domestic political programme and a move towards a foreign policy based on interparty consensus. Of particular note was the clear affirmation of West German membership of the Western Alliance at the party conference at Hanover in November 1960, where Brandt was chosen as the SPD candidate for the chancellorship. There were also indications that the rigid rejection of nuclear weapons was being modified to accommodate the existing arrangements for the defence of West Germany.

Although the issue of direct contacts with the East German regime and the recognition of the existence of two German states had been raised during the debate about the new foreign policy profile of the SPD, most of the party was not yet ready for such a radical shift. It was the traumatic experience of the erection of the Berlin wall which finally convinced Brandt that the Soviet Union was determined not to release East Germany from its sphere of influence and that the Western powers could not be counted on to support an active *Deutschlandpolitik*.[21] A foreign policy based on the Hallstein doctrine and thus the diplomatic isolation of the GDR was no longer sustainable. It took a number of years for this perception to become politically acceptable and it was operationalized in various stages. Initially Brandt's efforts were directed at mitigating the effects of the severed links between East and West, culminating in the 'passage agreement' in 1963. It was Brandt's aide Egon Bahr who spelt out the elements of the new direction in *Deutschlandpolitik* most explicitly in the course of his famous speech at Tutzing in July 1963.[22] He explained that the division of Germany, as symbolized by the Berlin wall, could not be overcome by a policy of confrontation, but only by a relaxation of tension between the two Germanies, a long 'process of many steps and stations' which he characterized as 'Wandel durch Annäherung' ('change through rapprochement'). By not endeavouring to change the status quo for the time being, the status quo could ultimately be overcome. Willy Brandt explained it in the following terms:

> There is a solution to the German question only with the Soviet Union, not in opposition to it. We cannot give up our rights, but we must recognise that a new relationship between East and West is imperative, and with it a new relationship between Germany and the Soviet Union.[23]

The statements by Bahr and Brandt provoked general political debate, encouraged among others by the writings of Peter Bender who explicitly advocated the recognition of the GDR as part of an 'offensive detente' to overcome the division of Europe.[24] The federal elections of 1966 resulted in a Grand Coalition between the CDU/CSU and the SPD with Willy Brandt as Foreign Minister and Kurt Georg Kiesinger as Chancellor. Although the *Ostpolitik* of the Grand Coalition did not go as far as an explicit renunciation of the claim to sole representation of the German people, it declared an interest in improved East–West relations (including arms control agreements) even without progress on the German question. The principal vehicle of *Ostpolitik* was a dialogue with the Soviet Union about an agreement on the renunciation of force. Relations with Eastern European countries continued to be pursued, while the Federal Government signalled its fundamental preparedness to accept the East German government de facto and enter into a European agreement on the renunciation of force to which both German states would be signatories. The exchange of letters between Chancellor Kiesinger and the head of the East German cabinet, Willi Stoph, although it produced no progress on any substantive issues, constituted an important direct contact with East Berlin. As the policy of isolating the GDR diplomatically began to be abandoned in the course of Bonn's policy of 'opening to the East', the GDR attempted to blunt the West German initiatives by trying, for its part, to impose a form of diplomatic isolation on the FRG. It demanded that no socialist country should establish diplomatic relations with Bonn until it was prepared to recognize the GDR, accept the territorial status quo in Europe, give up any form of nuclear sharing and recognize West Berlin as a separate political entity.

This policy enjoyed some success on the basis of bilateral agreements between the GDR and Poland, Czechoslovakia, Hungary and Bulgaria. The *Ostpolitik* of the Grand Coalition thus resulted in a considerable reduction in the isolation of East Germany, whose position on the German question and the issue of Berlin was now being supported by a multilateral treaty framework. On the positive side, it could be mentioned that diplomatic relations were established with Romania in 1967, with Yugoslavia in 1968, and a trade mission was established in Prague in 1967. On the whole, the domestic political room for manoeuvre in relations with the East was not sufficient during the period of the Grand Coalition to permit a kind of breakthrough in *Ostpolitik*. The Soviet intervention in Czechoslovakia in August 1968 was a blow to European detente and temporarily prevented any further progress. Its main long-term impact consisted in the realization that the approach based on a multiplicity of bilateral relationships with Eastern Europe could not be successful without establishing a new framework of Soviet–German relations.

The implementation of Ostpolitik

The formation of the coalition of SPD and FDP after the 1969 elections removed the domestic political barriers to a successful policy of detente. When Chancellor Willy Brandt introduced his government programme on 28 October 1969, he stated that with regard to the renunciation of force, the policy of his government would be based on the realities created by the Second World War and the territorial integrity of all states in Europe including the GDR. Foreign Minister Walter Scheel described the position as follows:

> The renunciation of force... bases itself on the situation as it is. It does not fix it, but describes it without attaching any value judgements to it... it bases itself on the geographical status quo and offers a political modus vivendi within the boundaries of the status quo. It respects and accepts reality. It does not undertake to recognise it in international law and thereby legitimise it.[25]

The principal ambiguity of this approach comprised the fact that although it involved the prospect of a de facto recognition of the GDR, including direct contacts with the East German government, and the practical renunciation of the claim for 'sole representation', it nevertheless clearly fell short of a recognition of the German Democratic Republic in international law. The formula which the Federal Government continued to use referred to 'two states within Germany'. The *Ostpolitik* of the social–liberal coalition had the following principal objectives:

- to reduce the East–West confrontation in Central Europe and establish co-operative relationships with Eastern Europe, including the Soviet Union and the GDR, provided the status of West Berlin and its connection with the Federal Republic were recognized
- the promotion of improved human contacts between the two Germanies and improved conditions within East Germany
- to avoid isolation from the Western Allies who were themselves pursuing a policy of detente and who were unwilling to pay the political price for a continued support of the West German claim for sole representation and allow West Germany to participate in the creation of a new European peace order
- to create a political basis for better trade and economic relations with Eastern Europe.[26]

The concrete implementation of this policy first of all consisted in the resumption of talks with the Soviet Union on the renunciation of force on the basis of these principles. The Soviet Union for its part initially pushed for the recognition of the GDR in international law and the inviolability of existing borders. Thus while the Soviet Union was seeking a formal recognition of the status quo in Europe, the West German objective consisted in a normalization of its relations with Eastern Europe while preserving its existing rights and future interests.

The principle of renunciation of force provided a suitable vehicle whereby a compromise between these two positions, which were still far apart in principle, could be found. Thus West Germany declared that it had no territorial claims against any country and agreed to the inviolability of the borders of all states in Europe now and in future, including the Oder–Neisse line and the frontier between the FRG and the GDR. This aspect of the German–Soviet Treaty which was signed in August 1970, and whose general outline first became public knowledge through the so-called 'Bahr paper', created a controversy in the Federal Republic as a public which had always been told that the current state of German affairs was provisional was finally confronted with the reality of *Ostpolitik* – the renunciation of territorial claims for all time. But nevertheless there was widespread support for the assessment by Chancellor Brandt that 'nothing was lost with this treaty that was not gambled away long ago'.[27] While the treaty itself laid down the general principles, the West German government sought to preserve its essential interests in two documents attached to the treaty:

- the 'Letter of German Unity' in which the Federal government maintained the right to 'work for a state of peace in Europe in which the German nation will recover its unity in free self-determination'[28]
- notification that West German ratification of the treaty would be subject to a satisfactory agreement on Berlin which would confirm the Four Power status of Berlin and its ties to the Federal Republic of Germany.

Berlin had been the point where the instability of the status quo during the cold war, which the policy of detente was designed to overcome, had been most acute. In return for the abandonment of the challenge by the Federal Republic to the status quo in Europe the Brandt government demanded the abandonment of the challenge to the status quo in Berlin. This would mean a general agreement among the Four Powers and an agreement between West and East Germany with regard to access to Berlin. Even this involved a substantial shift from the position previously maintained by West Germany insofar as any endeavour to have West Berlin recognized as an integral part of the Federal Republic was abandoned (it was by definition incompatible with the reassertion of the Four Power rights). The Quadripartite Agreement took 18 months of intensive negotiation and finally resulted in essentially securing the existing status quo of Berlin, including the guaranteed right of access to West Berlin without affecting the position taken by the Soviet Union with regard to the legal status, thereby regulating the transit between the Federal Republic and West Berlin.

The Federal Republic also negotiated treaties with Poland and the CSSR which were based on the renunciation of latent German territorial claims. But central to *Ostpolitik* was the agreement with the GDR. The Basic Treaty eventually negotiated with the Honecker leadership satisfied the East German demand for recognition, only insofar as each state recognized the equal status, boundaries and territorial integrity of the other. The West German government no longer insisted on the unqualified right to represent all Germans, while the issue of German citizenship remained unresolved. Given that there was no full legal recognition of the GDR, the two Germanies agreed to exchange permanent representatives instead of ambassadors. They also declared that in the course of the normalization of their relations they would be prepared to resolve practical and humanitarian issues and conclude a number of agreements on co-operation in various areas.

The debate about the Eastern Treaties was the culmination of the domestic political discussion of the change in the direction of West German foreign policy. Initially, the CDU/CSU opposed the Soviet–German treaty primarily on the grounds that it enhanced the status of the GDR, that it put at risk the rights of Germans to self-determination, that the issue of the future security of Berlin remained unclarified, that it did not substantially improve inner-German relations and that it put West Germany's policy with regard to the NATO Alliance at risk. It must be added that there was a strong undercurrent of opposition in principle to the Eastern treaties in all the parties, which made it difficult for either government or opposition to reach an agreed position and resulted in uncertainties about the voting position in the Bundestag. The quadripartite agreements however showed that some of the CDU/CSU objections were groundless. The principle conditions for opposition consent to the treaties remained a declaration on the self-determination of Germans and measures to improve the flow of people, information and goods. The effort by CDU caucus chairman Rainer Barzel to depose the SPD/FDP coalition by a vote of no-confidence failed. In the end the CDU decided to support the Eastern treaties, but found itself unable to do so because of its own internal opposition. The treaties were adopted by the Bundestag with most of the opposition abstaining.[29]

The international context of Ostpolitik

West Germany's *Ostpolitik*, although driven by very specific German concerns, was embedded in and a response to a much larger international context. In the course of the 1960s, the Soviet Union had developed a strategic nuclear arsenal to a rough level of parity with the United States and, in the opinion of some American analysts, was poised to overtake the US. The Warsaw Pact's capabilities for a conventional war in the European theatre were considered to be superior to those of the NATO Alliance. The Soviet Union was extending its influence in the Third World. At the same time, the global containment policy which had been, in varying degrees, been pursued by American administrations since Truman, was foundering in the morass of the Vietnam War. While the moral legitimacy of American military commitments abroad was under severe domestic political challenge, the economic costs also became increasingly burdensome. American economic leadership of the Western world was being challenged by a resurgent Japan and West Germany. The policy of detente pursued by President Nixon and his National Security Advisor Henry Kissinger was based on the assessment of a long-term change in the international system which made it impossible to continue a global policy of containment of the Soviet Union.

The Kissinger conception of detente was simply a form of containment by other means. The Soviet Union was to be involved in a network of agreements covering arms control (in order to regulate the arms race), recognition of the territorial status quo in Europe (that is spheres of influence – a Soviet agreement not to challenge the areas of American 'core interests') and trade. There was also an implicit assumption, not shared by the Soviet Union as it turned out, that within the framework of global detente the Soviet Union would exercise 'restraint' in its relations with the Third World (that is limit its endeavours to expand the influence of communism and its support for 'national liberation wars'). It is evident that there was a fundamental dichotomy between the public presentation of detente as a policy of 'peace' and 'rapprochement' in East–West relations and its objectives as perceived by the policymakers themselves, which, in the words of Kissinger, were to 'reconcile the reality of competition with the imperative of coexistence'.[30]

Similar factors and motivations were driving the Soviet interest in detente. Initial discussions about negotiations to limit strategic nuclear forces had already begun during the time of the Johnson administration. Only as the Soviet Union was well under way in the acquisition of a large-scale strategic nuclear missile force did a serious interest in strategic arms control emerge.[31] On the global level, the need to contain the Sino-Soviet conflict and the importance of trade relations with the West in the light of a stagnating economy and the requirements of access to Western technology constituted the political imperatives for detente from Moscow's point of view. Detente and arms control, furthermore, would recognize the status of the Soviet Union as a superpower on a par with the United States, which the Soviet Union had earned by virtue of the development of its strategic forces, and thus enhance Soviet influence in the world. On the European level, the consolidation and stabilization of the status quo had been a long established objective in Soviet foreign policy. The most vulnerable point had been East Germany; this is where the legitimacy of the Soviet presence was most severely tested, while the flow of talented people to the FRG until the erection of the wall in 1961 threatened the internal stability of the GDR. As the 1956 intervention in Hungary and that of 1968 in the CSSR indicated, there was a persistent potential for instability in Eastern Europe. The stabilization of relations with Western Europe and the diminution of Western pressure on the status quo in Eastern Europe was the principal motivation for Soviet *Westpolitik*.

For the Soviet Union therefore, detente was also in some ways the pursuit of the same policy objectives as before. The basic principle of competition between different social systems was not altered. Detente was entirely compatible with the principle of 'peaceful co-existence' as it had developed during the Khrushchev years, which shifted the competition with capitalism to the economic and political spheres while at the same time allowing for the extension of Soviet influence in the Third World through the support of National Liberation Movements.

Although *Ostpolitik* got under way before the Nixon/Kissinger policy of superpower detente began to take shape, nevertheless it was in accordance with the fundamental direction of United States policy. In Europe, additional factors promoted a greater emphasis on detente. The Western Alliance was showing signs of dissolution, with the French withdrawal from the integrated command and a general unwillingness by Alliance members to continue to shoulder the economic burdens of maintaining high conventional force levels.

This tendency was strengthened by a combination of a reduced threat perception and general economic difficulties. The United States was seeking to reduce its commitment to Europe owing to the balance of payment problems associated with the cost of the Vietnam War. On 14 December 1967 the NATO Council adopted the Harmel Report *On the Future Tasks of the Atlantic Alliance* which stated that in addition to the provision of military security against external aggression it was the task of the Alliance to seek progress in the establishment of enduring relations with the East to enable the solution of fundamental political issues. Thus the entire Alliance, including the Federal Republic of Germany, was officially committed to a policy of detente in Europe.[32]

The European level of detente found its principal expression in the Conference on Security and Cooperation in Europe (CSCE). The concept of a collective security regime in Europe and a pan-European Security Conference had been advocated by the Soviet Union since the mid-1950s and was being pursued with greater diplomatic effort from 1964 onwards. The Erhard government was rather critical of the idea. In the autumn of 1966 the Federal Government stated that the objective of such a conference would have to be to overcome the division of Germany by means of the establishment of a just peace in Europe, or at least take irrevocable steps in that direction. The GDR could not be a participant in such a conference. At the same time, the United States would have to be involved. The Federal Government itself recognized that this assessment amounted to a rejection of the basic concept itself.[33]

The Grand Coalition government reviewed the issue of a Conference on Security in Europe and concluded at first that it was unlikely that the deep divisions between East and West about the future of Europe could be overcome in a multilateral forum. It saw greater promise in bilateral negotiations with the Soviet Union. At the same time, Willy Brandt promoted the concept of negotiations on mutual troop reductions in Europe as a means of promoting detente and security within the Alliance framework. Towards the end of the Grand Coalition however the SPD began to take a more positive attitude towards CSCE as the Budapest Appeal by the Warsaw Pact in March 1969 indicated a less rigid attitude and interest among other West European states began to manifest itself. As Brandt cautiously began to welcome CSCE, the issue became very divisive within the coalition and restricted Brandt's freedom of action.

As *Ostpolitik* got under way on a bilateral level with the SPD/FDP coalition in government, CSCE became an instrument of *Deutschlandpolitik* insofar as West German co-operation became dependent on the successful conclusion of the Eastern Treaties, which in turn were made dependent on a satisfactory arrangement with regard to Berlin. The conclusion of the Soviet–German Treaty meant that the principal stumbling block of CSCE, that is its relation to the German question, had been resolved. Thereby the Soviet Union had achieved already much that it had set out to achieve in CSCE, while in the perception of the Federal Government CSCE had lost most of its potential danger to West German security interests.[34]

The Foreign Ministers Conference on Security and Cooperation in Europe opened in Helsinki in July 1973 with 35 participating nations. It resulted in a set of agreements concluded by August 1965 called the Helsinki Final Act. In many ways it can be seen as the continuation of *Ostpolitik* on a European scale. It accepted the *de facto* status quo in Europe without according it *de jure* recognition (Basket I on security), it provided for co-operation in economics, trade, science and technology (Basket II) and contained commitments with regard to the free flow of people and information (Basket III).

West Germany's *Ostpolitik* can therefore be explained in two different, but complementary ways. The most immediate one is that of *Ostpolitik* as a new concept of *Deutschlandpolitik*. As we have explained above, the SPD concept had proven as untenable as Adenauer's *Politik der Stärke*. In a sense *Ostpolitik* implied the abandonment of an active policy of reunification in return for Eastern guarantees of the preservation of status quo. At the same time it allowed for a more realistic pursuit of the objectives of *Entspannung* and disarmament which had been central to the political values espoused by the SPD, since they were now freed from the burdens of the German question. There was, however, also a subversive element in *Ostpolitik* insofar as it aimed at increasing human contact, trade relations with Eastern Europe and, through Basket III of CSCE, provided an instrument to promote human rights. *Wandel durch Annäherung* expressed the hope that through a network of political, economic and human relationships there would be convergence between both Germanies in the long term which would allow the division of Germany to be overcome. This could also be applied to the entire process of detente on the European level. After the Eastern Treaties had been signed, this aspect of detente in Europe (except for MBFR negotiations on conventional force reductions)[35] was the most important one for the Federal Government. The objectives underlying *Politik der Stärke* and *Ostpolitik* were not dissimilar, even if the means by which they were pursued were very different.

On another level, *Ostpolitik* was simply the adaptation of West German foreign policy to the changes in the international system. Although bold and courageous in terms of its domestic political operationalization, there was really no other policy for the Federal Government to pursue if it wanted to avoid political isolation, East and West – but the Gaullist alternative did not really exist for West Germany given its dependence on the Western Alliance and had been laid to rest by the time the SPD/FDP coalition assumed power. The German question was a crucial factor in the entire Western framework of security policy, given that Soviet European security policy was based on the containment of Germany. Thus West German participation in multilateral arms control negotiations, such as the PTBT, the Nuclear NonProliferation Treaty and the Mutual and Balanced Force Reduction talks all involved both the status of East Germany and West Germany (the latter insofar as Soviet proposals were usually designed to impose limitations on West Germany). As the continual erosion of the endeavour to isolate the GDR during the 1960s indicated, it was simply no longer possible to pursue a policy that threatened to derail the framework of security policy which West Germany's principal security guarantors sought to establish.

The decline of detente and the continuation of Ostpolitik

The signing of the Eastern Treaties marked a watershed in the domestic debate about the future of *Deutschlandpolitik*. From then on, a basic consensus existed with regard to *Ostpolitik* which lasted beyond the Brandt and Schmidt governments into the era of Helmut Kohl and Hans-Dietrich Genscher.[36] However, while the efforts to implement detente in Europe persisted, superpower detente went into decline from the mid-1970s on. The problem was in many ways one of perception of the meaning of detente. Detente, as conceived within the Nixon administration, was a complex policy rooted in the realpolitik of a changing international system. It essentially ignored the issue of the moral legitimacy of Communist regimes and did not attempt to eliminate the fundamental ideological antagonism between East and West, but rather sought to impose certain restraints and limits, and redirect the systemic competition into different channels and thus make it more manageable and less dangerous.

In terms of the American political system, the fundamental problem was that this approach was basically alien to the American political culture which saw American foreign policy in terms of a morally defined mission. It also engendered expectations with regard to Soviet–American relations and Soviet international behaviour (particularly in terms of relations with the Third World and arms control) which went far beyond the basic principles of detente. It was further undermined by the inability of the White House to operationalize the concept of linkage between the various areas of detente which it had sought to incorporate.[37]

In as far as the policy of detente was generated by changes in the international system and the strategic balance of power, it is not surprising that at the periphery of superpower influence where the balance of political power remained fluid and indeterminate, superpower detente was unable to provide the sort of stability which its American architects had hoped for.

For the American critics of detente, Soviet and Cuban involvement in Angola beginning in 1975 was evidence of continuing Soviet efforts to exploit regional instabilities and was interpreted as a violation of the spirit of detente, even though the crises were the result of events in Europe and American policy could not stand the scrutiny of rational political, let alone moral, analysis. Similar conclusion were withdrawn from events in the Horn of Africa. The Soviet intervention in Afghanistan finally marked the end of superpower detente and forced a public reappraisal of Soviet–American relations.[38] Strategic arms control also proved disappointing as both superpower's arsenals dramatically increased during the 1970s and in the deteriorating climate of Soviet–American relations President Carter decided not even to submit the SALT II Treaty for ratification to Congress.

The Reagan Administration was determined to make a clean break with its predecessor's foreign policy and take a clear stand against communism and the Soviet Union. It was extremely critical of the SALT II Treaty, in particular, and the whole process of arms control and detente in general. The main criticisms of the Administration's spokesmen, notable among them Richard Perle (a former aide to Senator Henry Jackson, one of the principal opponents of the Nixon/Kissinger policy of detente), were directed against arms control as a political process. Perle rejected Kissinger's notion of detente and the pursuit of arms control agreements for political purposes. The goal of American arms control negotiating strategy as conceived by

Perle should be nothing less than a complete restructuring of the Soviet nuclear arsenal to eliminate its perceived first-strike capability against the US ICBM force. Many in the Administration however had a more basic bias against arms control. They believed that the Soviets were violating existing agreements, and that concluding agreements with them was useless. Furthermore, Perle pointed out the failure of the arms control process to restrain the growth of the superpowers' nuclear arsenals – in particular of course the Soviet arsenal, thus leading to what they alleged to be US strategic inferiority. Indeed, the threat of an emerging Soviet first-strike capability against American ICBMs was proclaimed as 'the window of vulnerability'.

The Reagan administration was also extremely critical of the process of détente and rejected many of the basic assumptions underlying the relationship between the superpowers since the late 1960s. In particular, it was quite uneasy about the notion of strategic parity which was intrinsic to the arms control process. In Republican circles there was a growing feeling that what was really needed to keep the Soviets at bay was a return to American strategic superiority, since as a result of strategic nuclear parity the credibility of the American threat to use nuclear weapons in response to limited Soviet aggression had substantially declined. American conservative critics of detente fundamentally objected to the basic moral equivalence which in their view detente conferred on the Soviet Union and its allies.[39] There was a belief in the administration that the Soviet Union could be forced to behave by economic sanctions, the pressure of military power and the demonstration of political resolve. Some, such as Richard Pipes, went so far as to advocate that internal political change in the Soviet Union should be the objective of US foreign policy.[40]

Europe could not remain unaffected by the decline in East–West relations which has since been called the second cold war. However, the perspective from which the Reagan administration approached East–West relations in its first term was not widely accepted in Europe. Many of the perceptions which were driving American policy seemed to bear no relation to reality. While the rise in Soviet strategic power was real, there was no meaningful Soviet superiority. ICBM vulnerability was a purely theoretical problem that could never be solved. Despite the intense political struggle unfolding over the deployment of long range theatre nuclear forces (LRTNF) in Europe, this did not in itself imply that all of the achievements of the detente process had been lost. From the European perspective, there was no fundamental change in the international system which required the abandonment of detente. It was not evident that the confrontational course pursued by the Reagan administration would have the desired consequences. Quite to the contrary, it was precisely because of the fundamental strategic realities that the Soviet Union could not be coerced into accepting political change in Eastern Europe or engage in a constructive process of reducing the military confrontation in Central Europe.

While Western security interests had to be upheld, and while because of the nature of the 1979 NATO 'dual track' decision NATO really had to deploy LRTNF unless there were meaningful concessions from the Soviet Union, nevertheless in the West German perspective the way forward in East–West relations lay in more and not less detente. This reflected not only the conviction of the Schmidt government and its successors, it also reflected a fundamental shift in the basic political consensus of the West German population. The political conscientization of the younger generation during the era of the Vietnam War and the left-wing student revolts in Europe, which coincided with the process of *Ostpolitik* and thus a fundamental reorientation of West German foreign policy, had an enduring effect. The intense public controversy over the 'neutron bomb' changed the political climate to such an extent that the Federal Government insisted on an 'arms control track' to the LRTNF modernization decision because it felt that otherwise deployment could not be supported. The INF controversy resulting from the 'dual track' decision altered the basic consensus about the legitimacy of nuclear defence.[41]

In the midst of this intense controversy, the two German states endeavoured to protect their relationship. Intensified cultural and scientific contacts, greater opportunities for travel for East and West Germans, expanded trade and various other practical areas of cooperation continued to be pursued. The determination to maintain intra-German relations was such that it engendered considerable criticism for the weak German response to the imposition of martial law in Poland in 1981.[42] It continued into the Kohl era, where the FDP, which under Foreign Minister Genscher saw itself as the guardian of *Ostpolitik*, and the moderate CDU leadership protected West German detente policy from the more conservative elements.

New Thinking and the transformation of Europe

Mikhail Gorbachev's accession to power in the Soviet Union in 1985 was followed by an ambitious programme of political and economic reform. In its foreign policy dimension it involves the assumption that a genuine and enduring relaxation of tension in East–West relations and a significant restraint in the arms competition is an important prerequisite for the success of the policy of domestic perestroika. The driving force behind the new thinking is the long-term unsustainability of competing with the United States for military power on the basis of a weak economy.

The accommodation with the West that Gorbachev was seeking was of a different nature from that of detente during the Brezhnev period. Its conceptual basis was that of peaceful relations and interdependence instead of an international class struggle. Instead of basing arms control on the concept of 'parity', 'reasonable sufficiency' was advocated as a standard for force structure development which would allow asymmetrical arms reductions in Europe. The first concrete result of this new approach was the INF Treaty in 1987. The real test of Soviet willingness to move away from the military confrontation in Central Europe, however, was in conventional arms control. It was the announcement of significant unilateral force reductions in Gorbachev's speech to the United Nations General Assembly in December 1988 which convinced many in the West that Gorbachev was to be taken seriously on this, in contrast to Soviet behaviour during the MBFR talks which went on inconclusively for more than a decade.[43]

The perception of Foreign Minister Hans-Dietrich Genscher, who very early recognized new opportunities in Gorbachev's foreign policy, was not universally shared. There were voices in West Germany that agreed with American critics who saw Gorbachev's policy as the old Soviet policy pursued by different means. The CDU arms control expert Jürgen Todenhöfer expressed the view that the INF agreement was in the Soviet security interest and not in the German interest. The decoupling effect of removing Pershing II and Cruise Missiles from Germany was particularly emphasized. The concern that the United States, in its endeavour to come to a successful arrangement with the Soviet Union was ignoring European interests, was shared both by UK Prime Minister Thatcher and Chancellor Kohl. The internal tensions over defence policy and the perceptions of the remaining Soviet threat resurfaced during the debate over the modernization of short range nuclear forces (SNF) when Genscher forced the coalition to go back on a compromise agreed within NATO.

Everything changed, however, in 1989. The deliberate relaxation of bloc discipline by the Soviet Union in Eastern Europe aimed at a transition from relations based on coercion to relations based on consent and responsibility. The emphasis on reform and the un-willingness to use force precipitated the rapid changes in Eastern Europe and the collapse of the SED regime in East Germany in a manner which no-one, least of all Gorbachev, had foreseen.[44] After initial objections to putting the German question 'on the agenda', Gorbachev eventually accepted that German unity was inevitable after the Federal Government undertook to fulfil the trade obliga-tions which the GDR was no longer in a position to do.

The changes in Eastern Europe and German reunification had profound implications for the European security environment. They represented a significant diminution in Soviet political influence. There is no question that the Soviets found the prospect of a united Germany in NATO rather alarming. This was partly due to the his-torical pattern of relationships with Germany, partly due to residual fears of NATO and partly the overt way in which German reunifi-cation demonstrated defeat in the cold war. Nevertheless, these fears were set aside in the course of the 'two-plus-four' negotiations which settled the external aspects of German unification mostly on Western terms, but making concessions to Soviet security concerns by putting a ceiling of 370 000 on German armed forces in the future, an agree-ment not to deploy non-German NATO forces in the former territory of the GDR and generous economic assistance from Germany.

Conclusion

How are we to interpret the West German approach to national security in terms of the theoretical models under discussion? *Politik der Stärke* seems at first glance an archetypical realist concept. One important distinction that has to be made, however, is that whereas realism in its various forms does not consider the structure of the international system dependent on the nature of the regimes governing individual states, the threat to European security posed by the Soviet Union was very much seen by Western political lead-ers, including the political élite of the Federal Republic of Germany, as a consequence of the nature of the Communist regime. This threat was seen as posed by the accumulation of military power, economic power and the use of political subversion. The ideological basis of Soviet expansionism meant that, given that the ultimate objective was the establishment of world socialism and by implication the eradication of liberal democracy, the threat posed by the Soviet Union went far beyond the traditional security dilemma. The consequence of this was that the conflict with the Soviet Union was not amenable to an institutionalist approach. The Soviet Union could not be reasoned with or bargained with, it could not be socialized, it could only be contained. Detente was a delusion, because it merely softened the Western response, whereas the objectives of the Soviet Union remained the same. Detente was dangerous therefore, because it undermined Western resolve, it would undermine the policy of not giving any diplomatic recognition to the GDR, without contributing to a resolution of the cold war.

While the nature of the Soviet state meant that power politics was the only option, the opposite was true in relations with liberal democracies. *Westintegration* in Adenauer's conception went beyond the realist concept of Alliance formation. *European integration* in the form of the European Community was designed to overcome the ancient hostilities in Europe, particularly between Germany and France. This was an explicitly institutionalist approach to European security. This is not to say that the leaders of the Federal Republic had no conception of Germany's national interest. Quite to the contrary, they had a very definite view of Germany's political, economic and security interests. These were located in the creation of a prosperous, liberal democratic state that gradually achieved the status and role of a major regional power, the preservation of the security of the state against an enormous military threat, and in the long-term reunification with the East. They saw integration in the Western Alliance and the European Community as the only way that these interests could be actively pursued in a manner acceptable to the international community. But it would not do the Federal Republic justice to reinterpret its institutionalism simply in terms of national interest. The commitment to integration went much deeper than can be explained purely in terms of national interest.[45] The objective of German policy was at every end and turn the emergence of a genuine supranationalism in Europe. This was in direct opposition to the French vision of a *Europe des nations*. The West German concept of institutionalism went beyond mere intergovernmental co-operation towards a gradual and to some extent open-ended movement towards supranationalism which would result in a much deeper convergence between the national interests of European states.

The Brandt/Scheel era of *Ostpolitik* constituted a radical departure from the Adenauer approach to Germany's security dilemmas. It was recognized that in the nuclear age power politics alone was insufficient to achieve Germany's objectives. While the nuclear stalemate created a stability of sorts, it prevented any movement to overcome the division of Europe. For this reason an explicit institutionalist agenda for European security was adopted. However, in terms of contemporary international relations theory, constructivism provides more appropriate categories for describing this approach. *Wandel durch Annäherung* was essentially a very ambitious programme of international socialization to change the norms and values governing international behaviour and thereby reduce the threat to international security. The CSCE was the culmination of efforts to regulate the East–West conflict by creating institutions that would not only reduce tension, but had the more ambitious objective of inducing the East European states and the Soviet Union to adhere to certain norms in international relations and observe principles of human rights domestically.

The Federal Republic was not deterred by the fact that many of the more ambitious goals of the CSCE process were not achieved and that detente went into serious decline in the late 1970s. During this period the FRG saw itself as the guardian of detente and continued to promote co-operative security as the way forward. During the postwar period a deep aversion to war and militarism had taken root in West Germany, which was encouraged and consolidated by the social radicalism of the 1960s and the policies of detente of the 1970s. The decline of detente towards the end of the 1970s and the struggle of theatre nuclear force modernization resulted in a very deep and bitter controversy in West Germany about defence and nuclear weapons policies which fundamentally altered the basic consensus on these issues. The deployment of INF in 1983 was phyrric victory for the West German political élite. While the NATO Alliance held together and prevailed, at the same time a consensus was established in West Germany that from now on there could be no further deployment of land-based nuclear weapons system.

If the early 1980s put the previous efforts to regulate relations with the Soviet Union on hold, the appointment of Mikhail Gorbachev as General Secretary of the CPSU soon gave them a new lease of life. New Political Thinking was a mix of idealism and institutionalism, which in its final consequence seemed to aim at the demilitarization of East–West relations. This produced an interesting cleavage in West Germany's political élite; as the conservative/liberal coalition was in power, the initial reaction was one of suspicion. But soon the liberals who were in charge of the foreign ministry pushed forward with a return to the agenda of the 1970s. The debate about the INF treaty of 1987 once again opened up these cleavages, as some conservative politicians revealed themselves as strong adherents to a neorealist approach. Holding on to land-based missiles on German soil was deemed more important than grasping the chance for change in the nature of international relations in Europe. However the domestic political situation in Germany would not have permitted a return to *Politik der Stärke* and nor did the international environment. Foreign Minister Genscher pushed forward the agenda of demilitarization and change in Europe relentlessly. The peaceful dissolution of the Soviet empire and German unification could be interpreted as an extraordinary vindication of the German approach.

On one level it would be tempting to interpret this as a final vindication of Adenauer's *Politik der Stärke*. His prediction of a fundamental change in Soviet foreign policy as a result of a failing Soviet economy and the emphasis on the resolution of the German question in the context of a change in the whole of Eastern Europe is uncanny in the light of events. Nevertheless this does not imply the correctness or sustainability of *Politik der Stärke*. Certainly from the late 1950s the Soviet Union proved itself not to be an expansionist power in Europe, but a status quo power. Not only was *Ostpolitik* necessary to maintain West German interests in the international environment in which they had to be defended, but the whole process of detente and arms control kept the East–West confrontation within limits that significantly reduced the threat of war. Furthermore, it created a diplomatic and intellectual framework for East–West relations which provided the necessary basis for the Gorbachev leadership to move forward in the endeavour to transcend the impasse in East–West relations. To what extent 'Wandel durch Annäherung' was successful is another issue. Clearly many people benefited from the humanitarian aspects of detente. As Timothy Garton Ash has pointed out, however, there was an inherent contradiction in detente insofar as the reduction of external pressure of Eastern European governments resulted in increased internal pressure to which the authorities reacted with severe clampdowns.[46] The implementation of Basket III was generally very disappointing from the Western point of view. The detente process nevertheless contributed to the creation of a culture of dissent and provided international legitimation for it which was of great importance in itself and played a significant role in the downfall of the East European regimes at the end of the 1980s.[47]

It is important to note that for all the domestic and external pressures on the Soviet system, it was not anywhere near the point of collapse at the time when Gorbachev came to power. Although the Soviet Union was losing ground in the technological arms race, it had more than sufficient conventional and nuclear weapons to sustain its position for a long time to come. The collapse of Soviet power and the dissolution of the Soviet state itself fundamentally appears to contradict neorealist analysis, according to which the perpetuation of their own existence and the maximization of their power is the most fundamental objective that states pursue.[48] Indeed, in line with the long-established parameters of Soviet foreign policy, a greater assertiveness abroad and a more sustained endeavour to improve the economy by a more determined use of the authoritarian instruments of government and the ideological structures for political socialization, would have been expected. It is both the timing and *peaceful* nature of the end of the Soviet empire that defy explanation by the neorealist or the structural realist paradigm. The changes in the international system were not inevitable consequences of changes in the balance of power.[49]

It appears on the face of it that the cold war ended because the Soviet leadership decided that it wanted to end the cold war. The first indications that Gorbachev wanted to end the cold war came early during his tenure as Soviet leader, and soon he and his foreign minister Shevardnadze pursued this goal relentlessly. The *New Political Thinking* which formed the ideological justification and underpinning of the new foreign policy was based on the abandonment of the international class struggle in favour of universal peace and human rights. This of course begs the question as to what caused it to pursue this objective. There is as yet no complete answer to this question. However, it seems that a generational change occurred in the Soviet élite and that the new leaders were principally concerned to deal with the economic decline, with the failure of the Soviet Union to become a modern industrialized country, the social disintegration and the disillusionment among the intellectual élite.

The transformation of relations with the West was an integral part of this process but not the primary objective. The opportunity for the new generation to assert itself came as the older generation allowed the Soviet Union to fall into a state of complete political paralysis. The international environment undoubtedly played a part. The intensity of the hostility in East–West relations was perceived as extremely dangerous in the Soviet Union, but the previously established means of reducing tension proved wholly inadequate. A completely new departure, a whole-scale revision of the intellectual framework that defined Soviet foreign relations was required. The Gorbachev programme, even though it lacked precise objectives and was inconsistent in its implementation, had the very far-reaching goal of completely redefining the values on which the political systems inside the Soviet Union and consequently Soviet relations with the outside world were to be based.

Gorbachev, Shevardnadze and many of the younger academics who acted as their advisers had come to recognize the absurdity of continuing relations with the West on the basis of an international class struggle. In the first place, they recognized that the West had no interest in a military conflict with the Soviet Union and that the perception of an outside *military* threat was in fact an illusion, perpetuated by powerful interest groups inside the Soviet Union. This explains how quickly the conviction that there was no real threat from the West was adopted by the military establishment once the Soviet positions in Eastern Europe had been given up and the cold war was declared to be over. The real threat to Soviet security lay in the militarization of the Soviet economy and the detrimental consequences that resulted from the arms race. In the second place, they believed that the West was the place 'where civilization lies'. In other words, they believed that the Soviet Union needed to adopt many of the values on which Western political systems and societies were based, such as democratic freedoms and human rights, albeit tempered by socialist values. The full meaning of this programme did not become clear for some time. But between 1987 and 1989 it came to be recognized that arms control was only the first step and that one of the fundamental causes of the cold war, namely Soviet domination of Eastern Europe, needed to be removed.

To what extent this analysis of the end of the cold war is correct remains open to question, and without doubt this a complex issue that will occupy scholars for a long time to come. The point here is that on the face of it a good case can be made that the institutionalist/constructivist approach turned out to be extraordinarily successful. The Soviet Union was in fact successfully socialized and locked into international institutions, with the result that its foreign policy behaviour changed dramatically. The end of the cold war is perhaps the most dramatic example of a state doing precisely what constructivist theory claims is possible, namely to deliberately abandon a policy based on neorealist principles and thereby overcome the security dilemma that is the consequence of anarchy in the international system. It is not surprising that those in the German political élite who had put their efforts into *Wandel durch Annäherung* felt vindicated. Indeed, there was now a deep sense that all international problems would be capable of peaceful resolution through international institutions based on international law.

After the cold war: Germany in the international system

Can Germany adapt to its new role in the international system? While some fears about the growth of German power and influence have been expressed, there has also been the expectation that Germany should now assume greater responsibilities concomitant with its new position. This will require Germany to formulate its national interests and achieve a consensus on the political and military instruments required to secure them. Uwe Nerlich has succinctly expressed the problems confronting Germany's leaders:

> The Federal Republic is not only not prepared for this new situation. . . . It also can no longer simply take for granted those things that were previously axiomatic for our policy: the stability of our standard of living; progress toward European integration; a consensus for continuing integration; our ability to pursue out national interests without ever explicitly defining them; a preferential relationship with France; the balanced engagement of the United States; and the politically motivated desire to renounce the use of force. . . . This also means that the Federal Republic will have to develop its own political and security strategy in order to retain its ability to act within multilateral structures. . . . But this requires political and strategic behaviour and therefore a strategy. And for this the Federal Republic is not prepared – neither politically, conceptually, nor operationally.[50]

In particular, the role and the use of power in the international system is one that the Germans find very difficult to come to terms with, since the exercise of such power was politically and morally restrained as a consequence of the Second World War. This applies in particular to the use of force. The profound rejection of militarism was part of the process of international rehabilitation. The Bundeswehr was developed as a force whose sole purpose was to make sure that it would never be used.

The response of the political élite to this issue was a reaffirmation of many of the principles that guided German foreign policy throughout the postwar period. Its essential character was captivated in a phrase coined by Hanns Maull from the University of Trier who described Germany as a 'civilian power' whose main purpose is to contribute to building and international order that rests on norms and values rather than power. The basic principles are (i) the acceptance that international co-operation is necessary to achieve security and other basic objectives; (ii) the primacy of nonmilitary means (for example econonomic) to achieve security and other national goals, with military force as a residual instrument of last resort; and (iii) the willingness to develop intergovernmental and supranational institutions to deal with essential issues of international order, even when this is not necessary for a state to achieve its own national objectives.

Although there is no official statement of Germany's national interests, one can determine a cluster of fundamental interests:

1 The preservation of the freedom, security and well-being of the citizens of Germany and the inviolability of its territory.
2 Integration with the European democracies in the European Union.
3 A permanent transatlantic Alliance with the United States as a global power based on a community of values and common interests.
4 The involvement of Germany's Eastern neighbours in Western structures and the creation of a new comprehensive co-operative security order.

This formulation, albeit in rather general terms, sets out the basic foreign policy orientation of the Federal Republic at the beginning of the post-cold war period. Essentially this is a very explicitly institutionalist agenda (which IR theorists, however, would more likely categorize as constructionist), with multilateral co-operation as the fundamental means to construct a new world order. Germany is to play a major role as a regional civilian power, mostly by making a leading contribution to the unification of Europe and the integration of the European Union.

The following chapters will examine in more detail the meaning of these rather generalized statements of the principle of German foreign and security policy after unification. Chapter 2 will examine how the European international security developed since the collapse of the Soviet Union and how the united Germany perceives it and the threats to its national security. The following elements of foreign and security policy are then examined in turn in the following chapters: Chapter 3 analyzes German defence policy after the cold war, with particular focus on the issue of the use of force and German participation in UN or Alliance peacekeeping and peace-enforcement missions; Chapter 4 looks at the question of collective security and pan-European security regimes; Chapter 5 considers more specifically the role and the future of NATO. European integration and the role of the EU in European security is considered in Chapter 6. The final chapter will consider how Germany has adapted to the new European security environment and to its new role, as the Kohl era has come to an end. It will look at how Germany has fared in developing its position as a 'civilian power' in the context of the future prospects for European security.

2
European Security after the Cold War

For over four decades, the Federal Republic of Germany was at the frontline of the military confrontation in Central Europe. As the postwar European security architecture, dominated by the cold war and the confrontation between two blocs dissolved at the end of the 1980s, the structure of the international system of states in Europe and of European security had begun to undergo a complete transformation. What would happen after the end of the cold war and the dissolution of the Warsaw Pact? If the Soviet Union was no longer a threat, what kind of threats to national security would there be, and how could they be addressed? More importantly, what would the European system of states look like with the Soviet Union and the East European states no longer being opponents of the West, but partners. How could the West make sure that the transition from adversaries to partners would be successful, and not fall foul of new authoritarian regimes, brought to power by economic and social chaos? From 1990 onwards German policymakers (and especially Foreign Minister Hans-Dietrich Genscher) were conscious of the need to transform the collective defence structure of the cold war era into pan-European collective security structures. This was in part motivated by a sense that the end of the cold war and the withdrawal of Soviet/Russian forces from Central Europe was an uncertain process and that everything possible needed to be done to ensure that it was completed and that the realignment of international relations moved in the right direction. The objective was that, with the end of the bitter political and military confrontation of the last 40 years, Eastern Europe including the former Soviet Union, would become part of a system of democratic states united by a common set of values and principles.[1]

Indeed, this hope was expressed not only for Europe but for the global international system. The phrase 'New World Order' was used by President Bush in the context of the Gulf War in 1990/91. It referred to a new international system of states to replace the bipolar cold war order based on a consensus among the major powers on international norms, principles of international law and human rights that should govern relations among states.[2] The 'New International Order' has been derided from all sides. There are those who see Bush's 'New International Order' merely as a framework in which the United States, as the sole remaining superpower after the cold war, can pursue its national interests and preserve its dominant role in the international system.[3] This is, for example, a common interpretation of the Gulf War of 1990/91. Neorealist analysis, such as it has been recently expounded by, for example, John Mearsheimer and Kenneth Waltz,[4] takes a fundamentally sceptical view of collective security. It explains the cold war on the basis of the basic principles of how states interact in the international system and the role of the balance of power. According to realism, anarchy prevails in the international system and therefore relations between states are inherently prone to conflict. This manifests itself in the behaviour of states to maximize power and security. Since no international organization is ultimately capable of enforcing order, every state has to provide for its own security. In order to achieve this a state constantly seeks to improve its relative power position. This requires building up military capabilities and at times the use of military force.[5]

In the neorealist understanding of international relations, the East–West conflict which emerged in the aftermath of the Second World War was a natural consequence of the postwar balance of power and is best understood as the rivalry between two great power systems.

This interpretation of the cold war leads to a very specific analysis of the post-cold war security environment. The collapse of the bipolar system may result in instability and large-scale conflict if no balance of power emerges that can hold the emerging interstate rivalries in check. The policy prescription advanced by Mearsheimer is that to reestablish the stability of the international system in Europe, the United States and the Western European states (in particular Britain and Germany) should balance the multipolar system emerging in Europe with military (including nuclear) forces against states that threaten war. This implies a new balance of power arrangement to compensate for an apparent Russian inability to continue to function as a great power. John Mearsheimer suggests for example the acquisition of nuclear weapons by Germany. Together with a continued American commitment to Europe and a continuation of NATO these are the conditions deemed necessary for coping with ethnic conflicts, potential interstate rivalries in Europe and for maintaining stability in the region as a whole.[6]

However, as discussed in Chapter 1, the interpretation of the nature of the cold war by neorealists is open to question. In particular the timing and manner in which the cold war ended is a problem for the neorealist approach. A different interpretation of the nature of the cold war and the reasons for its end leads to a completely different characterization of the system of states in Europe after the cold war. The potential for interstate conflict predicted by John Mearsheimer is no where apparent in Europe except in the territory of states which have now fallen apart, such as certain parts of the former Soviet Union and the former Republic of Yugoslavia.[7] These conflicts can be interpreted either as civil conflicts or postcolonial conflicts. What we are witnessing in Europe are the consequences of the collapse of the Soviet Union and the Yugoslav state, where stability on their territories had been created by the constant threat of force and the removal of that threat has resulted in instability and conflict. However, generally speaking post-cold war European states do not seem to be naturally prone to military conflict. Quite the opposite appears to be the case: the principal objective of virtually all Central and Eastern European states appears to be to join various Western multilateral organizations such as NATO and the European Union and thereby accept international norms with regard to the use and the threat of the use of force and other consequent constraints on their foreign and domestic policies.

Whereas for neorealists the principal consequence for the international system of the end of the cold war is the collapse of the bipolar structure of power and the reemergence of a regional multipolarity, other perspectives provide a sense of a deeper change. These range from Samuel Huntington's *Clash of Civilisations*, which sees the bipolar global power struggle replaced by new patterns of conflict and co-operation emerging along cultural lines,[8] to Francis Fukuyama's belief in the final triumph of Western liberalism and the *end of history*.[9] It is not necessary to accept the whole of Fukuyama's framework or the triumphalism of some of his adherents to conclude that a major paradigm shift has occurred with regard to the role of military force in the international system and that we are indeed in a new era in which war between the major powers has become unlikely, or, as some would say, obsolete.[10]

There are several developments throughout the 20th century that point in this direction.[11] The first is that the cost of war has dramatically increased to the point of rendering war unprofitable. The last major systemic conflict between major powers was a *cold* war precisely for that reason. The destructive power of nuclear weapons was such that their large-scale use would threaten the very existence of the societies that would engage in such a conflict. But the destructive power of conventional forces is now such that an all-out conflict between major powers would result in unacceptable losses on both sides. This is illustrated by the fact that during the 1980s the Soviet leadership concluded that any war in Europe would be literally impossible because attacks on nuclear power stations would render Europe uninhabitable.[12] The vulnerability of high-technology societies and their high standard of living has resulted in an unwillingness to support the costs of war, both in terms of casualties and damage to the society itself.

The second factor is that the currency of power in the security space occupied by the Western powers and to some extent also Russia and China has changed.[13] The collapse of an empire controlled by a nuclear superpower with the military capacity to destroy every country on earth is a powerful symbol of this trend. During the 1970s and 1980s it was already observable that economic capacity and commercial competitiveness were becoming more important. These trends accelerated as the cold war ended, both in the West and also now in the East, where the survival of the post-Communist states was not endangered by external military threat but internal societal and economic collapse.[14]

Another aspect of this is a phenomenon referred to as globalization.[15] There is now a high degree of global economic interdependence. Financial collapse in one country can affect the wealth of people, companies and societies on the other side of the globe. The abandonment of the centrally planned command economy by the former Communist countries is of major significance for international security. Russia and China are no longer attempting to develop autonomous, socialist economies. Instead both countries have committed themselves to develop market economies. Wealth is no longer dependent on the possession of land or natural resources, but on the intellectual capital and social organization to produce high quality, high technology products. Such wealth cannot easily be acquired by war or conquest.

The third factor is based on the observation that even in an anarchic international environment, not all states are the same and that the nature of the domestic political regime has an important influence on foreign policy behaviour. This is important in explaining the dynamics of the cold war, but is also significant in understanding the emerging environment after the cold war when some of the main protagonists have radically changed the nature of their domestic political system. A number of scholars have argued that a neo-realist approach to international relations based on the Hobbesian analogy is not readily applicable to relations between liberal democracies.[16] Not only have there been no wars between liberal democracies, but neither are they perceived to threaten one another and the balance of power between liberal democracies has been relevant only in the context of responses to other external threats.[17] Although a common external threat and the conscious endeavour to overcome the national enmities in Europe which resulted in two world wars were undoubtedly important factors, a deeper structural principle seems to be necessary to account for this difference in the role of military force. Among the factors that may be part of the explanation are:

- a shared value system which includes the acceptance of international norms;
- the existence of institutional mechanisms for the resolution of conflicts;
- the more diffuse nature of political power in liberal democracies makes it difficult to sustain military conflicts, unless they are relatively limited in time and their objectives are widely accepted by the population.

This generally rules out the acquisition of territory by force owing to the difficulties of absorbing hostile populations in the political system and the violation of political norms involved.[18] It also means that domestic consent to a war is highly dependent on the nature of the regime against which war is to be conducted – that is, it has to be credibly described as an aggressive and authoritarian (non-democratic) regime.[19]

This analysis can be related to a constructivist approach in that democratization becomes a way to socialize states to adopt new norms of international conduct and become part of the international regimes that enable the security dilemma to be overcome. There are such regimes in place in Europe which regulate the military arsenals of all European states and create transparency about military potentials and strategic planning that allow for building a high degree of confidence. The Conventional Forces in Europe (CFE) Treaty, initially designed to reduce fears about large-scale conventional conflict between NATO and the Warsaw Pact, places strict ceilings on the tanks, armoured vehicles, artillery and aircraft each state is allowed to deploy. The CFE 1A agreement, albeit non-binding in international law and non-verifiable, limits the military manpower of all European states.[20] This means that all European states have signed up to a treaty regime which provides full information on the strength and capability of all armed forces and prevents the competitive increase of military potentials. The limits are designed to provide for defensive capability without enabling states to acquire the quantitative and qualitative superiority required for aggression. The scope and frequency of military exercises is also regulated in order to prevent exercises from being used as a cover for actual military operations. The strict verification procedures involving satellite observation and on-site inspections provide the regime with a high degree of credibility. The importance attributed to this regime is indicated in the fact that despite the pressure exerted by its military to find various reasons to break out of the CFE regime, the Russian government firmly held to its obligations and sought to redress grievances within the treaty regime rather than to abandon it.[21] The CFE treaty regime therefore stands out as a shining example of the success of a constructivist approach, whereby states which based themselves on the principle of total security (that is, the ability to totally defeat all conceivable enemies) changed their approach and adopted the principle of 'reasonable sufficiency' in the framework of a substantive regime of confidence-building measures, thereby ending both a military confrontation and a persistent arms race.

The notion that major war has become unlikely and is becoming obsolete as an instrument of policy does not amount to saying that wars will no longer occur. The Gulf War, although on the surface a contradiction of the notion that the world may be moving towards an inherently less conflictual state, is a good illustration of these principles. Iraq was in the grip of a tightly controlled dictatorship which imposed its own agenda on the Iraqi population by means of terror. It did so without any regard to the possibility of casualties or damage to the civilian economy. The United States and its allies were only able to muster a determined response because the Iraqi annexation of Kuwait constituted a clear enough violation of international norms for sufficient acceptance of military action by the populations of the Allied states. The war plans were designed to ensure the absolute minimum of casualties on the Allied side and contain military operations to the territory of Iraq, to the extent of introducing sophisticated tactical anti-ballistic missile systems in the (not wholly successful) endeavour to defeat Iraq's sole means of striking at surrounding states.[22] Opinion remains divided on whether the Gulf War demonstrated a 'New World Order' and whether it was justified. The point here is that the case of the Gulf War confirms, rather than refutes, the existence of the kinds of constraints on the use of force imposed on liberal democratic political systems outlined above.

All this suggests that the neorealist approach underestimates the potential for international co-operation to resolve the new security dilemmas and that co-operative collective security regimes can be established to incorporate newly emerging international norms, a commonality of values among new and old democracies, as well as increasing functional interdependence.

The new range of threats to international security

If the preceding analysis is correct, then it follows that the threats to European security are not a consequence of the characteristics of the new system of states, which requires the formation of new alliances and a new balance of power. Instead, we are confronted with problems which arise out of the specific conditions of the collapse of a political and economic system. The following areas of potential concern can be identified.

The first is a resurgence of conflict with post-Communist states, in particular Russia. The problem here is that the transition to a liberal democracy and a successful market economy is far from complete in the states on the territory of the former Soviet Union. Indeed, as far as Russia is concerned, with the loss of power of the CPSU and the disintegration of the union Russia became a territory that lacked many fundamental institutions of state and the process of state-building is still on-going, without any certainty as to its end.[23] The endeavour to construct institutions of government that allow political decisions to be reached and implemented without recourse to the instruments of coercion of an authoritarian state has so far been largely unsuccessful. Although there can be no return to the cold war that existed in Communist times, Eastern Europe remains an area of concern, especially while the transition to a liberal democracy in the Eastern European countries, and especially those of the former Soviet Union, is not complete.

There are a range of potential dangers. However, first of all it is important to stress that a reemergence of the old confrontation in Central Europe is now unthinkable. The reemergence of the kind of military threat Western Europe faced during the cold war is a remote contingency. Russia will not pose a direct conventional military threat to the West for the medium term at least.[24] What has to be taken more seriously is the attempt to reestablish an authoritarian regime along nationalist and anti-Western lines. Fortunately this is not a very likely development; the Russian Federation is too fragmented for an authoritarian regime to be able to establish itself easily. Also Russia's dependence on the international economy puts strict limits on anti-Western policies. Indeed, the history of the last six years has shown that while anti-Western rhetoric is often part of the Russian domestic debate and the occasional anti-Western political gesture is made, in the end a pro-Western line and adherence to international regimes prevails. A good example of this are debates over NATO enlargement, which were fiercely and bitterly resisted by Russia, accompanied by a whole plethora of threats resulting in eventual acquiescence. The conflict in Kosovo initially led to a breakdown in relations with Russia, which were at least partially restored very quickly after the end of the conflict. The year 1999 saw the unfortunate juxtaposition of the Kosovo crisis and the renewed attempt by Russia to bring the Chechen republic under control. By the end of the Yeltsin presidency US–Russian relations were at a low point, but nevertheless the Putin government was giving clear indications that it wanted to resume relations with the West on a co-operative basis.

The opposite possibility would be the further disintegration of Russia and the Balkanization of the former Soviet Union; many of the current trends point in this direction and the on-going Chechnya crisis could be seen as the first stage.[25] The NATO Alliance might come under very considerable pressure to provide security guarantees to the countries of Central Europe and the Baltic states at least. Although such a development will threaten current NATO members directly only if control over nuclear weapons was lost, the threat to the entire region would be of such a scale that the indirect effects on the West would be very substantial. Certainly neighbouring countries could be drawn in, resulting in the destabilization of much of the southern periphery of the former Soviet Union. It is clear that it must be the highest policy priority for Western Europe to prevent such an outcome.

A critical element in all this is the collapse of the former Communist economies. The transition from a stagnating command economy to a market economy has created conditions of severe economic dislocation in parts of Eastern Europe and the former Soviet Union which threaten societal stability. The financial collapse in Russia in 1998 was a stark reminder of the fragility of the transition economies. From the perspective of the West, therefore, the principal security problem is no longer perceived as stemming from the threat of military invasion, but the consequences of ethnic implosions and economic chaos in Eastern and Central Europe. Mass migrations from Eastern and Southern Europe as a result of political upheavals and economic deprivation could have serious repercussions on the economy and social cohesion of Germany and other West European countries.

Recreating a military balance of power in Europe?

The build-up of substantial conventional forces to create a military balance of power within Europe is not in the interests of future European security. First of all, it would not be required in terms of the military security of NATO Allies. One of the reasons why NATO members were initially reluctant to extend full membership to Central European countries is precisely that it was not perceived as enhancing the security of the Alliance as currently constituted, and only when it was judged that the *political* benefits for systemic stability in the region outweighed other considerations was NATO enlargement embarked upon. Second, it would reintroduce security dilemmas in the region. The recreation of a military confrontation at the Russian border would not enhance the security of East European countries; quite the reverse would be the case. Moreover this would destroy the CFE Treaty, which is in principle capable of preventing local arms races in Central and Eastern Europe and particularly constrains Russian military deployments west of the Urals. It is in the security interests of all European countries that this regime remains in place and that Russia remains an adherent to it.[26]

Critics of NATO enlargement have argued that however it is dressed up, NATO enlargement is a move towards reestablishing a new military balance of power in Europe. There is no question that this process is ambiguous. It extends a security guarantee to the new members which involves a commitment to use nuclear weapons in their defence if necessary. In order to dispel the impression that this process constitutes that creation of a new system of collective defence directed against the countries of the former Soviet Union, NATO has made a number of commitments. The first is that the actual balance of forces in the Central European region will not be altered. NATO will not forward deploy troops (except small numbers of military personnel to enable the co-operation of armed forces) and, most importantly, will not base nuclear weapons on the territory of the new members. The CFE agreement will remain intact and NATO members will observe its provisions. Thus in terms of the forces on the ground there will be no significant change. The second is that there will be extensive military co-operation between NATO and East European countries through the Partnership for Peace programme. The third is the Russia–NATO Founding Act (and a similar agreement with Ukraine) that establishes a permanent framework for consultation and co-operation with Russia, thus extending a form of close co-operation to Russia which gives Russia a voice (but not a veto) in NATO affairs.[27] The attempts to avoid the creation of a new divide in Europe through NATO enlargement have so far been successful and have survived even the stresses imposed by the NATO intervention in Kosovo.

There remains the issue of the use of military force in crisis regions in Europe, that is in the former Soviet Union and the former Yugoslavia. As far as the latter is concerned, the reluctance by leading members of NATO to assume a peacemaking role did much to discredit the idea of collective security.[28] The reluctance of Western European states to get involved in anything other than peacekeeping and humanitarian actions is a consequence of the perceived difficulty of legitimizing such potentially costly and controversial actions at home and of the fact that at present West European and US security interests are not directly affected. The Dayton Agreement which ended the war in Bosnia marked a turning-point, insofar as severe political pressure backed up by the threat of the use of military force was applied and NATO put forces on the ground to support the implementation of the agreement.[29] The Kosovo crisis and the NATO campaign against Serbian policy in Kosovo is a dramatic turning point in the development of the post-cold war security system in

Europe, given that NATO used substantial force to bring about a resolution. For the first time since the Second World War German armed forces were involved in active combat missions. However even in this case the constraints placed on NATO (such as the unwillingness to engage in ground operations) were a major factor and resulted in much criticism. Whether it will result in the both the legitimization and the practical establishment of effective collective security in Europe remains to be seen.

The principal point to be made here is that in the German view the use of the military instrument in Europe should in future be strictly limited to crisis management sanctioned by international institutions. In this way military confrontations between states should not arise. This will also affect the kinds of military instruments to be developed and deployed.

The argument can thus be made that end of the cold war is something more fundamental than a shift in the balance of power. It constitutes a change in the nature of international relations. The purpose of Western security policy must be to prevent a return to an international system dominated by the military factor. The only alternative is a political order based on international norms and institutions which provide a framework of collective security and economic co-operation. This is why the failure of Western policy in former Yugoslavia, even though it may not touch vital Western concerns directly, is potentially dangerous.

Conclusion: Germany's security challenges after the cold war

It is a striking feature of the security policies of Western countries that whereas during the cold war period they were defined on the basis of a specific substantial military threat, with forces deployed and configured to meet this threat, this is no longer the case now. Very soon after unification a consensus emerged that Germany was no longer facing a serious military threat. As former defence minister Volker Rühe has stated quite categorically, there is 'no enemy' as such any longer.[30] A book length study by a German military officer on the role and tasks of the German armed forces published in 1997 makes no reference to a military threat to national security, but discusses a range of diffuse 'Challenges and Interests'.[31] The concept of national security was broadened to include non-military issues that may threaten German society as the purely military threats diminished. The potential security threats to Germany arise as a consequence of ethnic implosions and economic chaos in Eastern and Central Europe.

Mass migrations from Eastern and Southern Europe as a result of political upheavals and economic deprivation could have serious repercussions on the German economy and social cohesion if Germany proves unable to control its borders. Here Germany saw itself once more on the frontline, because of its geographical proximity, the peculiarities of the legislation governing political asylum, high standard of living and generous social service provisions, Germany became the principal destination for immigrants from the East.[32] By 1995, the foreign population in Germany amounted to 8.8 per cent of the total, with the majority of the asylum seekers being located in East Germany. An unprecedented wave of violent incidents directed against foreigners raised questions about social stability in Germany, as it was trying to come to terms with unification and all the associated issues of national identity that this raised, especially for the Germans in the Eastern part. The potential for mass migrations from Eastern Europe and the former Soviet Union has so far not been realized, and there are good arguments to say that the worst case scenarios are highly improbable.[33] Nevertheless there is no question that this issue was at the top of the agenda of Germany's concerns with regard to national security.

There was also a recognition of the danger that Germany could be drawn into civil wars in Eastern and Southern Europe, either as mediators, as part of a collective Western response, or to protect a threatened German minority. Indeed, this is what did in fact happen in the case of the conflict in Kosovo. While the Kosovo conflict did not directly threaten German security, it presented the possibility that Germany would have to become involved in actual military operations which exercised the German political establishment.[34]

The proliferation of terrorist groups operating in Germany and organized crime moving in from Eastern Europe is also an increasingly significant issue. The devastation of the environment in the countries of Central and Eastern Europe and the former Soviet Union is another non-military security issue, with the fate of nuclear power stations of Soviet design and nuclear weapons on the territory of the former Soviet Union as the most acute cases.[35]

The German government was perhaps the most supportive of all Western governments of the general ideals of a New World Order, although due to the sensitivity of this issue in Germany the collective enforcement of international law was not given so much emphasis. The neorealist approach, despite having adherents among parts of the CDU (Christlich Demokratische Union)/CSU (Christlich Soziale Union) and more conservative academics, did not sit well with the general consensus on multilateralism and institutionalism that had become entrenched in German foreign policy in the last two decades of the cold war.[36] Overcoming the division of Europe through international regimes (detente and arms control) and institutions (CSCE, NATO, the European Community) had become central to the foreign policy of the Federal Republic. The end of the cold war served to strengthen this consensus in a number of ways. In the first place, the strategic changes in Europe and the peaceful manner in which they came about could be easily interpreted as a triumph of this approach. If the strategic confrontation with the Soviet Union could be resolved in this way, then anything seemed possible. The successful integration of Western Europe through the European Community pointed in the same direction. As we discussed above, there was a widespread perception that the end of the military confrontation in Europe marked a deeper shift in the international system, from a competing to a shared sense of values, and from military force as the determinant of international relations to the international economy. What Hanns W. Maull has called 'the obsession with stability and peaceful change'[37] was confirmed by the peaceful end of the cold war and German unification. The preservation of stability through collective security in Europe therefore assumed a central place in German foreign policy regarding the post-cold war order. Another element of the German foreign policy consensus was the commitment to democratic values, self-determination, nonviolence and human rights. Again international organizations were considered an important instrument for pursuing this commitment on a pan-European or even a global scale.

The optimism of the immediate period following the collapse of the Berlin wall was rudely shattered by the Gulf Conflict in 1990/91 which proved stubbornly and dangerously impervious to political instruments alone. Even worse were the conflicts in the former Yugoslavia and the former Soviet Union which, as has been discussed above, brutally exposed the inadequacies of European collective security arrangements and raised profound questions about the very concepts underlying them. These were of particular relevance to Germany since they raised the uncomfortable issue of a German role in the use of force to deal with instability and armed conflicts in Europe and beyond. As a consequence, the confidence in pan-European collective security and a New World Order declined even in Germany.[38] This does not mean that German policymakers will ultimately fall back on a neorealist analysis based on the balance of power. The commitment both to liberal democratic values and multilateralism politically is too deeply embedded in Germany.

A higher degree of institutionalization of the relationship of strategic co-operation, and the more Russia and other states from Eastern Europe can get locked into a system of collective security involving international institutions, norms and instruments of enforcement of human rights and international law, the greater the likelihood that the resurgence of fundamentally antagonistic relations based on a military confrontation could be prevented. A successful political and economic partnership with the West is the best hope of preventing the resurgence of authoritarian and nationalist regimes, or the descent in to chaos. In Germany, these concerns have had particular impact. There is no question that Germany has sought to project economic power in order to achieve a peaceful transition to a new European order and address the new security risks it has perceived. The whole structure of the 'two-plus-four agreements' on the external aspects of German unification, for example, can be interpreted as trading military for economic security.[39] In 1991, Germany accounted for over 56 per cent of financial aid to the Soviet Union and 32 per cent of aid to the rest of Eastern Europe.[40] This can be explained by the recognition that the economic stability of Eastern Europe and the former Soviet Union is of fundamental significance to German security. The geographical proximity and existing economic relations put Germany into a leading position to supply the emerging East European markets. But Germany is now facing substantial economic difficulties as a result of unification which will limit its capabilities to use economic power for political purposes and led former foreign minister Kinkel to look for burdensharing in supporting the restructuring of the Eastern European economies. Other West European economies are also experiencing great difficulties, however. Thus the constraints of domestic economies will limit the extent to which Western Europe can engage in direct financial assistance as an instrument to prevent economic and societal collapse in Central and Eastern Europe. German policymakers continue to believe that economic assistance and co-operation is an essential, if not sufficient, element in the economic recovery of Central and Eastern Europe, including the former Soviet Union, and thus a crucial nonmilitary instrument of West European security policy.

It would be fair to say that German policymakers share the view that after the cold war the nonmilitary aspects of security are likely to assume much greater importance. There are two key aspects to this. First of all, the instruments of foreign policy and power projection have changed. Economic power has become the key to political influence in the restructuring of international relations. The second aspect is that the threats to *societal security* are primarily nonmilitary, resulting from economic dislocation, ethnic rivalries and, as a consequence, large migratory movements. This has important implications for Western Europe. It has to face a new role arising from the fact that Eastern Europe sees it as the source of its future economic security. At the same time, it is facing new sources of insecurity, which question the existing political philosophy based on the ideas of tolerance, human rights, social justice and the welfare state and require new and politically unpalatable means to deal with them.

The international system in the early post-cold war era therefore faces the enormous paradox that while, on the one hand virtually all the states in the region have abandoned older forms of international conduct in which military force played a dominant role, at the same time the transition of the European system of states requires a system of collective security with effective military instruments to enforce and keep the peace. This is what we might term *the central dilemma of European security*. The problem results from the fact that while a value-free commitment to balance of power politics is deemed unacceptable, there is neither the intellectual analysis nor the political commitment to build effective structures of collective security in Europe, either in Germany or in its partner countries. As long as this is the case, the countries of Europe, and Germany in particular, are helpless as new conflicts erupt, and remain unable to take the necessary steps that it takes to ensure effective conflict prevention and management. This the real challenge for German security policy after the cold war.

3
Defence Policy in Transition

Among the changes in Germany's position as a result of the end of the cold war, the role and the use of power in the international system is one that the Germans find very difficult to come to terms with, since the exercise of such power was politically and morally restrained as a consequence of the Second World War. This applies in particular to the use of force. West Germans born after the war without the direct sense of a military threat to West German security arising from the experience of the Berlin air-lift, the division of Germany, the crushing of the uprising in East Germany, the erection of the Berlin wall, that is the development of the cold war in Central Europe where Germany was on the frontline, were socialized in a different manner from the older generation. Their parents which experienced the formation of the Federal Republic whose political culture developed on a foundation of the rejection of Nazism and the rehabilitation of West Germany in the international world, the rebuilding of the shattered German economy on the basis of high German productivity and generous American aid (Marshall Plan) and the reliance on an American security. The United States thus was seen both as the protector of West Germany as well as the model for democratic values. Part of the process of international rehabilitation was the profound rejection of militarism. The Bundeswehr was developed as a force whose sole purpose it was to make sure that it would never be used.[1]

The requirements of the new international situation have given rise to a wide debate in Germany about these issues. During the cold war the perceived external threat provided the rationale for West Germany's defence policy and served to define the parameters of force planning. What are the requirements for defence in an era where Germany is facing no military threats?

At one end of the spectrum is the view that Germany has now been rehabilitated in the international community; it must become a 'normal' state. Furthermore, in view of its economic and military resources and its location in the centre of Europe, Germany has to play a leading role in Europe, East and West. Its economic and political weight means that Germany will have to assume greater international responsibilities. This includes international security. Germany has to come to terms with the fact that it is a major medium-range power. For Germany to assume its responsibilities in the international arena will require the use of influence and power, including, if necessary, military force, although the use of force is envisaged not as a tool of power politics, but rather as a contribution to peacekeeping and intervention in conflicts in Europe. This view has been articulated by some prominent academics such as Michael Stürmer, the former Director of Stiftung Wissenschaft und Politik, and Hans-Peter Schwarz from the University of Bonn,[2] and it was widely shared among the political élite in charge during the early post-cold war years, especially those close to the government. Former Chancellor Kohl, President Herzog and former defence minister Rühe all made explicit statements along those lines.[3]

Quite a different perspective is based on the definition of Germany as a 'civilian power'.[4] The implication is that Germany, like Japan, has a unique experience as an economically successful state, rehabilitated from its former aggressive nationalism. During the rehabilitation period it was constrained in its foreign policy and thereby forced to adopt instruments of foreign policy that did not involve military force or the exercise of power. Germany should continue to play the role of a 'civilian power', based on the reality of international interdependence, with a strong emphasis on multilateral security arrangements and settlement of conflicts by negotiations. It should continue to rely on political and economic instruments as a way of conducting foreign policy.[5] This notion, with the implication that Germany should abstain from military action abroad, was adopted by many on the left of the political spectrum, including the 'realist' branch of the Green Party.[6]

Much of this debate focused rather narrowly on the question of whether Bundeswehr can be used in combat missions outside the NATO treaty area. It is therefore necessary to look in some detail at this debate and its outcome so far.

The Bundeswehr out-of-area

As a result of the catastrophic consequences of German militarism in the first half of the 20th century, those who framed the constitution of the FRG (the Basic Law) sought to restrict the role of the armed forces to defensive purposes by the maintenance of strict civilian control and thus prevent the armed forces from ever again becoming the instrument (or instigator) of territorial or hegemonic ambitions.

In the early decades of the cold war era, such constraints conformed to the interests of the Western Allies in containing Germany while involving it fully in the defence of Western Europe. The Carter doctrine of 1980 established a link between the stability of the Persian Gulf region and the security of Western Europe and Japan. The Reagan administration developed a global strategic concept for the confrontation with the Soviet Union. One of its central elements was the development of capabilities to resist Soviet expansionism in every part of the world and to assert American and Western vital interests by military means. The creation of a *Rapid Deployment Force* for intervention in areas of crisis, in particular the Persian Gulf, was part of the implementation of this strategy. The Reagan administration also put much stress on involving the European Allies in sharing its global responsibilities. As a result, the Federal Government led by then Chancellor Helmut Schmidt conducted a review of the German position with regard to the new strategy and in particular out-of-area involvements. In this context, an interministerial working group undertook an analysis of the legal position. It concluded:

- the basic law permits the use of the Bundeswehr abroad, outside the context of joint NATO operations, if there is an armed attack against the Federal Republic of Germany on the basis of the right of self-defence under Article 51 of the UN Charter.
- the basic law also permits military action in self-defence and the fulfilment of obligations under the WEU and NATO treaties.
- the basic law does not allow any military action solely for the purpose of safe-guarding economic interests.

The participation in UN operations in the Persian Gulf was ambiguously described as 'not covered' by the constitution. Even with regard to UN peacekeeping missions the paper merely recorded differing views in the various ministries. The internal review was concluded in November 1982, during the first months of the Kohl government. The official policy emphasized two areas in which the Federal Government would support allied forces engaged in missions out-of-area:

- support for the Allies directly involved. This support would take the form of providing sea and air transport, granting basing rights in West Germany and the support of NATO infrastructure programmes.
- economic and political support for states in the Gulf region as required to maintain their stability.[7]

At the same time, the participation in military operations out-of-area by the Bundeswehr was completely excluded, on the basis that the basic law prohibits Bundeswehr operations outside the NATO treaty area, unless it is in response to a direct attack against the FRG.

During the 1980s there were two specific occasions when the Federal Government had to respond to requests for assistance in out-of-area missions. In June 1985, after it was suspected that the Libyans or associated terrorist commandos had sown mines in the Red Sea, minesweeping operations were conducted by the United States. The Federal Government refused to participate. In the summer of 1987, when large-scale minesweeping operations became necessary to clear the Persian Gulf at the height of the war between Iran and Iraq, the West Germans once again refused any involvement. This time, however, a public debate ensued in which prominent politicians, such as the leader of the CSU, Franz-Josef Strauß, and Chancellor Kohl's foreign policy adviser, Horst Teltschik, raised the question as to whether the interpretation of the basic law on which the existing policy was based was correct, and whether the FRG could continue to avoid taking on international responsibilities.

These issues confronted the German public and political élite much more sharply during the Gulf conflict of 1990/91. Many of the current questions about the nature of the New World Order that seemed to be emerging in the first half of 1990 with the reunification of Germany, the end of the cold war and the implications of full sovereignty for Germany's role in the international systems were brought into focus. It is therefore useful to consider the German response to the Gulf crisis in some detail.

The Gulf crisis which coincided with the shift to the right in the Soviet Union had a traumatic effect on Germany. The new era of peace and co-operation seemed to end as quickly as it had emerged.

The crisis came at a time when Germany had not yet come to a clear view of its new national interests. This contributed to the great difficulties of the Kohl administration, which was still largely preoccupied with the enormous economic and political consequences of reunification, to arrive at a coherent response. The degree to which the end of the cold war had substantiated the conviction that even the most protracted political problems were capable of peaceful and negotiated resolution contributed to the inability of the German policymaking establishment to read correctly the developments in the Gulf crisis. Until the very last moment both the Chancellor and the foreign minister were convinced that the outbreak of hostilities could be avoided. Consequently the Federal Government was surprised and politically wrong-footed by the beginning of Operation Desert Storm.

It was clear from the outset that Germany would not deploy troops in the Gulf. The policy laid down in 1982 was followed implicitly in this regard. The large demonstrations against the war however were an indication of the political pressures against any direct involvement. The maximum the Germans were willing to allow was the transfer of 18 Alpha Jets with 270 support personnel and the deployment of the Allied Mobile Force in the region (that is Turkey), as well as providing minesweeping support. The United States administration was not concerned about this and indeed did not expect direct German participation in either Operation Desert Shield or Operation Desert Storm.[8] It was not so much the lack of the physical presence of German troops on the ground generated public criticism, especially in the United States, but the unwillingness to share the political burdens and the responsibility that the United States and other members of the coalition undertook, in what was understood to be the common interest of the West; much was manifest in the debate as to whether an attack on Turkey would invoke the NATO commitment and the initial reluctance to make available equipment (ammunition, missiles, Patriot air defence systems).[9]

The policy of the Federal Government from the beginning of the crisis was that it had to be resolved by full implementation of the UN resolutions, which meant the total and unconditional withdrawal of Iraq from Kuwait.[10] Defence Minister Stoltenberg made it clear from early on that the constitutional restrictions would not allow participation of German forces in military operations in the Gulf, but members of the Federal Government reassured the United States and other Allies that the Federal Government would seek amendments to the Constitution at the earliest opportunity. In any other respect the government pledged its full support to the Allies. It provided air and naval transport at a cost of DM 400 million, made available equipment for the protection against chemical and biological weapons and sent a minesweeper to the Persian Gulf. As Knut Kirste has observed, the Federal Government was very uncertain about its role in the conflict. It assumed that its allies and neighbours expected a very low profile with regard to such an international crisis and was surprised that this turned out not to be the case.[11] In response it engaged in various efforts to reassure them that Germany was a dependable ally and that after the next elections in December 1990 the necessary constitutional changes could be achieved. Thus Chancellor Kohl lamented to US Secretary of State Baker in September that he was 'dismayed that we are not completely free to act in the community of nations in the way we would like to act.'[12]

In reality Bonn was using the constitutional issue as a way of deflecting allied expectations in view of the domestic political resistance it perceived in support of any direct participation. In September 1990 72 per cent of the German population supported the sending of US troops to the Gulf, but only 23 per cent expressed support for German participation, 42 per cent took the view that Germany should keep completely out of this conflict and only 28 per cent supported (Allied) military action if Saddam Hussein did not withdraw from Kuwait.[13] The Federal Government remained largely in the background, but nevertheless it was clear that Bonn was pushing for a diplomatic resolution. This was both an issue of principle and of possible repercussions for relations with the Soviet Union, thereby endangering the process of unification. Bonn was still very nervous about the withdrawal of Soviet troops.[14] German diplomacy was very active in international institutions, especially the European Political Cooperation and the WEU, contributing to various diplomatic initiatives. The United States feared that these activities would serve to undermine the resolve of the international community to stand up to Iraq and Kohl had to reassure Baker on this point. This effort was undermined by the visit of former Chancellor Willy Brandt to Iraq in order to obtain the release of hostages. Although the visit was not an initiative of the Federal Government, it had to support it, thereby violating the international consensus against any negotiations with Iraq on this issue. Moreover, the Bonn government became associated with efforts to promote diplomatic initiatives at a time when President Bush was seeking to prepare the international community for the likelihood of war. As a result deeper divisions about the strategy for dealing with the Iraq crisis became apparent.[15]

In the run-up to the Federal elections in December 1990 the Iraq issue had a high profile, with all parties portraying themselves as advocates of peace. Genscher pursued further diplomatic efforts. In January 1991 he strongly supported a diplomatic initiative by the European Community to achieve unconditional withdrawal from Kuwait. At a time when the US government had already decided to move ahead with the strike against Iraq Germany was still pleading for a peaceful resolution, thus putting both governments at odds and creating the impression that Bonn was pursuing a policy of appeasement. The lack of clarity at the official level gave the impression that Germany was principally against the use of force and thus created a moral distance with the other allies. While many German politicians responded to the outbreak of hostilities negatively, Foreign Minister Genscher maintained complete silence. However, in the course of the conflict German attitudes changed. Support for *Operation Desert Storm* reached a level of 75 per cent after Scud missiles had been launched against Israel.[16] The Federal Government provided critical logistical support and permitted Allies to use military bases and installations in German without restriction. Moreover, for the first time it broke its own guidelines against supplying weapons to third parties engaged in military conflict by delivering weapons and munitions to Israel. The public statements of the government remained very muted until it had gained some reassurance about the reactions of other countries, especially the Soviet Union, before taking a more forthright position on its involvement. Germany also provided substantial funds to support the Allied effort (DM 13.5 billion).[17]

The Gulf war raised a number of issues which had been a central preoccupation of adherents of the peace movement in Germany for some time:

- the resolution of conflicts by non-violent means (in this case sanctions)
- the dangers of weapons exports to the Third World (in this case German exports of missile and chemical weapons technology to Iraq)
- the dangers of Western dependence on oil
- the ecological catastrophes that might be caused by this war.

The result was a large popular response against the war without a clear focus or political base, given that party leaders across the political spectrum, including some prominent leaders of the Greens, supported the war or at least declined to oppose it outright. It also forced a debate about Germany's role in the international system, with which the government had to engage both at home and in the international arena during an election period, but for which it was not ready.

The Gulf crisis made manifest a whole range of political issues related to Germany's role in the new security political environment. Of particular significance is the opening up of the debate on the constitutional implications for the use of force, especially with regard to out-of-area commitments, and the resulting implications for future military planning. The lines of the debate were drawn along party lines. In the CDU/CSU there was a wide consensus that Germany should be prepared to become involved in a wide range of out-of-area operations in a strictly multilateral context (although such actions necessarily would not have to be covered by a UN mandate). There was also consensus in the CDU/CSU that a constitutional change is not required to permit such involvements. The FDP, the liberal partner of the CDU/CSU in the governing coalition, adopted the position that participation in 'out-of-area' missions should only be permitted within a United Nations framework. This could also involve combat missions carried out without direct UN control, but on the basis of UN Security Council resolutions, such as the Gulf War 1990/91. Hans-Dietrich Genscher reflected the dominant view in the FDP when he stated that a change in the Basic Law was necessary for this purpose.

Opposition to 'out-of-area' involvements by the Bundeswehr was very strong in the SPD. Although some leading SPD figures, such as Egon Bahr and Karsten Voigt advocated involvement in combat missions authorized by the United Nations security council, the party conference in Bremen in May 1991 would only go along with participation in UN peacekeeping operations (so-called 'blue helmet' missions). Further to the left of the political spectrum, the Greens/Alliance 90 and the PDS (the successor to the former East German Communist Party, SED) rejected any form of Bundeswehr operations out-of-area.

The pressures of external events and popular opinion moved this debate in conflicting directions. The reaction to the Gulf war indicated unmistakeably that the commitment of Bundeswehr troops to combat out-of-area politically would be extremely difficult to support.[18] These results are well in line with any other surveys that were conducted at the time. Accordingly, Defence Minister Volker Rühe developed a dual-track approach to deal with the legal and political obstacles. As far as the legal situation was concerned, Rühe promoted a change in the constitution to give any government a free hand to become involved in multilateral military operations out-of-area. Many conservative commentators, including most of the leading figures in the CDU/CSU, did not believe that such a change in the Basic Law was actually necessary. The principal restriction on military action is contained in Article 87 of the Basic Law: 'Except for defence armed forces may only be used as expressly permitted by the Basic Law.'[19] Article 26 also prohibits a war of aggression.[20] However, Article 24, paragraph 2 reads:

> To preserve the peace the Federal government can take part in a system of mutual collective security; it will agree in the process to such inroads into its sovereign rights as bring about and safeguard a peaceful and lasting order in Europe and between the nations of the world.[21]

Some, like the former defence minister and law professor Rupert Scholz, argued that Germany is not only permitted, but even required to support Allied and UN out-of-area operations with its own forces. In 1973 the FRG joined the United Nations Organization without any preconditions. This means that on the basis of Article 43 of the UN Charter the Security Council could require Germany to provide troops for measures to keep world peace and international security. It has also been argued that Article 87 was introduced into the Constitution in 1968 in connection with the legislation about 'states of emergency' and was not intended to prevent German involvement in military actions led by the Alliance, but rather restrict the use of the military in domestic conflicts.[22] One aspect of this issue which has so far received little public attention is that the constitutionality of 'out-of-area' operations is not a purely German domestic affair. Article 2 of the Soviet–German Treaty of 12 September 1990 contains the following commitment:

> The Governments of the Federal Republic of Germany and the German Democratic Republic declare that the united Germany

will never employ any of its weapons contrary to its constitution and the Charter of the United Nations.[23]

A gradual erosion of the constitutional restriction may therefore at some point result in the breach of an international treaty.

In view of this controversy, the Federal Government had three options. The first was to adopt the more liberal interpretation of the Basic Law and leave it up to the opposition to challenge any action in the Federal Constitutional Court. The second was to co-operate with the FDP and the SPD in changing the constitution to allow participation in UN 'blue helmet' missions. The third was to seek a sufficient political consensus between the parties to allow a broader change in the constitution. Some voices in the CDU/CSU supported the first option on grounds of principle. The reason was explained by Jürgen Rüttgers (CDU) in a paper on *Elements of a New Peace Order*:

> German and European security must not depend on the uncertain decision-making in the UN security council. Germany and the other countries of the EC cannot rely on the notion, that the USA or the UN would intervene in every European conflict outside the NATO area as ordering powers. The civil war and genocide in the former Yugoslavia demonstrates this without doubt. . . . A European Security Union must be capable of action – independent of any deadlock within the UN security council – if conflicts or wars threaten European security, without triggering the classic NATO or WEU treaty obligations.[24]

Certainly there is a broad consensus within the CDU/CSU that the government could not accept an amendment to the constitution which would limit German out-of-area involvement to United Nations peacekeeping or peace-making operations. Foreign Minister Kinkel stated his clear preference for the third option. He adamantly rejected a constitutional restriction to UN 'blue helmet' missions, but reflected the FDP consensus that the Basic Law had to be amended before any out-of-area involvements could take place.[25] Thus there was no unified approach to the issue in the government.[26]

The fundamental political dilemma was that any change in the Basic Law required a two-thirds majority in the *Bundestag* and therefore could not take place without support from the SPD. The SPD leadership on the other hand was unable to obtain internal party consensus on the kind of changes the CDU/CSU demands, even if they had been supported by the party leadership. The conflicts over this issue at the party-political level were a reflection of deeper uncertainties in the German population. Volker Rühe therefore embarked on a long-term strategy to resolve this problem politically. He started with a recognition of the anti-militaristic attitudes which have grown-up in the German population over the last 40 years which will not permit the involvement in out-of-area conflicts such as the Gulf War for some time to come. According to Rühe 'The instincts of people that have developed over 40 years cannot simply be ordered to disappear.'[27] Assuming greater international responsibility is, according to Rühe, an organic process which takes time. He emphasized that German participation in UN 'blue helmet' missions should however begin in the very near term. As a first step he announced the sending of a medical support unit in aid of UN troops in Cambodia. Rühe suggested a separation of the legal and political issues by proposing a change in the Basic Law to allow multilateral 'out-of-area' combat engagements by the *Bundeswehr*, accompanied by a political agreement among the main parties to limit such involvement to UN 'blue helmet' missions for a certain period of time.

The political impasse on this issue could not be resolved. However, there were some indications that popular opinion might change. The events in the former Yugoslavia and the perceived weakness of the Western response provoked wide-spread press comment about the untenability of Germany's position.[28] This was particularly the case given that the Germans had taken a particularly forthright line on the Balkan conflict, first by Genscher's insistence on the recognition of Croatia and Slovenia and subsequently by Kinkel's calls for actions against Serbia. The first out-of-area in which Bundeswehr personnel participated actively was the UNTAC mission in Cambodia in May 1992 where 140 soldiers took part in a UN peacekeeping mission. This action found broad support in the Bundestag. Things were different when Germany decided to send the destroyer *Bayern* to support the United Nations mandated sea and air forces deployed to enforce sanctions against Serbia (although the *Bayern* was not in fact permitted to engage in any hostile action). The decision was made as the result of an acrimonious debate in the Bundestag on 23 July 1992 in which the various positions were aired in some detail. Rühe defended the involvement of the federal navy as necessary, because Germany should not become incapable of pursuing a foreign policy and assume its responsibilities in Europe. He and Kinkel specifically excluded any direct involvement in the Yugoslav civil war. SPD Party Caucus chairman Hans-Ulrich Klose accused the government of sending soldiers on a mission the legality of which was unclear.[29] The SPD responded to the decision by instituting proceedings in the Federal Constitutional Court and formally filing an application for a change in the Constitution which would permit participation in UN peacekeeping operations only.[30] When surveillance of the embargo was stepped up to a blockade, the fissures in the Federal Government over this issue reopened. Kinkel tried to get the destroyer *Hamburg*, which by then had replaced the *Bayern*, withdrawn. This was successfully blocked by Defence Minister Rühe.[31]

Meanwhile the SPD leadership recognized, however, that its own position was not sustainable in the long term. At a meeting at Petersberg on 22/23 August 1992, where the party leadership sought to hammer out its new political programme, the then leader of the Party, Björn Engholm promoted the notion that German armed forces should be able to participate in combat operations under *United Nations command*. This was made conditional on a reform of the United Nations that would allow such operations under Article 43 of the UN Charter. On the assumption that such reforms would take a number of years, Engholm pledged that the party was prepared to decide on the participation of German forces in 'unforeseen conflicts'.[32] What line will ultimately prevail in the SPD remains to be seen. But it is interesting to observe that even the Greens were not immune from the effects of the suffering in Bosnia. Thus in an interview with *Spiegel*, billed as 'the end of pacifism', Helmut Lippelt, member of the Federal Committee of the Greens, accepted the need for protecting aid transports with military force and liberating the 'camps of hunger', having seen the results of 'ethnic cleansing' for himself.[33] While not representing official policy, Lippelt's comments were an indication of how the pressure of external events influenced the debate and shifted established political boundaries.

The approach which was finally adopted by the Federal Government consisted in the gradual extension of the government's freedom of action until stopped by the Federal Constitutional Court. Thus Chancellor Kohl announced the decision on 17 December 1992 to send 1500 German troops to Somalia to assist in a humanitarian mission after the arrival of US troops. The *Bundeswehr* soldiers were be armed to defend themselves against attack. Kohl also stated that the German air force may participate in the enforcement of the no-fly zone over Bosnia, but emphasized no German ground forces would be deployed in the former Yugoslavia. The German air force personnel involved in policing the no-fly zone were in AWACS aircraft which guided fighter planes towards any moving object that violated the non-fly zone. This was considered by many in the Bundestag as a combat mission, requiring an amendment to the consitution. The FDP ministers voted against the Cabinet decision on 2 April 1992 and later the FDP brought a case before the Constitutional Court against the government of which it was a part. In this it was supported by the SPD.[34] The CDU/CSU strategy proved successful, insofar as the Constitutional Court at first refused to grant temporary injunctions against the government's actions and decided that the Federal Government had the right to deploy German air force personnel to support the implementation of the UN Security Council Resolution 816. The SPD subsequently went to the Constitutional Court again over the decision by the government to send troops to Somalia in support of a peace-enforcement operation called 'Restore Hope'. This operation was based on the establishment of a Unified Task Force (UNITAF) under US command. In response to a request by UN Secretary General Boutros Boutros-Ghali, based on UN Security Council Resolution 814, for troops to support the United Nations in Somalia (UNOSOM), the German government decided to contribute 1640 men for logistics, transport and engineering. The failure of this mission, which raised serious questions about UN peace-enforcement operations, did not have any significant impact on the debate in Germany. At this stage the Constitutional Court was the focus of the debate and it finally ruled in July 1994 that participation in operations outside the NATO area under a UN mandate were not a violation of the Basic Law and could be approved by a simple majority of the Bundestag.[35]

In the proceedings on the dispute over the deployment of German armed forces the Federal Constitutional Court (Second Panel) has ruled that the Federal Republic of Germany is at liberty to assign German armed forces in operations mounted by the North Atlantic Treaty Organization (NATO) and Western European (WEU) to implement resolutions of the Security Council of the United Nations (UN). The same applies to the assignment of German contingents to peacekeeping forces of the UN.

... The Court also finds that, however, after thoroughly analysing the provisions of the Basic Law relating to the status of the armed forces in the constitutional system, that the Federal Government is required to obtain the Bundestag's explicit approval for each deployment of German armed forces. Such approval must in principle be obtained prior to their deployment, The Bundestag must decide on the deployment with a simple majority.[36]

Contrary to perceptions outside Germany, this did not resolve the issue politically even if the Basic Law could no longer be used as an instrument in the debate. Opinion surveys still indicated deep-seated reluctance for German involvement in military actions. A RAND survey indicated wide support for NATO's involvement in crises on Europe's periphery (74 per cent). At the same time, 55 per cent of those polled agreed that Germany's allies should assume responsibility for such missions and that the role of the *Bundeswehr* should be restricted to territorial defence.[37] A poll by Infratest Burke Berlin conducted in October 1994 indicated a high level of support (up to 75 per cent) for the use of military force in humanitarian and peacekeeping operations. When asked about specific scenarios involving combat actions, a strong aversion to military action became evident.[38] The perception persisted that it would be difficult to obtain domestic political support for military operations.

The Federal Government was soon confronted with further external pressure on this issue when on 30 November the Supreme Allied Commander Europe (SACEUR) General George Joulwan asked Germany to provide six ECR *Tornado* fighter bombers to support NATO operations in the event of a withdrawal of UN peacekeeping forces (UNPROFOR) from Bosnia. On 8 December 1994 there was another request from General Joulwan regarding Bonn's contribution in the event that NATO was asked by the UN to protect the withdrawal of UNPROFOR troops. The political reaction in Bonn revealed quite clearly that the decision of the Constitutional Court had changed the terms of the debate, but not the substance, and that arguments for restraint were now based on political, rather than legal, criteria. The government responded that it would provide logistical assistance and air cover, but that no German ground troops would be deployed in the event of a complete withdrawal of UNPROFOR from Bosnia.[39] This policy came under pressure from the left, which opposed even the limited involvement promised by Bonn, and from the Allies, as events in Bosnia deteriorated and the withdrawal appeared to become a likely contingency.[40] Fortunately for the Federal Government, they were never put to the test, even though the Bundestag did in the end approve the deployment of the Tornado and support forces for the rapid reaction force in Bosnia.[41] The Dayton Agreement provided a safer context for Germany to prove that it was a reliable ally. It provided 4000 troops for the Implementation Force (IFOR), but only in support roles such as transport, medical and logistical specialists, as well as Tornado fighter bombers, in a context where direct engagement seemed unlikely.[42]

The other external challenge to German policy after the court decision came in the form of UN requests for participation in peacekeeping missions. A split developed between Minister of Foreign Affairs Kinkel and Defence Minister Rühe about the scope of out-of-area involvements. Kinkel wanted to support Germany's claim for a permanent seat on the UN Security Council with the willingness to participate in peacekeeping operations all around the globe. Rühe sought to limit involvements to Europe or areas close to Europe and was adamantly opposed to assign German peacekeeping forces to NATO for use at the discretion of the Security Council. Rühe outlined the following criteria for the employment of German peacekeeping forces:

- military actions should be confined to Europe and its periphery
- actions can take place only on the basis of a UN mandate and in conjunction with other allies
- special care needs to be taken regarding territories which were occupied by German during the Second World War
- the involvement of German forces must have broad public support in the Federal Republic
- there must be a clear threat to international peace, stability in Europe or Germany's security.[43]

The extent to which Germany will participate in UN peacekeeping missions thus remains unresolved. It is unlikely that this will satisfy Germany's partners for long, but it also remains unclear as to how this is going to be resolved, and how and when Germany is going to take a significant step towards taking on what its partners and allies consider its international responsibilities.

The debate which is ultimately about the redefinition of Germany's national interests and role in the international system focused narrowly on legal issues for a number of years. Now that the legal issues have been resolved, the political questions have come to the fore. It is evident that official statements to the contrary notwithstanding Germany's participation in the United Nations, NATO and European organizations will remain circumscribed for the time being. This is even more likely to remain the case since the centre-right coalition led by Chancellor Kohl lost the Federal Elections in September 1998 and a SPD/Green coalition came to power with Gerhard Schröder as Chancellor. As we have already pointed out, the future military tasks of the Alliance will most likely be outside the traditional treaty area. The Eurocorps founded by Germany and France is designed to be used under the direction of NATO or WEU; in either case however out-of-area contingencies are the most likely. The current situation means that the Eurocorps is in practice unavailable for European crisis management tasks. However, other European states will become increasingly intolerant of a German *Sonderweg* which consists of a politically leading role in the reshaping of the European security environment with all the dilemmas and crises that face us, while refusing to accept the associated military risks. Thus Germany will find it is unable to play a full leading part in the emerging security architecture in Europe until it has resolved the political and legal issues with regard to the role of its own armed forces.[44]

The new government with Foreign Minister Joschka Fischer (Greens/Alliance90) and Defence Minister Rudolf Scharping (SPD) emphasized the continuity of German foreign and security policy, German commitments to NATO and German involvement in peacekeeping and even peace-making operations.[45] However, one important new emphasis was on the role of the United Nations. The SPD and the Alliance90/Greens agreed on a formulation to the effect that the UN should have the monopoly on the use of violence in international affairs, just like a government has in domestic affairs. In other words, any use of force has to be in accordance with international law, and must be sanctioned by the United Nations.[46]

In this context the establishment of mechanisms to 'civilize' international politics were announced as a central goal of German foreign policy. That the Alliance90/Greens were uneasy about the use of force did manifest itself quite clearly. Thus they called for cuts in the Bundeswehr to a level of 200 000 and the abolition of so-called Crisis Intervention Forces, demands which were rejected by the SPD. The first major test for the new coalition was a Bundestag vote on a decision to send troops to Kosovo, an issue inherited from the previous government. In the event the Bundestag did agree to send

350 personnel from the armed forces to Macedonia with the task to support NATO's surveillance of the implementation of the Kosovo agreement by the use of unmanned observation drones.[47] While the new coalition government surmounted this hurdle, the first real test was yet to come. When the Kosovo situation finally reached an impasse NATO began to implement its threat of air strikes, German participated with 14 Tornado strike aircraft (including four electronic reconnaissance planes). For the first time since the Second World War, Germany's armed forces were engaged in military combat actions without equivocation. German troops subsequently joined KFOR, the peacekeeping force that was deployed in Kosovo after the Serb withdrawal.

The German involvement in the Kosovo conflict is discussed in more detail in Chapter 4. The important point to note here is that the coalition survived the severe stresses of German participation in the NATO force intact. More importantly, the German population supported it. This means that Germany has come a long way towards being a full partner in out-of-area operations of the Alliance. But one should strike a cautionary note. Throughout the crisis there was a consensus right across the political spectrum that a ground war in Kosovo would be unacceptable. Conservative spokesmen, including the previous Defence Minister Volker Rühe, Greens and even Chancellor Schröder himself declared their opposition to ground operations. Indeed the German role in the military operations was so limited that it could almost be called token. There may be further tests ahead of the German willingness to risk the lives of German soldiers in the name of peace and security.

The future of the Bundeswehr

When considering the role of military force as an instrument of foreign policy, it is necessary to think about the military resources. The armed forces of the Federal Republic of Germany are substantial. But like the political system, the armed forces have had to undergo a painful process of adaptation to the new environment, which is not yet complete. The armed forces of the united Germany are subject to a long-term reduction programme agreed by treaty (the 'two-plus-four agreement'). On 18 February 1992 the government approved a statement by the Ministry on Defence on the future tasks of the Bundeswehr which incorporated the following elements:
- to protect the national territory of Germany and its citizens against

external aggression or the threat of aggression (in co-operation
with Allied forces)
- to enable Germany to participate in the Alliance and international
politics by providing appropriate military instruments
- to contribute to pan-European stability by the maintenance of a
security political balance, closer co-operation within the Alliance
and close co-operation with all European partners
- to take part in collective operations outside the NATO treaty
area within the framework of the Charter of the United Nations.[48]

Within this framework, a substantial restructuring of the Bundeswehr
had to be undertaken in order to fulfil the following objectives:
- the absorption of the East German army (NVA) and the effective
extension of the Bundeswehr to the territory of the former GDR
- adaption to the new strategic situation. This implies reduction
to an overall force level of 370 000, and the adoption of the
new NATO strategy based on greater flexibility and mobility, including the creation of rapid reaction forces.
- operate within a declining defence budget.

Although Germany has substantial military forces, these were
designed to counter a massive land offensive in Central Europe.
The Bundeswehr was built up as a deterrent force on the assumption that it would never have to be used. It is largely a conscript
army. No effective crisis intervention force can be created by the
German armed forces that does not include conscripts. This creates
the following problems:
- the ethos of the Bundeswehr has to undergo a profound change.
The current generation was still brought up to believe that Germany
would never be involved in war again.
- it is a generally accepted principle that conscripts cannot be used
in combat actions, unless they volunteer for it.
- the *right for conscripts to refuse combat duty* is deeply enshrined
in Germany. Soldiers can refuse right up to the last moment to
take part in combat.
- as Germany has had to drastically reduce the level of its armed
forces because of the Soviet–German agreements in 1990, the
conscription period has been reduced. This means that *conscripts
may be inadequately trained* for serious combat.
- civil conflicts abroad raise complex political issues. It may be
hard to explain to the troops who the 'enemy' is and why German
forces are involved. This will create problems of morale and
motivation.

For Germans brought up with an antipathy to militarism these may be especially hard to address. Political controversy about the involvement at home will exacerbate such problems.

One possible way to resolve these problems is to abolish conscription and create a professional army. This is resisted by politicians. Ever since it was founded in 1955, the Bundeswehr has been primarily a conscript force. There are a number of reasons why the principle of universal conscription has been central to civil–military relations in the FRG, despite its unpopularity with the population. After the experience of two world wars, the creation of the armed forces ran counter to the instincts of the population and the political leaders. In order to prevent the emergence of the 'military' as an independent political force, it was decided to root the Bundeswehr firmly in society by means of conscription, thus keeping the professional element at a minimum. Moreover conscription creates a high degree of awareness in society of security and defence and emphasizes the common responsibility of all citizens for national defence.

This concept of civil–military relations accord to the values and norms of the democratic consitutional state and the principles of the armed forces are institutionalized in the principle called *Innere Führung*.[49] The main elements of *Innere Führung* are:

1 Education about the political and legal reasons for the armed forces and military service. In this way soldiers can appreciate the rationale for their mission and their service to society.
2 Internal discipline within the armed forces should be based on the values of the German legal and political system.
3 Personnel of the armed forces have responsibility for the freedom and human dignity of all citizens. Soldiers are politically educated and morally aware. The individual soldier has to accept the consequences of military actions he engages in.[50]

Although *Innere Führung* would not have to be abandoned entirely with the creation of a professional army, the perception in the German political and military élite is largely that the bond between the people and the armed forces will be weakened and that the perceived educational and socializing effects of military service will no longer be provided. Other arguments against the abolition of conscription are that a professional army is expensive, that conscription creates a pool of trained reserve personnel that can be rapidly mobilized in times of crisis and that the Bundeswehr has a very poor public image and it is therefore difficult to recruit professional soldiers. Presently there is a shortage of officers and it is feared that many professional soldiers find themselves socially alienated.

In the new environment, there are a number of difficulties associated with maintaining the principle of universal conscription. For this reason, a public debate about the future of the conscript army is now taking place. The principal problems are:

- conscription is not popular and the poor image of the Bundeswehr exists partly because of conscription. Moreover, after the cold war it is difficult to maintain the political case for the need of a large conscription army.
- there are demographic problems. The Bundeswehr began a process of a phased reduction, with a ceiling of 370 000 that was achieved by 1994. The population from which conscripts were to be drawn, however, increased from 60 million to about 80 million as a result of unification. This means that the principle of *Wehrgerechtigkeit* ('justice of the draft') is difficult to maintain. It was estimated in 1991 that only about 50 per cent of those conscripted actually complete the basic training. The *Independent Commission for the future tasks of the Bundeswehr* estimated that this would reduce to 40 per cent. This damages the already strained political credibility of military service in Germany.
- the current structure of the Bundeswehr makes the use of conscripts necessary for any out-of-area operations. This could constitute another powerful political barrier to out-of-area operations. It has therefore been proposed that conscripts should be sent out-of-area only on a voluntary basis.[51]

The reality of the contemporary international environment is that in the absence of the threat of large-scale war conscription is becoming unfashionable and unsustainable. The United Kingdom, the United States and, recently even France, have abolished conscription. It is clear that conscription is no longer sustainable even for Russia, where financial problems and a lack of will political does not address the problems of a deteriorating army and constitutes the main barrier for resolving this issue.[52]

The decision to maintain conscription was accompanied by a reduction in the period of the draft from 12 to 10 months and more relaxed attitude to conscientious objectors. Indeed, press comments suggested that it had become a matter of personal choice – whether to sign up for military service or the alternative service of the conscientious objectors.[53] Two important trends coincided. On the one hand, the reductions in the defence budget made it difficult even to maintain a force level of 370 000. In 1991 the defence budget was DM 53.6 billion; in 1996 it had been reduced to DM 47.1 billion. The 1998 defence budget was slightly lower still at DM 46.7 billion[54] and the size of the German armed forces had been reduced to 333 500. In July 1999 it was announced that the Bundeswehr would have to cut its expenditures by another DM 18 billion over the next four years.[55] The second trend was the increased number of conscientious objectors. In 1996 160 658 were granted exemption from the military service on the grounds of conscientious objection; the total number of conscripts serving in the armed forces was 137 500. Instead of a surplus of conscripts, the Bundeswehr is now confronted with a persistent shortage.[56] These trends, the requirements for out-of-area missions and the announcement by President Chirac that France will end conscription, has put renewed pressure on the Federal Government to follow suit. So far the hard decisions are still being postponed. Another consequence of the budgetary squeeze is that operational budgets are cut to a point where the capability of the Bundeswehr to carry out its task is put at risk. In other words, there is a widening gap between planning ambitions and actual operational capabilities.

In order to adapt for the new tasks, the Bundeswehr has recently established a crisis reaction force consisting of 50 000 troops that can be used for crisis management in conflicts out-of-area. It is claimed that all troops assigned to the crisis reaction force are professional soldiers or have volunteered. The entire force consists of the following elements:

Army
3 paratroop brigades
2 tank divisions
The Franco-German Brigade

Air Force
2 Tornado squadrons (electronic warfare and reconnaissance)
2 Tornado squadrons (fighter bombers)
2 F4F Phantom squadrons (fighter bombers)

Air Defence
6 Patriot batteries
4 Haw batteries
1 Roland battery

Navy
6 frigates/destroyers
15 minesweepers
13 speed boats
8 submarines
1 tanker/supply ship
6 submarine hunter killers
1 squadron of naval bombers

Although during the cold war Germany became the largest conventional military power in Western Europe, these capabilities were developed for high intensity warfare jointly with other NATO forces. The logistics were organized on the basis of stockpiles placed in Germany and rapid reinforcement capabilities from Britain and the United States. Among the now obvious gaps in intervention capability are:

- lack of strategic reconnaissance and command and control capability
- lack of air transport capability to move large numbers of forces rapidly into a crisis area
- lack of logistic support over long distances.

Thus at present Germany is able to play a support role, but not a leading role in conflict intervention. Such operations remain inconceivable without substantial involvement of the United States, which can provide the necessary airlift capabilities as well as satellite reconnaissance and communications. The Bundeswehr is seeking to redress this situation by the acquisition of a range of new equipment which includes:

- the future large aircraft to provide new transport capability
- a new support helicopter (to be built in co-operation France)
- satellite reconnaissance capability (possibly controlled by the WEU)
- a multi-role ship that can carry an entire battalion including heavy armour and helicopters
- various frigates, submarines and 15 Corvettes.

In the current political and economic climate it is unlikely that most of the equipment on the Bundeswehr shopping list actually will be funded.[57]

When the SPD/Greens–Alliance 90 coalition took office in 1998, future force planning was to be examined by a Defence Structure Commission. The Green Defence expert Angelika Beer demanded that the armed forces should be reduced to a level of 200 000. This has been adamantly rejected by Defence Minister Scharping, who stated that the Commission would not be a cover for decimating the armed forces. Moreover, he reconfirmed his commitment to the principle of conscription. Whether the Defence Structure Commission, which is supposed to provide an agreed framework for force planning in the long term will face up to the contradictions between resources and ambitions remains to be seen.

Conclusion

During the last ten years since unification, the German political élite has grappled with defining its perceptions of German national interests in a transformed international environment. The new challenges of the post-cold war situation have been unexpected for the entire world and have created new dilemmas in different regions. But as is the case for Russia, Germany's identity as a state, as well as its immediate environment, has been affected more profoundly by these changes than other countries like the United Kingdom, France or the United States.

Germany has emerged from the cold war not only regaining the lost elements of its sovereignty (including unification with its eastern part), but also as the third largest economy in the world and the economic leader of Western Europe. The section of the political élite that is holding the reigns of power is dominated by the consensus that Germany should match its international role and influence after the cold war with its economic power. Taking this view, Germany must assume its international responsibilities and play a leading role in the construction of the new political, military and economic order in Europe. There is, however, a lack of consensus in the political élite as a whole and in the general population. This is particularly true with regard to the use of military force for purposes other than the territorial defence of the Federal Republic. Although the constitutional barrier against the use of German armed forces out-of-area, especially under a UN mandate, has been shown not to exist, and the German participation in the Kosovo conflict marked a decisive transition in Germany's preparedness to contribute to allied military operations out-of-area, political barriers still remain that may come to the surface during other crises. For any effort by the German government to play a leading role in the development of European security this issue remains a critical and sensitive one.

The future development of the Bundeswehr needs rethinking in the light of the new realities. Defence budgets have shrunk inexorably during Rühe's tenure, to the extent that there is now a serious mismatch between resources and commitments. Conscription is becoming increasingly untenable, although the political élite has yet to face this reality.

German defence policy remains in transition. The political élite needs to muster the political will to address the fundamental contradictions and problems of the present situation. Nevertheless it is clear that Germany has already taken some decisive steps in the process of adaptation to the European security environment after the cold war.

4
The Dilemmas of Collective Security

A prominent feature of the cold war regime was that it defined a very definite structure for European security. This was based on a fundamental systemic conflict which expressed itself in the deployment of military forces on a substantial scale, held in check by the nuclear strategic stalemate. At the same time, as we have seen, a political process of consultation and co-operation between the two sides developed, for which the Conference on Cooperation and Security in Europe (CSCE) provided the institutional framework. Embedded within the larger framework of East–West detente of the CSCE was Germany's *Ostpolitik*. Both *detente* and *Ostpolitik*, just as West Germany's alliance and European policies, were based on an explicit institutionalist approach, with elements of what we now would call constructivism. The essence of this approach was that the tension between East and West could be mitigated by the absolute gains both sides made as a result of participation in the institutions of detente. As a result, they would have a stake in the continuation of these institutions and this would, in the long run, transform the nature of the relationship itself. This was called *Wandel durch Annäherung*.

The end of the cold war was the ultimate triumph of this philosophy and the peaceful end to this monumental global struggle was perceived as an extraordinary vindication of this approach.[1] With the end of the fundamental conflict of interests and values between East and West, the future security environment was not defined by a highly militarized confrontation, but by bilateral, subregional and intrastate conflicts of interest. The central task of foreign and security policy was seen to be to construct a pan-European security system that included Russia and that would be suited to the new international situation. This was no easy task. Indeed the institutionalist agenda foundered quickly for several reasons:

1 The relative security of West European states after the collapse of the cold war regime resulted in a deep-seated unwillingness to get involved in conflicts and security risks that did not affect them directly.
2 Russia was not prepared to subordinate its own security problems to a collective security regime.

The failure to resolve the most basic questions of the principles according to which a new European security order should be created meant that no functional collective security institutions could be created. Hence we arrived at what I have called *the central dilemma of European security*. It is the enormous paradox that, while on the one hand virtually all of the states in Europe have abandoned older forms of international conduct in which military force played a dominant role, at the same time the transition of the European of states some of which are now quite unstable due to a mismatch between territorial boundaries and social/national identities. The reemergence of ethnic conflicts suppressed during the cold war period requires a system of collective security with effective political, diplomatic and military instruments to prevent conflict, and to enforce and keep the peace.

The conceptual basis of collective security in Europe

The concept of collective security is based on the notion of collective action to support international security against the violation of international law by individual states, in particular the violation of the principle of the renunciation of force to settle disputes. This obliges governments to collectively use force to support states under attack, while at the same time abstain from the use of force to support what they perceive to be their own national interest (except in the case of self-defence against aggression). The security of one state thus becomes the concern of all other states and an agreement of collective security implies that all states will defend the security of each state as if it was their own security that was under threat. A system of collective security requires a common understanding of a stable and just international order. It requires mechanisms whereby in a crisis situation states can agree on who is responsible for the aggression, the need to intervene and the appropriate political and military steps required to maintain or restore international order and peace.[2] In short, there are three operational requirements that are necessary to establish a working collective security regime: (i) effective and legitimate decisionmaking procedures (ii) a range of instruments to provide for early warning of emerging conflicts, and conflict resolution by non-violent methods; and (iii) overwhelming power to apply political, military and economic sanctions against aggressors.

The institutionalist answer to the problem of collective security is the creation of the appropriate institutional framework that commits all the parties to a common set of objectives and ultimately to joint, collective action. The most obvious framework for collective security on a pan-European scale in 1990 was the Conference on Cooperation and Security in Europe (CSCE). The main reason was the fact that it had been a pan-European institution created in the cold war period with a legitimacy that West European or transatlantic institutions lacked. For CSCE to be transformed into a collective security regime would have entailed a complete transformation of its basic functions. Instead of regulating competing norms, interests and objectives, its purpose would be to implement common norms, interests and objectives of erstwhile protagonists. At the same time its main objective would be to reduce the potential for conflict, prevent the outbreak of conflict through crisis management or bring about the cessation of hostilities if violent conflict had erupted and facilitate the resolution of conflicts.[3]

The Paris summit in November 1990, where the CFE Treaty was signed and the end of the cold war was declared, proclaimed a 'charter for a new Europe'.[4] The CSCE member states acknowledged democracy as the only legitimate form of government. They affirmed market economics and the safeguarding of human and minority rights as a guiding principle of their national policies. Despite the proliferation of activities and institutions, CSCE did not achieve a consensus to develop effective mechanisms for crisis management in Europe.[5] The notion of a security council in CSCE, much mooted in 1990, has not made any progress. The expansion of CSCE from 34 to 52 member states at the July 1992 summit in Helsinki has considerably exacerbated the problem of decisionmaking in CSCE. By the beginning of the CSCE review conference in March 1992, the endeavour to create a mechanism for the Peaceful Settlement of Disputes to be operated through the Conflict Prevention Centre had not moved beyond mediation by common agreement. All this must be seen against the background of a number of violent conflicts raging in Europe – in the former Yugoslavia, between Armenia and Azerbaijan over Nagorno-Karabakh, the Transdniestr dispute in Moldova, and Georgia. The United Nations and the European Community have played a much greater role in the former Yugoslavia than CSCE, and crisis management in the former Soviet Union is currently left to the Commonwealth of Independent States (CIS–Russia). The one area in which the CSCE has played a very effective role has been in moving forward the ratification and implementation of the CFE Treaty. The Provisional Application of the CFE-I Treaty signed by 16 NATO countries, six former Warsaw Pact countries and seven former Soviet republics at Helsinki on 10 July 1992 has brought the treaty into force.[6] Another important step was the signing of the Concluding Act of Negotiation of Personnel Strength of Conventional Armed Forces in Europe (also known as CFE-IA) which imposes limits on various categories of military personnel in the ATTU (Atlantic-to-the-Urals) zone.

The 1992 CSCE review conference held in Helsinki from March to June, prior to the July 1992 summit created a number of new institutions in order to provide new instruments to improve the hitherto clearly inadequate performance of CSCE as a pan-European collective security framework. Furthermore, the CSCE declared itself a regional security organization under Chapter VIII of the UN Charter. It was hoped that this would allow the CSCE to enhance its role in peacekeeping.[7] After the Helsinki conference, the CSCE underwent significant institutional development. The supreme governing body is the Council and the organization is led by the Committee of Senior Officials (CSO). The main functional agencies are the Conflict Prevention Centre (CPC) and the Office for Democratic Institutions and Human Rights (ODIHR), and there is a High Commissioner on National Minorities. The effectiveness of these institutions is limited by both structural and practical factors. Structurally, the CSCE remained an intergovernmental institution without independent power to take and implement decisions, and dependent on the consent of all member states. The practical constraints resulted from the low-level of personnel and other resources made available.[8]

A major factor that complicated the issue of collective security early on, was the problem of conflicts in the FSU and Russia's role in them.[9] It was generally accepted that only the military establishment of Russia has the means and the domestic political backing to engage in effective peacekeeping and peace-making operations in this region, and Western powers had no desire to become engaged militarily. However the nature of Russian policy towards regional conflicts and its international legitimization was controversial. The West resisted the concept of Russian hegemony in the FSU, but it proved difficult to develop a form of legitimation for Russian peace-keeping/enforcement that could serve to both support and restrain Russia.

Here collective security can come into play, given that Russia has asked to be mandated by the UN and/or the OSCE to provide security in the CIS. The Russian endeavour to obtain a UN mandate foundered on its insistence that only Russian/CIS forces should be involved in peacekeeping in the former Soviet Union and that the UN should only provide observers. This proposal raises a number of problems. Most obviously, it sets a question mark against the impartiality and neutrality of the forces. Moreover, UN mandated peacekeeping is traditionally carried out by fully multinational forces, under sole UN command. The formula put forward by Russia thus contradicts many of the essential requirements for UN mandated peacekeeping operations. Furthermore, in several of the crises in which Russian forces have been engaged, the task has been one not of peacekeeping (after being invited to do so by all the sides involved in the conflict) but rather of peace-making. Thus Western policymakers face a dilemma. On the one hand, Russia is asking for an international mandate, both to legitimize its actions and in order to obtain financial support. Such a mandate, if given, could be used to establish the framework and limits of Russian actions. Moreover, no Western state is willing to contemplate a substantial military engagement anywhere in the former Soviet Union. However, on the other hand, Russia remains unwilling to fulfil the conditions necessary to achieve a UN mandate and certainly would under no circumstances contemplate transforming the peacekeeping forces in the CIS into UN forces, evidencing continued unwillingness to permit international control over, or the involvement of foreign troops in, peacekeeping operations in former Soviet space. Nor is Russia's impartiality in its involvement in regional conflicts in Eurasia beyond question. The concept of CIS peacekeeping and the notion of recognizing the CIS as a regional organization that could engage in peacekeeping under a UN mandate also remains dubious as long as no CIS states other than Russia are involved in more than a token form in terms both of troop presence and of decisionmaking.[10]

Russia's endeavour to obtain a CSCE mandate for peacekeeping and peace-making operations in the former Soviet Union followed similar lines and encountered similar obstacles. In July 1992 the CSCE was declared to be a regional agency according to Chapter VIII of the UN Charter. This endowed it with the authority to carry out peacekeeping operations. The Rome Council meeting of the CSCE in December 1993 considered a Russian request for authorization to conduct peacekeeping missions in the CIS. This was not accepted. The meeting approved the concept of setting up a CSCE co-operative arrangement that would, *inter alia*, ensure that the role and functions of the third-party military force in a conflict area were consistent with CSCE principles and objectives.[11] In June 1994, however, Russia made it clear that it would not accept the monitoring of its forces by CSCE representatives.

It is ironic that the Budapest summit in autumn 1994, at which the CSCE was finally transformed into a security organization (the OSCE) and where a decision was made to prepare for its first major peacekeeping operation in Nagorno-Karabakh, took place shortly before the Russian military incursion into Chechnya. Discussions about an OSCE mandate for peacekeeping in the former Soviet Union were put on hold as a consequence of this crisis, in which international norms and humanitarian principles have been violated on a large scale. Nevertheless, the OSCE did assume a role in the Chechen crisis when the Permanent Council decided to deploy the OSCE Assistance Group to Chechnya.

The part played by the OSCE in the former Soviet Union thus has been a very limited one, confined mainly to observer missions and involvement in the negotiation of political settlements (for example in the Transdniestr dispute).[12] The OSCE still lacks the instruments for effective peacekeeping and enforcement, and Russia is as yet unprepared to give up control over operations in the former Soviet Union. It nevertheless remains imperative to make collective security in Europe effective, precisely in order to place constraints on Russian military actions in the FSU.[13]

A related issue is that of the extension of NATO membership. One of the reasons why, initially, NATO members were reluctant to extend membership to central European countries is that it was not perceived as enhancing the security of the alliance as then constituted. Indeed, the opposite might be the case, insofar as Western Europe might be drawn into conflicts from which it would otherwise remain isolated. Secondly, the extension of NATO membership to the Central European countries and the Baltic states without including Russia itself would lend strength to those forces in Russia that seek to hinder the process of political reform and integration in the world community.[14] Nor would recreation of a military confrontation at the Russian border enhance the security of East European countries; again, quite the reverse would be the case. However, to provide security guarantees without putting in place the means to support them would be irresponsible. There is currently in effect an extensive conventional arms control regime (the CFE Treaty) which is in principle capable of preventing local arms races in Central and Eastern Europe and particularly constrains Russian military deployments west of the Urals. It is in the security interest of all European countries that this regime remains in place and that Russia remains an adherent to it.[15]

By 1994 the Western reluctance to enlarge NATO had all but disappeared and the United States began to press for the rapid enlargement of the Alliance. This had the effect of galvanizing both Russia and Germany into support for strengthening and extending CSCE. Russia proposed the development of CSCE to a European system of collective security comparable to the UN, as an alternative to NATO enlargement, whereas the Germans supported the strengthening of CSCE in order to make the enlargement of NATO politically more palatable.[16] The United States agreed at the Budapest summit to the institutional changes that transformed the CSCE into the OSCE and nominally gave it an important role in the development of European security in to the 21st century. These changes, however, remained largely symbolic, without the transfer of power to the OSCE. All these agreements were of a political character and were not binding in international law. More importantly, the United States rejected Russian President's Boris Yeltins's vehement condemnation of NATO enlargement and insisted that this process would go ahead.[17]

The conclusion is that while CSCE/OSCE was in principle a suitable framework for collective security in Europe,[18] neither Russia nor the principal Western powers were prepared to give the OSCE the means to conduct not only crisis prevention but provide the political instruments and military resources to prevent conflicts or bring conflicts to an end. It is true that some European states, especially Russia and Germany, did at various points take initiatives to develop the CSCE/OSCE into a system of collective security. In 1990, the German government promoted the strengthening of CSCE as a way of inducing the Soviet Union to accept the NATO membership of a united Germany. Thus Chancellor Kohl indicated general support for the Soviet objective to develop CSCE into a pan-European, bloc-transcending security structure, while at the same time using the Helsinki Final Act to emphasize the sovereign right of all member states to join or not join any alliance. Subsequently, in the aftermath of the CSCE Paris Summit, Foreign Minister Genscher continued to promote CSCE and its institutional mechanisms with the ultimate objective of creating a security council within the CSCE that would take on the function of a European Security Council. While supported by the Soviet Union, the German feelers in this direction received a negative reaction from other leading Western states, especially the United States and the United Kingdom, but also France. Germany and the United States buried their differences over the matter in the joint declaration by Baker and Genscher in May 1991 and the Joint Communique of the NATO Council Meeting in June 1991 where all sides recognized the central role of NATO in European security. Germany decisively acknowledged the American order of priorities and was at pains to avoid any impression that its support for CSCE would result in a weakening commitment to NATO and the transatlantic Alliance.

The failure to establish a collective security regime at the end of the cold war, the conflicts in the former Yugoslavia and the general reluctance of Western states to become involved, and the downturn in relations with Russia in 1993, all combined to induce even greater scepticism about the feasibility and utility of a European collective security system. However, German diplomatic efforts to develop and strengthen CSCE continued and in 1994 there was a Dutch–German initiative, in the run-up to the Budapest Conference, to establish a regional arrangement under Chapter VIII of the UN Charter. For conflict prevention and crisis management the CSCE would become involved in the first instance (the 'CSCE first' principle), and only if the efforts of the CSCE failed or it became apparent that military forces would be required, would the matter be referred to the UN Security Council. Any findings by the CSCE regarding a crisis situation and referrals to the UN Security Council, according to the Dutch–German proposal, did not require the consent of the parties to the dispute or conflict. The Western permanent members of the UN Security Council were not very enthusiastic about the proposal, but accepted it eventually on the understanding that the 'CSCE first' principle did not affect the right of any state to refer a dispute to the UN Security Council under Article 35 of the UN Charter. Russian Foreign Minister Kozyrev proposed an Executive Committee resembling the Security Council for CSCE, and a 'co-ordinating role' between the various security organizations for the CSCE. The United States, however, while accepting the Dutch–German proposal, refused to entertain any notion of a CSCE security council or any widening of the institutions of the CSCE/OSCE.[19]

As we have seen, on the Russian side enthusiasm for the OSCE was tempered by an unwillingness to allow it to have a significant role inside the FSU. On the German side, the principal constraint was the reluctance of the Western Allies. However, the difficulties about Germany itself contributing military forces for peacekeeping and peace enforcement meant that there were fundamental problems about Germany taking a lead in the development of a collective security regime in Europe. The German attitude encapsulated the fundamental dilemma of the very principle of collective security: based on the precepts of international law and the peaceful resolution of disputes, it requires the willingness and the ability to use overwhelming force in the event of serious breaches of the peace. While Germany played a leading role in the promotion of the former, it found itself severely constrained in advocating the development of instruments for the latter.

In terms of the principal requirements for a collective security regime discussed above, the OSCE fails to fulfil them. While the decisionmaking procedures of the OSCE have legitimacy, they are not very effective and they are mostly irrelevant as the major powers do not use the OSCE framework to address serious security crises in Europe. In terms of the second requirement, the OSCE has engaged in substantial and pioneering work in developing mechanisms for the early warning of emerging new conflicts, as well as providing a forum for political consultation, and these have become the main functions of OSCE. However, while these are necessary for a system of collective security, they are not sufficient. Moreover, the role of OSCE even in this field remains too limited. As regards the third requirement, OSCE fails entirely as it has no military instruments at its disposal. The Helsinki documents of 1992 state quite explicitly that no military forces should be assigned to CSCE for peacekeeping. There was an agreement, however, that NATO forces could be made available for CSCE peacekeeping missions on a case-by-case basis and with the consent of member states. The possibility of CSCE having a role in peace enforcement was explicitly excluded in 1992.

The failure of European states and the North American members of the Alliance to agree on the creation of a regime of collective security in Europe has had far-reaching consequences for security in Europe since 1989. In order to understand these more clearly and the development of German policy towards collective security in Europe, this chapter now focuses on a case study of German policy towards the conflicts in the former Yugoslavia. This will allow for us to test the various explanations that have been advanced, to explain the evolution of the postwar system of states and the effect that events will have on shaping the future European security environment.

The Yugoslav crisis: the challenge and failure of common security

The conflicts in the former Yugoslavia could well serve to define the development of the international order in post-cold war Europe. It exposed both the inadequacy of the institutions developed to protect international norms and security, the lack of commitment of Western governments to support them and at the same time, paradoxically, their durability and persistence in the face of weak political support and determined violation of international norms through aggression. Like other leading Western nations, Germany was aware of the dangers of conflict in Yugoslavia, but for as long as they did not involve the outbreak of large-scale violence the situation seemed to be amenable to crisis prevention.[20] Germany pursued a rather low key policy, articulated and implemented virtually exclusively through the European Community and aimed at crisis prevention through economic incentives and potential sanctions.

The decisive steps toward ethno-nationalist conflict in Yugoslavia came in 1990 when the Serb-dominated government in Belgrade suspended the autonomy of Kosovo and Vojvodina. The drive towards Serbian domination of the Federal Republic of Yugoslavia under the leadership of Milošević and the ex-communist Serbian political élite propelled the federation towards a violent break-up. The collapse of the Yugoslav economy, which had been gathering momentum throughout the 1980s, was an important factor. Indeed, some analysts have described the transition from a centrally planned to a free market economy in Yugoslavia as one of the primary causative factors of the collapse of the state and the conflict between the republics of the federation.[21] During the 1980s, much of Yugoslavia's public debt was underwritten by the West, with Germany providing the major contribution. This was part of a general policy by the German government to prevent instability in Eastern Europe by the provision of aid, which became an important instrument of German security policy as the cold war system began to unravel.

German policy on the Yugoslav crisis in 1990–91 was low key and conducted through the European Community. When in June 1991 the regular Yugoslav army, now under Serb control, sought to enter Slovenia and met with armed resistance, the European Community was galvanized into action. This was a period when Germany was preoccupied with the building of European institutions, and the Maastricht process was underway. It was an important element of the approach taken to this issue that in the aftermath of the weakness of the European decisionmaking processes exhibited in the Gulf War the European Community could demonstrate that, as it sought to build its Common Foreign and Security Policy, it could act decisively and effectively on such matters. A meeting of European foreign ministers on 13 May 1991 where the United Kingdom had expressed the view that Yugoslavia should remain a loose confederation of republics without splitting into new independent states. The main planks of the European policy on Yugoslavia in 1991 therefore were the preservation of the Yugoslav federation as a state and the European Community as a model for the future of relations between its constituent republics. Both elements of the policy proved to be unsuitable for a proper foundation of the future of the region. The insistence on the integrity of the Yugoslav state was based on thinking inherited from the cold war period, where the maintenance of existing state borders was perhaps the most fundamental cornerstone of peaceful co-existence and stability. It was also informed by the possible risks of ethnic conflicts throughout Eastern Europe and the risk of other conflicts in Central Europe and, more importantly, in the Soviet Union. The Soviet Union only agreed to the establishment of a new political crisis mechanism in the context of CSCE in June 1991 because of an explicit reference to the integrity of the state of the Federal Republic of Yugoslavia. However, given the sentiments of the people in the various republics, the continued integrity of the Yugoslav state was not compatible with a transition to democracy, as the only means whereby it could be maintained was brute force. As it turned, out, the same proved to be the case with the Soviet Union. In both cases, the status quo was the objective of Western foreign policy until it became no longer tenable. Moreover, the model of the European Community, which is designed for countries that are in the process of integrating their institutions, was ill-suited for the condition of the Yugoslav Federation, which was in the process of disintegration and where the establishment of separate, rather than common, institutions was in progress.

On 25 June 1991 Slovenia and Croatia declared their independence, thereby undermining the very foundation of the EC approach to the Yugoslav crisis. The Yugoslav National Army (JNA) moved into Slovenia on 27 June in order to reassert federal authority, precipitating the war. The armed conflict in Croatia began on 3 July 1999. The EC dispatched a troika of Foreign Ministers to Yugoslavia (Gianni de Michelis, Italy; Jacques Poos, Luxemburg and Hans van den Broek, Netherlands). Their objective was to put pressure on Yugoslavia to end the fighting and they brought proposals which included the temporary suspension of the declarations of independence.

It was at this critical juncture that there was a fundamental policy shift in Germany. It came about partly in response to domestic political pressure, which expressed itself in a campaign in conservative newspapers and was echoed in demands by influential CDU spokesmen such as Karl Lamers and the then Party Secretary General (later defence minister) Volker Rühe. The demand was for the international recognition of Slovenia and Croatia. The high proportion of Slovene and Croatian populations (over the order of 90 per cent) supporting independence gave credence to their claim, just as East Germany's desire to be unified with West Germany had been legitimized by the overwhelming expression of the will of the population in a referendum. By May 1991 it was evident that the SPD, the largest opposition party, was moving in a similar direction. Foreign Minister Genscher visited Yugoslavia in early July 1991 and his visit convinced him of the need to stop Serb aggression. By now the German political establishment had achieved a virtually complete and unique consensus on this issue. The essence of this consensus was that the fighting must be stopped, that multilateral crisis management mechanisms must be invoked to achieve this objective, that Croatia and Slovenia (and by implication possibly other Yugoslav republics) had the right to self-determination, that they should be recognized as independent states and that Serb attempts to restore Belgrade's control by force was a form of aggression.

Genscher invoked the CSCE crisis management mechanisms and on 3 July 1991 the CSCE called for an immediate ceasefire in

Yugoslavia and an assurance the JNA was under political control.[22] This reflected Genscher's concerns that 'the federal army in Yugoslavia was "running amok"'.[23] Germany formally proposed EC recognition of Slovenia and Croatia on 4 July at the foreign ministers meeting in The Hague. However, some other members, especially France, but also Holland and the United Kingdom, were not willing to go along with this. Genscher backed off from recognizing the two republics immediately, preferring joint European action. However, the theme of self-determination for the Yugoslav people and by implication for their constituent republics became a dominant theme in German statements, including those made by Chancellor Kohl, on the crisis in Yugoslavia. The Federal Government was coming under substantial domestic pressure, which manifested itself in a unanimous vote in the Bundestag foreign affairs committee to investigate Foreign Minister's Genscher alleged policy of appeasement towards the Yugoslav government in Belgrade.[24]

As a consequence Bonn kept up the pressure for recognition if the fighting did not stop. The visit by Croatian President Tudjman and his meeting with Chancellor Kohl on 12 July was a highly symbolic gesture, criticized both in Paris and Belgrade. Among the various ways in which Germany sought to put pressure on Yugoslavia, was the refusal to issue any further export guarantee licences except to exports from Croatia and Slovenia and the threat of sanctions. The increasing violence, now focused on Croatia, also resulted in Genscher's call for a CSCE peacekeeping force and Security Council.[25]

On 7 September 1991 a peace conference was convened by the European Community in The Hague under the chairmanship of Lord Carrington as the fighting became more intense. The talks were based on three principles: no unilateral changes of borders, the protection of the rights of all minorities and the full respect of all legitimate interests and aspirations. Although Lord Carrington did manage to obtain, for the very first time, the concession from the Serb President, Slobodan Milošević, that all republics have the right to become independent, in the end Serbia refused to accept the peace plan, partly because of the lack of status accorded to the Serb minorities in the other republics. The conference adjourned on 8 November, having failed to achieve agreement. Attention now turned to the UN Security Council.

During the time of the EC peace conference and its aftermath, which saw a further escalation of the fighting in Croatia, political pressures inside Germany for recognition grew and were translated into increased diplomatic efforts. One of the arguments that came to be deployed was that it was necessary to recognize Slovenia and Croatia in order to turn the issue from an internal conflict into an international one, thereby enabling international organizations to become involved on a proper basis. The issue of self-determination was being addressed by the EC Arbitration Commission chaired by Robert Badinter which had been set up in August 1991.[26] The Secretary General of the United Nations, Javier Perez de Cuellar, warned against premature recognition of Slovenia and Croatia. Former US Secretary of State Cyrus Vance was appointed the UN envoy to Yugoslavia, with the task of mediating a cessation of the conflict. The deployment of UN peacekeeping troops remained out of the question until the fighting stopped and the political conditions for the acceptance of such a force were created. During the months of November and December the fighting in Croatia reached new levels of intensity.

Meanwhile Germany increased the pressure for recognition while at the same taking further measures against Serbia and Montenegro, such as cutting transport links, while the EC imposed economic sanctions. Other major EC member states began to fall in line with the German position, most notably Italy, France and Britain. The United Kingdom was initially opposed, partly because of its Northern Ireland experience, and partly because it simply wanted the Carrington mission to succeed. France retained serious reservations, but both France and Britain came to support the German position, partly as a result of German concessions during the Maastricht Treaty negotiations. The United States remained hostile to the idea of recognition, seeing a dangerous precedent that might affect another region that was more central to US strategic interests, namely the Soviet Union. There was good reason to make such a connection in the aftermath of the Moscow coup against Gorbachev. Indeed, such a connection was made by the Germans who openly supported independence for the constituent republics of the former Soviet Union, recognizing that any attempt to preserve the Soviet Union was as futile as the preservation of the Yugoslav federal state.

In early December Chancellor Kohl promised the Croatian President Tudjman that Germany would recognize Croatia before Christmas 1991. On 16 December 1992 the EC Council of Foreign Ministers came to an agreement on recognition. This envisaged common recognition after the assessment by the Badinter Commission had been completed, by 15 January 1991. But not only had Germany already committed itself to recognition before that date and regardless of the assessment, but Genscher reiterated that the Federal Republic of Germany would recognize Croatian independence irrespective of the deliberations of the Badinter Commission. In the event the Arbitration Commission found in favour of Slovenia and FYROM (the Former Yugoslavia Republic of Macedonia) but against Croatia. By 23 December 1991 the Kohl government announced its recognition of Slovenia and Croatia, although, in order to maintain some semblance of European unity, the implementation of this decision was delayed until 15 January 1992, when the other members of the EC joined in the process. In early January 1992 a ceasefire was achieved in Croatia, and the timing was not entirely coincidental. The military stalemate and the prospect of imminent recognition convinced the Serb military leadership that more was to be gained at the negotiation table rather than on the battlefield.[27]

While Chancellor Kohl celebrated the ceasefire in Croatia as a 'triumph of diplomacy', the consequences of this policy proved to be somewhat ambiguous. First of all, the assertive foreign policy stance taken by Germany resulted in widespread international criticism. This had the effect of inducing a more muted approach to diplomacy subsequently. Moreover, it raised questions about EC foreign policy decisionmaking processes and Germany's commitment to common decisionmaking.[28] A good case can be made that the EC policy and the policy of some of the major member states was based on untenable assumptions, namely the preservation of the political and territorial status quo in Yugoslavia and the Soviet Union. In this sense German policy was arguably based on a more accurate perception of political realities. However, having set up the Badinter Arbitration Commission the EC, under pressure from Germany, did not implement its conclusions. The Badinter Arbitration Commission made recognition dependent on the CSCE principles of human rights (including safeguarding the rights of ethnic minorities), democratic rule and inviolable borders. This is where Croatia was found wanting. Although recognition by the EC did impose conditions requiring adherence to these principles, the implementation was lax. Another major inconsistency was the situation in relation to Macedonia, which despite the recommendation of the Badinter Commission was denied recognition by the EC because of objections from Greece. Finally, criticism has centred on the issues left unresolved by recognition, especially the situation in Bosnia-Herzegovina which subsequently became the centre of conflict.

The issue of the right to self-determination and the status of the republic was more complex in the case of Bosnia-Herzegovina. Throughout 1990 and 1991 political parties in Serbia had lent support to the concept of 'cantonization' of Bosnia (a concept borrowed from the political system of Switzerland) along ethnic lines. The proposal offered in early 1992 by Lord Carrington and the Portuguese diplomat Jose Cutilheiro to create 'three constituent units' in Bosnia (Serb, Muslim and Croat) was also commonly described as 'cantonization', even though this term was never used during the negotiations. What James Gow has described as 'essentially a Serbian idea supported by some Croats'[29] found no support with Bosnian President Alia Izetbegović and among Muslims more generally. On 1 March 1992 a referendum was held in which 99.7 per cent of those voting voted in favour of independence for Bosnia. Only 64.4 per cent of the population took part in the election, which was largely boycotted by the Serb population. Subsequently hostilities escalated rapidly, with JNA forces and Serb irregulars in position to begin a systematic campaign of murder euphemistically known as 'ethnic cleansing', creating literally hundreds of thousands of refugees in addition to the tens of thousands killed.

The next major initiatives, after the United States and the EC recognized the republic of Bosnia-Herzegovina, were the London Conference in August 1992 and the Vance–Owen plan proposed in January 1993 by the UN envoy Cyrus Vance and the EU envoy David Owen (like his predecessor Lord Carrington a former British foreign secretary).[30] The Vance–Owen plan was based on the division of Bosnia into ten relatively ethnically homogenous areas while at the same time preserving some element of common statehood. Although the plan to some extent acknowledged the facts created by the fighting and the ethnic cleansing, the Bosnian Serbs opposed it, while the Croats and the Bosnian government were prepared, albeit unenthusiastically, to sign-up to it. In Germany the Vance–Owen plan was widely criticized from all sides because it seemed to legitimize Serbian atrocities. Nevertheless the German government supported it, however unenthusiastically, since for a short time, it was 'the only game in town'. The US government adamantly opposed the Vance–Owen plan on the grounds that it was not feasible to implement it and that it was unfair to the Muslims in Bosnia, but was persuaded to put its weight behind it, including the threat of air strikes against the Serbs if they did not sign it. The leader of the Bosnian Serbs, Radovan Karadjić, was persuaded to sign it subject to ratification by the Serb assembly in Pale. There the plan was made subject to a referendum among Bosnian Serbs, in which 95 per cent of those voting opposed it. It was followed by the Owen–Stoltenberg plan (Thorvald Stoltenberg replaced Vance as UN envoy in May 1993) in August 1993 which went even further than the Vance–Owen plan in consolidating the partition of the country. The resulting entity would be known as the 'Union of Republics of Bosnia and Hercegovina'. The Bosnian Serbs would end up controlling 52 per cent of Bosnia, the Croats 17 per cent, and the Muslims about 31 per cent of the territory. Negotiations on this plan came to a climax on 20 September 1992 on board the British aircraft carrier HMS *Invincible*. The agreement reached then was accepted by the Bosnian Serb and Croat assemblies, but rejected by the Bosnian Parliament in Sarajevo.

Despite these setbacks, the so-called Vance–Owen process continued, with the 'EU Action plan' proposed by the French and German foreign ministers (Alain Juppé and Klaus Kinkel). This plan was in essence a reworking of the 'Union' scheme, the central element being that the Muslim republic would get at least a third of the territory. The proposal that was eventually negotiated would have given the Muslim Republic 33.56 per cent and the Bosnian Croat Republic 17.5 per cent, but in December 1992 Izetbegović rejected it outright. Negotiations continued but by the end of 1993 it was not progressing anywhere. In April 1994 a new mechanism was set up, called the Contact Group. The Contact Group involved the United States and Russia, in the hope that Russia as a major power with good relations with Serbia would contribute to the negotiation. France, the United Kingdom and Germany were also part of the Contact Group; Germany had played an important role in the formation of the group in order to remain involved in the diplomatic process. Russia's influence on Serbia did not prove to be as significant as expected. The Contact Group produced yet another plan for the future of Bosnia based on a territorial division of 49 per cent for the Bosnian Serbs and 51 per cent for the Croat–Muslim Federation.

All of these plans came to nothing, because ultimately they did not conform to the war aims of the Bosnian Serbs. These consisted in the establishment of the borders of a Great Serbia or Union of Serbian states, to secure the territorial contiguity of Serb areas and render those ethnically pure. Efforts by the West to compel acceptance of a peace plan short of these aims failed because they lacked instruments to achieve this.[31] However, the situation began to change in two important ways. One was that as the Bosnian army was granted access to heavy weapons the military situation on the ground became less favourable to the Serbs. The second was that as a result of the situation in Sarajevo NATO had become increasingly involved. The Rapid Reaction Force supporting the UNPROFOR and the use of NATO air strikes against Serb positions on the hills surrounding Sarajevo struck a significant blow against Bosnian Serb capabilities and morale. Germany, although not actively engaged in air operations, nevertheless fully supported the use of force.[32] The willingness of the United States to deploy its own ground forces alongside other NATO troops to police any settlement was also a new factor. As a consequence the Serb government in Belgrade no longer saw the original war aims as achievable and was willing to cut a deal which the Bosnian Serbs had to accept. The peace conference held in Dayton, Ohio, eventually reached an agreement which was implemented with the deployment of the Implementation Force (IFOR), to be succeded by SFOR (Stabilization Force) after the first year. This was largely a NATO force, with Russian participation. German forces were also involved, but only in a nonmilitary role.[33]

The Dayton agreement held and thereby ended the war in Bosnia, but the worst was yet to come. The Dayton agreement had no effect on the situation in Kosovo, which until 1989 had been one of two autonomous republics in Serbia. Kosovo did not achieve recognition as an independent state in 1991 because it was not a separate republic. Since 1989 Kosovo had avoided the kind of armed conflict that devastated Bosnia and Croatia, in part due to the policy of the Albanian leadership of Rugova of nonviolent resistance. But in February 1998 the mounting oppression of the Albanian majority by the Serb government in Belgrade shattered the fragile peace when the government launched major offensives against ethnic Albanians. This in turn resulted in growing support for the Kosovo Liberation Army which by July 1998 had 'soft control' over about 30 per cent of Kosovo's territory. Increasing Serb offensives had the effect of killing hundreds of Albanian civilians and displacing tens of thousands. After the UN Security Council confirmed that the situation in Kosovo constituted a threat to international peace and security and hostilities intensified over the summer of 1998, the United States, with the support of the Contact Group, began an informal process of discussions led by the US ambassador to Macedonia, Chris Hill. The Hill process itself ran into a cul-de-sac, but the Contact Group persisted, resulting in the Rambouillet Conference in February 1999.[34]

By this time the pressure exerted by Serbia on OSCE observers and the Kosovo Verification Mission practically rendered them ineffective and the continuing violence, despite various undertakings by Yugoslav President Milošević, especially a massacre of 45 individuals executed by Serb forces in January 1999, brought NATO to the point of threatening military action in the form of air strikes in support of the demands by the Contact Group for specific measures to resolve the crisis in Kosovo. Western governments were spurred on by the increasing perception of the potential for a massive humanitarian catastrophe in Kosovo and the desire not repeat the mistakes in Bosnia. The Rambouillet conference eventually reached an agreement that was signed by the Kosovar delegation but rejected by the Serbs, at least in part because it called for severe restrictions on Serb forces in Kosovo and the presence of NATO peacekeepers to enforce the agreement (a KFOR along the lines of SFOR in Bosnia).[35] The refusal by Serbia to accede to the Rambioullet accords and last minute diplomatic efforts by Richard Holbrooke to persuade the Serb leadership that the West was serious about military action unless Serbia came in line with the demands of the Contact Group led to the point where a complete impasse was reached and the leading Western nations saw no alternative but to make good their threat of military action.[36]

A long campaign of NATO airstrikes followed which initially failed to compel the Serbs to meet NATO's demands and resulted in an accelerated process of ethnic cleansing whereby hundreds of thousands of ethnic Albanians were forced to flee into neighbouring states. Having begun an air campaign, NATO was now well and truly locked in, as Serbia continued with its campaign in Kosovo undeterred by the prospect of a looming ground war. However, eventually the scale of destruction in Serbia and Kosovo reached such a level (with no respite in prospect) that even Milošević was compelled to cut his losses and agree to the NATO demands which were then agreed in terms of a UN Security Council resolution.

The crisis in the former Yugoslavia forced the West European states, and Germany in particular, to face the panoply of issues and dilemmas in the post-cold war security environment. The first issue was the nature of the international system that began to emerge from the shadows of the cold war. The consensus among Western states was that the territorial status quo in Europe should not be disturbed. The British Prime Minister Margaret Thatcher had gone so far as to recommend the continued existence of the Warsaw Pact. Stability was the watchword, the disintegration of states and especially that of the Soviet Union was seen as the likely source of dangerous instability. The key problem was that the continued existence of the Soviet state, or the Yugoslav state, was not compatible with democracy, not to mention human rights. The German political élite was less obsessed with the preservation of the status quo than other leading Western powers. This was a consequence of reunification, which was the supreme example of the redrawing of territorial boundaries on the basis of the self-determination of peoples.

The German perception of the conflicts in the former Yugoslavia was, from the outset, that it was a war of territorial redistribution between ethnic groups.[37] The Serbs were identified as aggressors, engaging in attacks against the civilian population and ethnic cleansing. Germany's role in the crisis evoked interesting parallels with its fascist past. The Serbs constantly drew this connection, referring to the fascist Croat puppet regime of 1941–45 and its links to Hitler's Germany to explain Germany's support for the Croats, and describing Germany's objectives in terms of a new imperialism and racism. The German political élite saw this connection in precisely the opposite way. It was the behaviour of the Serbs, characterized by authoritarianism, grandiose ideas about a Greater Serbia and the violent suppression and extermination of other ethnic groups that evoked the image of Nazism. The German press, especially the conservative broadsheets in Germany seemed to exhibit a distinct pro-Croat bias in the early stages of the conflict. This was explained in various ways, for example by the large number of Croatians living in Germany (about 700 000) and their political clout, and the dependence (for a short time) of Bonn on the President of Croatia to permit Bosnian refugees in Croatia. It is clear that Bonn had a special relationship with Croatia and its President, Franjo Tudjman. This, however, did not mean that it supported him blindly, and Germany sought unsuccessfully to restrain him when he escalated tensions and attacked besieged Muslims. The most compelling explanation for Bonn's behaviour is that notwithstanding the fact that there were many villains and many acts of brutality in the former Yugoslavia, Serbia was identified as the principal aggressor who was ultimately to blame for what James Gow has called the 'the war of dissolution'.

The conflict in Yugoslavia was a severe test for the multilateral mechanisms which were at the heart of Germany's foreign policy orientation. There were several reasons for this. The most immediate problem was, as has been outlined in detail above, that the existing multilateral mechanisms were simply inadequate for such a task. Or, in other words, a European system of collective security to deal with such a crisis did not exist. Consequently Bonn turned to the existing structures of the Atlantic Alliance and the European Union. There were several fundamental problems that affected German policy on the Yugoslav crisis:

1 The structure of the European system of states after the cold war was only beginning to emerge. This means that the balance of power between the major powers (and indeed the question of who the major powers might be), the nature of alliance and other relations between the states, the nature of and the role of individual states in the system, especially Russia, remained unclear for some time. The same was true for the roles and functions of NATO, the OSCE and other institutions. Even more important, the role, the influence and the responsibilities of Germany itself were uncertain as Germany, like all other states, was in a process of adaptation to the new environment.

2 The European Community, in the process of becoming the European Union, was the immediate focus of Germany policy. But the relative role of Atlantic and European institutions had not been redefined. The United States saw the Yugoslav crisis as a European problem and wanted the Europeans to resolve it. This on one level was favourable to Germany's ambitions as it would enhance the pressure on the European Union to operationalize the Common Foreign and Security Policy and even to move towards a common defence policy. Germany therefore seemed to prefer, at the early stages of the crisis, European over transatlantic frameworks. The European Union did indeed engage in substantial diplomatic efforts but these proved ineffective. Moreover, when it became increasingly clear that a substantial military engagement was necessary the Europeans were unable to proceed without a substantial US involvement, both for political reasons and for the simple lack of military resources. The fact that a settlement of the Bosnian conflict was not possible without US leadership and military engagement was a massive defeat for Europe.

3 The Yugoslav crisis fundamentally challenged the *Weltanschauung* of the German political élite whose enlightened liberalism and

institutionalism believed that just as the cold war had ultimately been resolved, the future of international system was one of peace and prosperity in which conflicts would be resolved through international negotiations and institutions within a framework of internationally recognized norms and procedures. Germany saw itself as a 'civilian power' with foreign policies moulded in this way of thinking. It had developed policy instruments that were designed to operationalize this concept, which involved the development of multilateral institutions, the extension of membership of these institutions to promote stability and the use of economic aid and sanctions as a means to induce or compel conformity with international norms. For most of Central and Eastern Europe (excluding Russia and Belarus), these instruments proved extraordinarily effective and without doubt played a key role in the stabilization of the region. In the former Yugoslavia, however, they failed dismally. This made the recourse to military instruments increasingly necessary, putting Germany in a very difficult position. Having forged ahead with policy on Yugoslavia and by pushing the EU into recognition of the former Yugoslav republics, it then was unable to continue a leading role given that it would be unable to contribute to any military forces that would have to be deployed. This was both a consequence of fear about Germany's image abroad and the domestic political and constitutional difficulties which led Kinkel and Rühe to exclude the involvement of the Bundeswehr in combat actions in the former Yugoslavia. Although Germany maintained a high level of involvement through its membership of the Contact Group, many grand designs of German foreign policy after the cold war were shattered by the Yugoslav conflict, demonstrating impotence rather than a new assertiveness and the failure of new political mechanisms and instruments.

Before drawing some conclusions about the implications of the Yugoslav 'war of dissolution' for German foreign and security policy and European security more generally, it is worthwhile taking another look at the Kosovo conflict and Germany's role in particular. By the time the Kosovo conflict broke out, many lessons had been absorbed from the Bosnian war. More importantly, the Dayton agreement had created precedents and institutional mechanisms that could, it seemed, be adapted to the situation in Kosovo. The United States was fully prepared for NATO to provide the military back-up for diplomatic initiatives. The Contact Group was ready to spearhead the diplomatic efforts. Germany had resolved the constitutional debate and to a large extent the political debate on the use of force in support of collective security. The Kosovo crisis occurred as the political transition from the Kohl era to the Red–Green coalition took place. A fundamental question mark was placed over whether the foreign policy course of the long-standing Kohl government would continue, given that both the SPD and the Greens had bitterly opposed central elements of it in the past. Any fears other governments might have had in this regard were quickly dispelled, despite a foreign minister (Joschka Fischer) from a party that had espoused an anti-nuclear, anti-NATO and pacifistic line on international politics. Moreover, the transition from passive to active participation in military operations still had to be made. The Kosovo crisis and the responsibility of the EU presidency which Germany assumed in January 1999 both had a galvanizing effect on a government that in its first months after the election in September 1998 appeared confused and without direction. Chancellor Gerhard Schröder appeared positively presidential as he led Germany into its first military campaign since the Second World War and presided over the European Union's activities in the crisis. Fischer became a stalwart supporter of the Western Alliance and carried a traumatized Green Party through all the vital decisions as German planes participated in the bombing of Serb targets. Defence Minister Rudolf Scharping, dismissed as a lightweight after his unsuccessful stint as SPD leader enthralled with his passionate speeches in the Bundestag detailing the nature of the unspeakable acts that Serb security forces were committing in Kosovo on a daily basis. The only serious opposition to the NATO air strikes within Parliament came from the PDS. Party leader Gregor Gysi's visits to Belgrade and his handshake with Milošević earned him a lot of criticism, but his Party's position was popular in East Germany. Indeed the war opened up a division between east and west, with only 41 per cent in the east supporting Bundeswehr participation in the Kosovo operation, compared to 70 per cent in the west.[38] When the air campaign seemed to be failing to produce results and the flood of refugees from Kosovo was reaching nightmare proportions, there was a debate right across the west about the use of ground troops. The opposition parties, including the CDU leadership, and also the Greens were adamant in their rejection of a ground war. As a result Schröder adopted this as the official position of the federal government; fortunately it was never put to the test as the Serb government capitulated without a ground offensive. German ground troops were sent into Kosovo as part of KFOR and participated fully in armed peacekeeping.

The Yugoslav conflict and especially the war over Kosovo has had profound implications for European security policy in general and German security policy specifically, some of which are not yet fully apparent. The European security institutions were tested and their limitations were fully exposed. It did add significant pressure to the development of European security cooperation, and the OSCE and the WEU were given important tasks, but in terms of the central political and military negotiations their role was marginal. The United Nations, the Contact Group and NATO were ultimately the key players.[39] The fall-out from the Kosovo crisis still remains to be seen, but the pattern which established itself in Bosnia and Kosovo is likely to remain the most likely model of the medium term. There would be two separate foci for diplomatic endeavours to deal with a crisis – a European focus, centred around the European Union and making full use of the OSCE crisis management mechanisms, and a global focus, centred around the United Nations, based on US leadership, with NATO providing any military force required to support efforts to resolve the crisis. Such a set of arrangements is very untidy, to say the least. It lacks both the conceptual clarity and the political legitimacy of a proper institutional framework for collective security in Europe. It remains hostage to the real or perceived vagaries of public opinion, especially in the United States. Moreover, it perpetuates the perception that the post cold war international system is dominated by the United States. The challenge to develop a new regional system of collective security therefore remains.

For Germany, the Yugoslav conflict had a major impact on the process of geopolitical maturation. It proved that Germany did have an important role as a major regional power, while at the same time establishing the limits of the leadership role of the Federal Republic in Europe. It forced a reappraisal of the diplomatic, economic and military instruments at Germany's disposal and how they could be deployed. Most importantly, it provided the political context in which a fundamental review of the use of military force could be accepted. One of the enduring legacies of the Yugoslav conflicts therefore is that the 'normalization' which the German political élite was calling for at the end of the 1980s has been achieved finally.

Conclusion

The purpose of this chapter was to look at the institutionalist agenda of the new Germany for European security, against competing neorealist perspectives. The neorealist prediction of a conflict prone Europe, riven by interstate rivalries and conflicts in the absence of a major ordering power in the East, has clearly not been fulfilled. Precisely the opposite has occurred. The military forces of states in the region have been reduced to ceilings agreed in a comprehensive arms control agreement. The major ordering factor in West, Central and Eastern Europe has not been military power, but the enlargement of Western institutions and the spread of 'norms of governance', which include democratization, the rule of law and the transition to market economies. The basic elements of Germany's institutionalist security policy proved to be very successful. Bilateral diplomacy, multilateral diplomacy and foreign economic policy were focused on supporting economic stability in CEE countries and drawing them into the Western community of nations. On all of those counts, all the states with the exception of the non-Baltic states of the former Soviet Union have made substantial progress. The first wave of NATO enlargement has occurred, with EU enlargement to follow. Effectively the threat of the return of communism, the emergence of authoritarian regimes and the spectre of regional conflicts among smaller states and new regional arms races have all been avoided.

The conflicts in the former Soviet Union and the former Yugoslavia cast a substantial shadow on this optimistic picture. They do not necessarily contradict the conclusion, however, that both an idealist and/or institutional perspective proved to be a better guide to the future of Europe than Kenneth Waltz's and John Mearsheimer's dire neorealist predictions. The first point to be made is that these conflicts were associated with the dissolution of states and were not interstate, but rather intrastate conflicts. They are therefore special cases that do not necessarily permit conclusions for the European system of states as a whole. The former Soviet Union and the former Yugoslavia otherwise are quite distinct. The conflicts in the FSU were concentrated in regions of the Caucasus and Central Asia in which central government had become incapable of enforcing order. This is the antithesis of the neorealist case, where a government fails to use all of its resources to maximize its power and authority. From a neorealist perspective the relatively peaceful dissolution of the Soviet Union is a remarkable and in many respects paradoxical event. There was no war of dissolution in the Soviet Union; to the contrary, the core state, Russia, was one of the principal agents bringing about its dissolution. It is true that since then Russia has sought to exercise a hegemonic influence over the former Soviet territory, and that its involvement in various conflicts (Georgia and Abkhazia, the Transdniestr dispute and the Tajik civil war) had the intention of consolidating its influence and support its perceived security interests as an important determining factor. But this was never pushed to the point of removing governments or destroying the national sovereignty of the newly independent states, and when push came to shove there was no appetite in Moscow for the re-establishment of the Soviet Union.[40] While democratization in the former Soviet states remains incomplete, and pockets of regional anarchy and potential conflict zones persist, the reality is that the newly independent states have integrated into the international system in a peaceful fashion and with an increasing acceptance of accepted norms of international conduct.

This in stark contrast to the dissolution of Yugoslavia which was resisted by the core state, Serbia, with ferocious violence. While the events in the former Yugoslavia have important consequences for the whole of Europe, they are not evidence that the international anarchy in Europe is going to be the norm, and that new balances of power and new nuclear weapons states to provide an ordering power will be required. In this sense the Yugoslav 'war of dissolution' is very much the exception rather than the rule. Neorealist analysis can draw more comfort from the failure to develop adequate institutional mechanisms for collective security and the reluctance of Western powers to commit to peace enforcement in the former Yugoslavia. This accords with Mearsheimer's and Waltz's belief that states will always prefer the maximization of autonomy and therefore pursue autonomy-seeking policies. Moreover, European states, and to a greater extent the United States, had difficulty identifying any national interest in the Balkans. But this leaves them with the paradox that European states ultimately behaved in a manner that is best explained by institutionalism, without the development of the necessary institutions. The United States eventually did commit its resources, including armed forces, despite the domestic political cost and the lack of perceived geo-political benefits. Hegemonic stability theory is also weak in its explanatory power because the major power saw the Balkan area as being outside its province.

Neorealist and institutionalist explanations fail because they ignore the importance of norms and values, especially in the post-cold war order. Try as they might, Western states could not in the end ignore Serb aggression, the persistence of conflict and massive human rights violations. While the institutionalist explanation is weak (given the weakness of the institutions), the constructivist explanation is attractive because it can explain both the behaviour of the West European states and the United States in the absence of either pressing risks to their national security or institutional commitments. The post-cold war systems of states has now settled down. Germany has clearly been forced to moderate its expectations both of a leadership role in the new Europe and the grand designs for European security institutions. It has successfully accomplished the transition to 'a normal regional power' that can play an important role in the diplomacy of security and contribute to peace-making and peace-enforcing operations when they are required. But it continues its efforts to develop a multilateral approach to international security and sees its role as that of a 'civilian power'. The door to a renationalization of German security policy remains firmly closed.

5
NATO: at the Heart of European Security

The end of the cold war, as manifested by the dissolution of the Warsaw Pact and the Soviet Union, was accompanied, as we have seen, by demands for the dissolution of NATO and the rebuilding of a pan-European security framework on a new basis. The failure to develop such a new framework for European security or even a commonly accepted general vision for the future of European security is closely connected with the preservation of NATO as the most important and indeed the only functioning integrated security structure in Europe. This chapter will look at how NATO sought to redefine its purposes and strategy, its role in the future of transatlantic relations, and will examine Germany's participation in the Alliance in the light of German perceptions in the role of NATO in the emerging European security architecture.

A new strategy for NATO

The Western Alliance since its inception in 1949 has had three fundamental tasks: providing for the security of Western Europe by means of the containment of the Soviet Union; integrating and containing West Germany within the Western Alliance; and keeping the Americans in Europe. The end of the cold war and the unification of Germany has rendered at least the first two of these objectives largely obsolete. The result is that the Western Alliance needed to redefine its purpose, objectives and strategy.

The principal task of the NATO Alliance, as defined in the *Alliance's New Strategic Concept* adopted by the North Atlantic Council in November 1991, remains the defence of the territorial integrity of the Alliance member states. However, it is recognized that there is

in the current environment no significant threat against the territorial integrity of the Alliance *per se*. Thus the NATO document
states in paragraph 10:

> Risks to Allied security are less likely to result from calculated
> aggression against the territory of the Allies, but rather from the
> adverse consequences of instabilities that may arise from the serious
> economic, social and political difficulties, including ethnic rivalries
> and territorial disputes, which are faced by many countries in
> central and Eastern Europe. The tensions which may result, as
> long as they remain limited, should not directly threaten the
> security and territorial integrity of members of the Alliance. They
> could, however, lead to crises inimical to European stability and
> even to armed conflicts, which could involve outside powers or
> spill over into NATO countries, having a direct effect on the
> security of the Alliance.[1]

The fourth and final of the 'fundamental security tasks' of the Alliance
listed in the document is therefore 'to preserve the strategic balance
within Europe'. This is a direct reference to crisis management in
Europe. Military intervention of any form other than in defence
against direct threats against the Alliance however, is not covered
by Articles 5 and 6 of the Washington Treaty which define the
mutual defence commitment of the Alliance members.[2] Article 4 of
the Washington Treaty provides for consultation among the Allies
about appropriate responses in such situations, but there is no treaty
obligation to participate in any such actions.

The crisis in the former Yugoslavia fits all the general descrip-
tions of a potential threat contained in the NATO document. It is
driven by ethnic rivalries and territorial disputes, poses a serious
threat to the stability of the entire subcontinent (with NATO members
Greece and Turkey being particularly affected) and has generated a
refugee crises that affects some NATO countries and Germany in
particular. It is remarkable that not only have all the various collective security fora failed to generate a coherent response, but there
has been a marked reluctance to classify the crisis as one that NATO
should be particularly concerned with. This can be explained by
the fact that despite the formulation of the Alliance strategic concept, there was no political consensus about the role of NATO in
crisis management. As we have seen, it was the German government in particular which was reluctant to involve NATO in such a

role and looked to the United Nations and the OSCE as the institutions that will assume the responsibility for crisis management. In terms of the strategic concept however, this is precisely the sort of threat that the Alliance should now address. Since the Kosovo conflict of 1998/99 NATO's role in crisis management has been very considerably enhanced. It remains the case, however, that decision-making on crisis intervention by NATO remains ad hoc, because there is neither a treaty obligation nor does NATO itself have the political and legal legitimacy to make such decisions.

Paragraphs 12 and 13 extend the remit of NATO even further, by reference to the implications of events in the Middle East for Alliance Security, and the threats emanating from 'the proliferation of weapons of mass destruction, disruption of the flow of vital resources and actions of terrorism of sabotage.' These paragraphs are clearly inspired by the Gulf conflict. Here the response has been markedly different from the crisis in the former Yugoslavia. There was a determined political and military response, *de jure* under the auspices of the United Nations, but in many ways reliant on NATO capabilities.

The collapse of the Central Front has of course profound implications for military strategy and force postures. During the cold war NATO's armed forces were preparing to counter a massive strategic assault across the North German plains consisting primarily of large tank armies and theatre-wide air strikes backed up by tactical and long-range theatre nuclear forces. The doctrine of 'flexible response' was developed which involved the explicit commitment to escalate to the level of nuclear strikes if and when deemed necessary.[3] In order to accommodate German concerns that large parts of West German territory should not be given up in the early stages of a conflict, NATO also adopted the principle that defence should begin at what was then the East German border and that no West German territory should be given up without a fight. This concept became known as 'forward defence'.[4] The concept of 'flexible response' as hitherto understood is now obsolete; the concept of 'forward defence' has been replaced by 'forward presence'. The diverse and multidirectional risks of the future mean that 'the maintenance of a comprehensive in-place linear defensive posture in the central region will no longer be required.' Instead, NATO's forces are now to be organized to be lighter, more mobile and flexible to be able to deal with a wide range of contingencies. 'Available forces will include, in a limited but militarily significant proportion, ground, air and sea immediate and rapid reaction elements . . .' For the purpose, the Allied Reaction Force (ARRC) was created under British command in October 1992.[5]

In January 1994 the North Atlantic Council adopted a new command-and-control concept known as Combined Joint Task Forces (CJTF). It was designed to make the NATO command structure more flexible in order to permit the greatest variety of possible missions that it might undertake, including missions not led by NATO itself, but by other institutions such as WEU. This would allow the use of NATO assets in circumstances where the United States was not directly involved. It should be noted, however the CJTF are still far from being an operational reality.[6] What is apparent from the description of the future tasks of the NATO Alliance in the *Alliance's New Strategic Concept* (1991) is that any military action by NATO in the future is likely to be, strictly speaking, out-of-area. This has put NATO into a paradoxical situation, where the Alliance has treaty commitments to its members to meet the least plausible threats to Western security, whereas there are no firm obligations to participate in any actions needed to deal with likely contingencies. To put it another way: the bi-polar security environment imposed a requirement on the Western states to unite in a system of collective defence against an overwhelming threat. The post-cold war security environment however requires the creation of an effective system of collective security.

On 24 April 1999 a new version of the NATO *Strategic Concept* was adopted at the Washington summit. The purpose of this summit was to celebrate NATO's 50th anniversary with the admission of three new members from Central Europe (Poland, the Czech Republic and Hungary). The summit was rather overshadowed by the fact that for the first time since its creation the Alliance was effectively at war as a result of the Kosovo crisis. The fundamental structure of the new *Strategic Concept* inevitably is similar in the absence of changes to the Washington Treaty. In view of the experience of the Balkan's conflict, the text of the *Strategic Concept* makes frequent reference to crisis management. NATO's 'essential and enduring purpose' is described as safeguarding 'the freedom and security of all its members by political and military means'.[7]

> The achievement of this aim can be put at risk by crisis and conflict and affecting the security of the Euro-Atlantic area. *The Alliance therefore not only ensures the defence of its members but contributes to peace and stability in the region.* [Emphasis added].

In order to achieve what is described as its essential purpose, the Alliance will perform the following tasks:

1 Security. The document does not actually set out how NATO provides security, but commitment to the growth of democracies and peaceful resolution of disputes is at the heart of its concept of security. The notion put forward by IR theorists that 'liberal democracies do not go to war with each other' appears to be operationalized here. In other words, the growth of democracy results in a reduced likelihood of armed conflict. Other instruments for providing security are arms control and confidence-building regimes in Europe.

2 Consultation. All members states have a right to make their voice heard on any decision.

3 Deterrence and defence. The new language of the *Strategic Concept* does not disguise the fact that collective defence is still at the core of what NATO is about, even though it is hinted in the document that this is fortunately not a current concern.

4 Crisis management. The document states that NATO's involvement in crisis management and crisis response according to Article 7 of the Washington Treaty is on a case-by-case basis. This makes it absolutely and unambiguously clear that NATO is not a collective security organization.

5 Partnership. Co-operation and dialogue with other countries in the Euro-Atlantic area (through the Partnership for Peace programme) are designed to enhance good relations, trust and security.

The manner in which NATO took the lead role in securing the Dayton agreement that ended the war in Bosnia-Herzegovina and the Kosovo conflict has resulted in a situation where NATO is now widely accepted as the main security organization in Europe by all states, including Germany. The Germans, among others, are however acutely aware that this has not resolved the contradictions that underlie such arrangements. NATO remains fundamentally an organization of collective defence, that is available for crisis management and response tasks when needed and if there is sufficient consensus among its members. While NATO has, in a manner rediscovered a role, this is no subsitute for a pan-European system of collective security.[8]

NATO and Eastern Europe

In the immediate aftermath of the dissolution of the Warsaw Pact in 1990 the question of how Central and East European countries could be integrated in a system of European security could not be clearly answered. NATO did not appear to be a suitable instrument for developing a pan-European security system at the time, because the Allies were not prepared to extend security guarantees to the former members of the Warsaw Pact. It was also recognized by the European members of the Alliance that the extension of NATO to Eastern Europe would not enhance the security of current members of the Alliance, but rather diminish it.[9] Indeed, Western Europe might be drawn into conflicts from which it would otherwise remain isolated. Second, if NATO membership was extended to Central European countries and the Baltic states without including Russia itself, this would promote those forces in Russia which oppose the process of political reform and integration in the world community.[10] The recreation of a military confrontation at the Russian border would not enhance the security of East European countries; again, quite the reverse would be the case. However, to provide security guarantees without putting the means in place to support them would be irresponsible. Moreover, there was an extensive conventional arms control regime in place (the CFE Treaty) which was in principle capable of preventing local arms races in Central and Eastern Europe and, in particular, could constrain Russian military deployments west of the Urals. It was considered to be in the security interests of all European countries that this regime remains in place and that Russia remains an adherent to it.[11]

Nevertheless, there was an awareness that in some way the Central and East European states had to be involved in a new security regime. This was an issue regarded with a high level of concern in Germany. As a gesture towards the Central and East European states, and in order to forestall application to join NATO with full membership, the German Foreign Minister Hans-Dietrich Genscher proposed the creation of a North Atlantic Co-operation Council (NACC) at the North Atlantic Council meeting in Rome in November 1991. All former WTO states including the former Soviet Republics (but only those with territory in the ATTU area) were invited to join NACC. The purpose was to allow NATO to offer a limited degree of partnership to the Central and East European countries without involving them fully in NATO's integrated military structure and, most importantly, without having to extend security guarantees. The first meeting of NACC took place in December 1991. At this meeting Genscher proposed the formation of a High Level Working Group (HLWG) to deal with the CFE Treaty and enable it to enter into force in the aftermath of the dissolution of the USSR. The importance that Germany attached to this in view of the gradual withdrawal of former Soviet forces from East Germany cannot be exaggerated.

All of this fell far short of the demands of the Central European states, and especially the Czech Republic and Poland for full NATO membership which were put forward increasingly stridently by presidents Havel and Walesa.[12] Among the principal arguments for NATO expansion put forward were the following:

- the expansion would project stability into the region of Central and Eastern Europe[13]
- Central and East European countries were to become part of the West. The most promising path is membership of the European Union, but these states will take many years to meet the economic and political conditions for EU membership. NATO membership will serve to integrate them into the West in the meantime. This argument became particularly urgent as Communists came back to power in some of the Central European countries.[14]
- the cooling of relations between Russia and the West after the assault on the Parliament and the rise of Vladimir Zhirinovsky gave rise to renewed fears about Russian intentions with regard to the former Soviet sphere of influence.

There remained a deep ambiguity in the Western debate about the wisdom and the purpose of future NATO enlargement. There were proponents of NATO enlargement on the Central European and Western side who argued for it on the basis of the security requirements of Central and East European states. This was based on concerns about Russia in some central European states, given the political instability of the Russian Federation and the rise of anti-Western and nationalist forces there. The need for a security guarantee against Russian hegemonic ambitions was stated most explicitly by Poland. In the United States Zbigniew Brzezinski advocated NATO enlargement on grounds of the geopolitical situation in Eurasia. Such arguments were considered dangerous and therefore were not repeated by government officials in the NATO countries, as these kinds of statement would support the Russian view that NATO expansion is directed against Russia. While not entirely without foundation, the basis on which NATO countries sought to persuade Russia to accept NATO enlargement was as a process that would not threaten Russian security, but enhance stability in Europe. Moreover, the end of the cold war also meant the end of the adversarial relationship between the West and Russia and therefore NATO could not possibly threaten Russia. The ambiguity about the issue of whether the principal motive for NATO expansion was to provide for the security of the new members, which would otherwise be under threat, undermined the central message that NATO leaders wanted to convey to Russia about the benign character of NATO enlargement.

The pressure from central European states for admission to NATO and the support in Western Europe derived primarily from their wish to be firmly integrated into the Western Alliance and thereby enabled them to deal with internal political elements that threaten the stability of the newly democratic regimes. The ideal solution for this problem would in fact be membership of the EU, but as a consequence of the difficulties associated with the transition to a modern market economy, and the structural changes the European Union itself would have to undergo, full EU membership was and remains more distant. NATO membership was therefore seen to some extent as a substitute.

The German Defence Minister Volker Rühe at an early stage made forthright statements in support of NATO membership for the Visegrad countries. Thus he stated before the Defence and Security Committee of the North Atlantic Assembly in Berlin on 21 May 1993:

> With their forthcoming association with the European Communities, the political foundations have been laid and for the Visegrad states – Poland, Hungary, the Czech Republic and the Sloval Republic. I therefore see no reason in principle for denying future members of the European Union membership of NATO.[15]

This derived from Rühe's view that political instability and economic dislocation in Central Europe were a threat to German security; Poland and the Czech republics should not become a source of refugees as a result of political turmoil or economic collapse. The enlargement of NATO was seen as one element in a grand strategy designed to draw these states into a close relationship with Western Europe. In the words of Rühe: 'If we do not export stability, we will import instability.'[16] The new purpose for NATO, in this context, was to act as a political framework to deal with the new, nonmilitary security threats affecting Germany.

There was a remarkable, gradual but definite shift in German foreign policy priorities in 1993. While from 1990 onwards the German–Russian relationship had first priority with regard to the development of a new security architecture in Europe, relations with its immediate neighbours, Poland and the other Visegrad countries, became more important as Germany began to push for the widening of the European Union and the NATO Alliance. This shift was due to the following reasons:

- The German perception of security risks from Russia had lessened considerably. All Russian forces had been withdrawn from German territory. No waves of mass migration from the former Soviet Union had occurred despite the severe social and economic problems, and none were expected in the foreseeable future. The disintegration of the Russian military (except strategic nuclear forces) had continued and it appeared unlikely that Russia will have the social, economic and military resources for a sustained major war with the West.

- On the other hand, the transition in Russia had proved more difficult that anticipated. Economic reform had been ineptly handled and the transformation to a democratic system of government remained incomplete. There was a distinct sense of disappointment about Russia, and a recognition that the transformation of Russia's political system and economy would take a very long time and require enormous resources. The German government let it be known that it could no longer assume additional burdens to aid Russia.

- All of this was exacerbated by the downturn in Russia's relations with the West. This was the result of a shift in the priorities of Russian foreign policy due to a complex range of factors. For example, closer co-operation with the West had not brought the anticipated economic benefits for Russia. The current political élite in Russia is dominated by people who are sceptical of relations with the West and who promote policies designed to promote Russia's own national interests. There was also a general consensus that Russia should play a more assertive role in the territory of the former Soviet Union (FSU), referred to as the 'near abroad'. The negative German reaction to the Chechnya campaign in particular led Russian policymakers to reassess the notion of a special relationship with Germany.

- The proposed expansion of the NATO Alliance to include members of the former Warsaw Pact has become a major issue of contention between Russia and the West. Germany became particularly concerned about developments in Central Europe. The German government appeared to be convinced by the argument that the expansion of NATO was one way to support democratic governments in the region by closer integration with the West. The strong German support for the expansion of NATO had negative repercussions for relations with Russia. The Russian government described the move to expand NATO as a violation of the commitments Germany made in the 'two-plus-four agreement' to settle the external aspects of German unification. This was exacerbated by the fact that Germany was adamant that Russia itself can never be a member of NATO. This was in marked contrast to the American attitude which wanted to keep Russian NATO membership open as a future possibility in the long term.

During 1994 the NATO Alliance took the first steps towards enlargement. In January 1994 the *Partnership for Peace* (PFP) was launched. At the time it was widely interpreted as a poor substitute for NATO membership, especially by some of the Central European countries such as Poland who were pushing hard for full membership. This was justified in part because PFP did not involve the extension of any kind of security guarantee. Nevertheless it was explicitly designed as preparation for membership and involved a commitment to the expansion of the Alliance.[17] It was offered to all members of the CSCE (now OSCE) and thus clearly would involve states that would not be offered NATO membership at an early (or any) stage. The rationale for the programme was described by US Deputy Assistant Secretary of Defence for European and NATO policy, Joseph Kruzel, in the following terms:

[It] offers a training ground for NATO membership. Provides a security home for those not in the first group of countries that became members – but still able to participate in 95 per cent of what NATO members do, and assures one country that will not be an early NATO member, Russia, that NATO expansion is not a threat to its security.[18]

The six areas of co-operation in PFP were as follows:
- facilitating transparency in national defence planning budgeting processes;

- ensuring democratic control of defence forces;
- maintaining the capability and readiness to contribute, subject to the constitution of participating states, to operations under the authority of the United Nations or the CSCE;
- developing co-operative military relations with NATO for the purpose of joint planning, training and field exercises in order to strengthen the ability to undertake missions in the fields of peacekeeping, search and rescue, humanitarian operations and others;
- developing, over the longer term, forces that are better able to operate with those of the members of the North Atlantic Alliance;
- consultations with NATO for any active participant if it perceived a direct threat to its territorial integrity, political independence or security.[19]

Intending partners join the PFP by signing a Framework Document. They then develop an Individual Partnership Programme (IPP) agreed between the individual partner and NATO. The Framework Document identifies the NACC as the institution in which the PFP has been established, in order to emphasize the PFP is an extension of the co-operation within the NACC.[20] The IPP allows each country to define the scope of its partnership and the pace at which it wants to develop it. The various elements of PFP were designed to increase co-operation between the partners and NATO both at an institutional and practical military level. All partners had permanent representation at NATO headquarters in Brussels. At the site of the Supreme Headquarters Allied Powers Europe (SHAPE) a Partnership Coordination Cell was formed. The most visible aspect of co-operation was the increasing number of PFP exercises where the partners were working together at the practical military level. Apart from fostering interaction between military personnel and thereby building relationships and trust, this activity was designed to develop a capacity for joint action with partners and allies. There was much emphasis on this in NATO,[21] and the involvement of PFP partners in the IFOR in Bosnia saw PFP making its contribution to European security in practice. The experience in Bosnia showed that PFP could make a substantial contribution to peacekeeping in the post-cold war international security environment. The promotion of interoperability of equipment, the increasing adoptions of standard concepts of operations and operating procedures and therefore a convergence of military doctrine is a central objective of PFP. A biennial Planning and Review process was established in

1995. Many aspects of PFP activities could be considered as part of the preparation for eventual membership. However, the level of participation in PFP did not reflect itself in the list of early candidates or NATO membership which was generated purely by political considerations.

Although the attitude of Western governments to NATO enlargement remained ambiguous at first, thereby strengthening the initial impression that PFP might be an alternative rather than a preparation for NATO membership, the commitment to enlargement was eventually reaffirmed and deepened at the December 1994 ministerial meeting when NATO decided to undertake a study on the scope and modalities of NATO expansion.[22] This study was completed in September 1995 and at that point it was generally accepted that at least some Central East European regimes would be invited to join the Alliance as full members in the near future.

The reaction from Russia was a firm and hardening opposition to the extension of NATO which was fairly uniform throughout the political élite. At one end of the spectrum of opinion it was presented as an aggressive move that threatens Russia's security and therefore demands a response. A detailed exposition of this view was given by Pavel Fel'gengauer, allegedly representing the scenarios developed by the General Staff. It states that currently the risk of war between Russia and NATO is low because of the geographical distance. After the inclusion of Central and East European states in the Alliance NATO operational plans would be revised and the infrastructure for a rapid forward deployment of NATO forces in Poland would be put in place. NATO would create a unified operational space in a territory reaching right up to the Russian frontier. Integrated mobile air and ground forces could be moved across a distance of thousands of kilometres in a short period of time in order to inflict massive and decisive strikes against Russia. In the view of the general staff, as reported by Fel'gengauer, this transformation of the strategic environment of Europe harbours a real threat of war. In the event of a crisis NATO might begin to forward deploy substantial forces in order to be able to exert pressure on Moscow. Russia would then have no choice but to react with a preemptive strike. If Poland were to become part of the NATO integrated military structure, then Russia might have to respond by deploying hundreds of tactical nuclear weapons in Kaliningrad in order to be able to target the infrastructure in Poland designed to support NATO mobile forces. This would also affect Russia's attitude to the integration of the Baltic countries in Western structures in whatever form.[23] The danger that the extension of NATO could provoke a new military confrontation and arms race in Europe has been emphasized by various military and civilian analysts and one that might lead to actual war has been reiterated by General Lebed and on occasion even by former president Yeltsin.[24]

A threat perception, of course, is not generated purely by military capabilities, but is also based on the interpretation and perception of the international political environment in which it occurs. The view that the extension of NATO represents a threat to Russia presumes the existence of an adversarial relationship with the West to the extent that the West may indeed have reasons to plan military strikes against Russia. On the surface this appears to be completely absurd and contradicts various assertions by Yeltsin and Kozyrev (post-Soviet Russia's first foreign minister) about Russia's relations with the West. While the military scenarios are dubious enough, given the risks that the West would run, not least because Russia is still a strategic nuclear power, none of the Russian statements that condemn the expansion of NATO suggest any political motives or even give a hint of how this could conceivably be in Western interests. Indeed, any objective analysis would suggest that the effect of the extension of NATO, at least to the Visegrad countries, would make very little difference to the European security environment. The threats that Russia faces to its security and stability derive from its internal problems and the conflicts at the southern periphery. The West is the principal source of stability and security even for Russia itself.[25]

Western attitudes however exhibit similar contradictions.[26] The principal argument in favour of NATO expansion has been that it would contribute to the stability of the former Communist countries in Central Europe. There have been voices, however, which have argued that the Central European countries do face a genuine security threat, especially given the prospect of a nationalistic and/or communist leadership in Russia.[27] The strident manner in which Lech Walesa and Vaclav Havel demanded NATO membership with reference to developments in Russia have encouraged such views. Republican members of the United States Congress have also treated Russia as if Russia was still the enemy and are dealing with security issues such as the ABM Treaty, strategic arms control and co-operation on nuclear safety on the basis of an adversarial relationship with Russia. They look at the issue of NATO expansion similarly as a means to deal with a potential Russian threat.[28]

If NATO expansion is designed to enhance political stability, then it is a questionable instrument to achieve this objective because it is difficult to see how it will affect the internal sources of instability in the CEE countries in a tangible manner. If on the other hand it is designed to address an external threat to the stability of the CEE region, then the Russians are correct to interpret it as a move against them (albeit defensive) and put it into the framework of a (potentially) adversarial relationship between Russia and the West. The conceptual contradictions in Russia's response mirror the conceptual contradiction in the process of NATO expansion itself.[29]

The principal reason for the strong reaction to NATO expansion is not just based on considerations of military security, but rather on the perceived political implications. The view of the Ministry of Foreign Affairs has been articulated in a planning document. It states that the expansion of NATO will create a new European security system which will ultimately embrace most Central and East European States, but not Russia. This will impede Russia's participation in a pan-European security structure and a full security partnership with Western states. The document reaffirms that a strategic partnership with the West is in Russia's interest. There is a discernible fear of isolation and the political consequences. These could involve the strengthening of anti-Western forces in Russia, the weakening of the democratic, pro-Western élite, leading ultimately to the 'Weimarization' of Russia. It could result in a significant downturn in relations with the West, one manifestation of which might be the breakdown of arms control regimes and efforts to restore Russia's military capabilities with devastating political and economic consequences.

The problem of Russia's potential international isolation is exacerbated by the ambiguous nature of the NATO enlargement process. The pressure from Central European states for NATO membership is primarily designed to integrate them firmly into the Western Alliance and thereby deal with internal political elements that threaten the stability of the newly democratic regimes. The ideal solution for this would be membership of the EU. As a consequence of the difficulties of the transition to modern market economies full EU membership is likely to be further in the future and NATO membership is seen to some extent as a substitute. However, there are also concerns in some Central European states about Russia, given the political instability of the Russian Federation and the rise of anti-Western and nationalist forces. The need for a security guarantee against Russian hegemonic ambitions has been stated most explicitly by Poland. Although Western leaders deny this, the Russian perception that NATO expansion is directed against Russia is not entirely without foundation. This is strengthened by the ambiguous position on Russia's potential NATO membership. While the United States has insisted on keeping this open as a possibility for the future, the European Allies and Germany in particular have insisted that Russia could never be a member of NATO. Although there are strongly conflicting views in Russia about the wisdom of Russian membership of NATO, these attitudes reinforce Russian perceptions of the hostile nature of NATO expansion.

In the Russian perception, the expansion of NATO has a fundamental impact on the future European security architecture that is at odds with the terms under which the cold war was ended. In this context, it must be remembered that there remains a widespread view in Moscow that Gorbachev's agreement that a united Germany could be a member of NATO was an historical mistake. Nevertheless it is believed that the extension of NATO violates the understanding that Gorbachev reached with Helmut Kohl at the time. Thus President Yeltsin wrote to the Heads of State of the United States, Great Britain, France and Germany that the extension of NATO contravened the 'two-plus-four agreement' of 12 September 1990. From a purely technical point of view, this is clearly not the case. However, the 'two-plus-four agreement' prohibited the deployment of NATO tactical nuclear weapons and the stationing of non-German NATO troops in the territory of the former GDR. In this sense there was a commitment not to extend NATO eastwards beyond its cold war borders, including the former inner-German border. It is quite undeniable that the Soviet Union was given assurances that NATO had no intention to extend eastwards.[30] Gorbachev has stated that there was a 'Gentlemen's Agreement' in the course of the negotiations of the 'two-plus-four agreement' not to extend NATO eastwards.[31] The Russian Ministry of Foreign Affairs and various specialists have therefore argued and continue to maintain that the plans for the expansion of NATO violate the 'spirit' of the 'two-plus-four agreement' and constitute a fundamental breach of trust.

This interpretation is not without some merit given the assurances the Soviets were given in order to obtain acceptance of full German NATO membership after unification. However, it is questionable that the intention was to preclude NATO membership for Central and East European countries indefinitely. The defining period was the first four years during which Soviet/Russian troops were withdrawn from Germany. Still, the Russian reaction may be an indication that the transformation of the international system in Europe after the cold war has not proceeded far enough and to proceed on the basis that these assurances are now no longer relevant.[32]

The Russian case is considerably weakened by the fact that the Soviet Union itself made a public declaration that all former Warsaw Pact states are free to decide to join any alliance. In the agreement of 25 February 1991 which dissolved the Warsaw Pact there was a final communique which declares that all states have the right to decide whether they want to be part of an alliance or not. Despite all other Russian protestations to the contrary, therefore, it would seem that the free choice of the Central East European countries to join NATO should be respected in the new international environment.[33] It is quite clear, however, that these arguments were not politically effective in Moscow. NATO enlargement has become a symbol of relations with the West more generally and a political instrument of those who support a more independent, less pro-Western or even anti-Western foreign and security policy. In other words, NATO enlargement has become a political wild card which has served to promote the interests of a range of political constituencies in the Russian political élite and therefore was not susceptible to rational counterarguments based on an 'objective' assessment of Russian national security interests. The attitude taken by the Russian government was that the decision to accept new members in the NATO Alliance was not final and therefore could be defeated. This meant that until the Helsinki summit in March 1997 there was no willingness to prepare fallback positions or develop political compromises.

On the other hand, ultimately Russia was not in a position to prevent NATO expansion. Among the possible Russian responses to any widening of the Alliance the following were mooted:

1 The creation of a military alliance in the CIS. This option was proposed by the then Russian defence minister Grachev but was widely considered to be unrealistic.

2 The strengthening of a special military relationship with Belarus. This appears to be in progress.

3 The deployment of tactical nuclear weapons in Belarus and Kaliningrad, and other forward base areas.

4 The renunciation of the INF Treaty, the redeployment of INF or/ and the targeting of strategic nuclear forces at military targets in the CEE.

5 The renunciation of the CFE Treaty and an all-round build-up of Russian conventional forces.
6 The end of strategic arms control (i.e. non-ratification of START II).
7 Disregarding Western concerns about arms exports to 'rogue states', including Iran and Libya, and collaboration in missile production with India.
8 The occupation of the Baltic states if they are to be accepted into the NATO Alliance.

Despite the generally uncompromising stance taken by all shades of opinion in Moscow, some possible avenues of solution were explored. From the Western side, there was the concept of a special partnership with Russia that recognizes Russia's special position as a great power and seeks to take the edge off NATO enlargement by reassuring Russia through a variety of consultative mechanisms. Such gestures did not appear to be enough to overcome Russian opposition. In the Russian foreign ministry there was the suggestion that Russia's principal concern is the deployment of nuclear weapons or nuclear infrastructure in the CEE states.[34] A commitment by NATO not to recreate a new theatre nuclear threat in Central Europe stood out as an important element of a deal whereby Russia would acquiesce in the extension of NATO membership to some CEE countries.

The German position on this issue created fundamental contradictions for German security policy. It could be argued that the debate about NATO expansion itself is a dangerous distraction. It deals with symbols, rather than the real and unprecedented security threats that Russia, and to a lesser extent, the rest of Europe are facing. The post-cold war environment requires a security architecture that provides collective security. NATO is a collective defence organization that still remains maladapted to the requirements of collective security despite the transformation of its military structure. The argument put forward by German government officials rests on the premise that the cold war is over and NATO expansion exports stability without threatening anybody's security. This failed to address the ambiguities inherent in this process, especially as regards Russia, and it did not resolve the question of NATO's role in the post-cold war era. Moreover, it put in question the special relationship between Germany and Russia which could well be fundamental to the new security architecture in Europe. The Russians clearly blamed the Germans for their role in the NATO expansion debate, especially in view of the 'two-plus-four agreement'. However, the Russian–German relationship remains so important that both sides placed it back at the top of their priorities during the presidential elections in Russia. In order to minimize the impact on relations with Russia, the German government sought to place the two processes of NATO and EU expansion in parallel as much as possible.[35]

Until the Helsinki summit in March 1997, despite the various hints of a possible resolution of this issue, a complete rejection of NATO expansion in all its forms remained at the core of the official Russian stance, as expressed by President Yeltsin himself:[36]

> I do not rule out the possibility that we [Yeltsin and Clinton] may disagree on something. The position of the Russian leadership is known: we do not intend to make concessions that would undermine the defense capability of the country. What the Americans are suggesting – the spread of conventional armaments to Eastern Europe – the effect of which would be to seal Russia off. We will not agree to that. . . . Our other categoric condition is that Baltic and CIS not be drawn into NATO in any form.

Clearly, the Russian leadership had become alarmed by NATO's contacts with the leaders of countries in the former Soviet Union, in particular the tour of several CIS nations by NATO Secretary General Javier Solana. Yeltsin furthermore dismissed any suggestion that Russia itself might join NATO.[37] Yeltsin also made it clear that Russia did not fear a military attack by NATO, but was seeking to prevent isolation as a result of NATO enlargement. But already prior to the summit his language became somewhat more ambiguous. Instead of a complete retreat by the American President, he merely demanded some unspecified 'compromise'.

In the course of the Helsinki summit, which took place on 20–21 March 1997, it became clear, if it had not been before, that NATO enlargement would proceed and Yeltsin was forced to acknowledge the fact that it could no longer be prevented. Indeed, to many in Russia the results of the Helsinki summit looked like a total surrender on the part of Yeltsin.[38] The principal objective of Russian policy became damage limitation. The most suitable device for saving face was an agreement between NATO and Russia that would in some way safeguard Russian interests and define the future relationship between Russia and the Alliance. For Russia, such an agreement had to have at least four basic elements:

- No nuclear weapons would be stationed on the territory of the new NATO members.

- There would be no substantial forward deployment of NATO conventional forces or NATO's military infrastructure.
- The adaptation of the CFE Treaty to take account of the changed international security environment in which Russia will find itself after NATO enlargement.
- Russia would have a voice in NATO decisions, especially with regard to those affecting relations with the East, so that diplomatic means would exist to prevent actions inimical to Russia's national security.[39]

Intensive talks were held between Russian Foreign Minister Primakov and NATO Secretary General Solana and also between Primakov and US Secretary of State Albright to finalize such an agreement. The principal point of disagreement right until the last moment was that Russia was seeking iron clad guarantees on the four basic elements outlined above. This was obviously incompatible with the obligations under the NATO Treaty, and in the end NATO did not budge from a formulation that conceded that these demands could be met under present conditions, but that NATO reserved the right to deploy its forces in whatever way it deemed necessary in the event of an emerging risk to international security in the region.

The *Founding Act on Mutual Relations, Cooperation and Security between NATO and the Russian Federation* was signed by NATO Heads of State and Russian President Boris Yeltsin in Paris on May 27. According to the document,

> NATO and Russia will help to strengthen the Organization for Security and Cooperation in Europe (OSCE), including developing further its role as a primary instrument in preventive diplomacy, conflict prevention, crisis management, post-conflict rehabilitation and regional security cooperation, as well as in enhancing its operational capabilities to carry out these tasks.

> NATO and Russia will base their relations on a shared commitment to the following principles:

> development, on the basis of transparency, of a strong, stable, enduring and equal partnership and of cooperation to strengthen security and stability in the Euro-Atlantic area; acknowledgement of the vital role that democracy, political pluralism, the rule of law, and respect for human rights and civil liberties and the development of free market economies play in the development of

common prosperity and comprehensive security; refraining from the threat or use of force against each other as well as against any other state, its sovereignty, territorial integrity or political independence in any manner inconsistent with the Charter of the United Nations and with the Declaration of Principles Guiding Relations Between Participating States contained in the Helsinki Final Act; respect for sovereignty, independence and territorial integrity of all states and their inherent right to choose the means to ensure their own security, the inviolability of border and peoples' right of self-determination as enshrined in the Helsinki Final Act and other OSCE documents; mutual transparency in creating and implementing defence policy and military doctrines; prevention of conflicts and settlement of disputes by peaceful means in accordance with UN and OSCE principles; support, on a case-by-case basis, peacekeeping operations carried out under the authority of the United Nations Security Council or the responsibility of the OSCE.

The agreement partially satisfies Russia's requirements, but in a way which does not bind NATO in the event of a real crisis in relations with Russia. Thus NATO has said that the deployment of nuclear weapons on the territory of future NATO members is not anticipated in the foreseeable future, but has refused to give a definite guarantee that this will never happen. Moreover, the Alliance has stated that it does not intend to deploy any significant combat forces on a permanent basis in these countries. On the basis of Article 5 of the NATO Treaty, the Alliance reserves the right to deploy whatever forces are necessary on the territory of all its member states in a crisis situation.

The creation of a NATO–Russia Council has the purpose of providing the forum for consultation to reassure Russia of NATO's intentions at all times. It even provides Russia with a voice – but no vote – on internal issues of the NATO Alliance. President Yeltsin and Foreign Minister Primakov heralded the 'consensus rule' as a veto on all NATO actions, but in reality the rule of consensus will only be applied during the adoption of decisions concerning bilateral co-operation between Russia and NATO.[40] The resolution of the dispute over the enlargement of NATO appears to have had the effect of creating an agreed framework for Russia's relations with the West and thereby improving relations considerably. However, NATO enlargement has the potential of reemerging as a political problem if countries of the former Soviet Union, such as the Baltic states or even Ukraine demand membership at a later stage.

Germany pushed very quickly for the implementation of NATO enlargement by direct bilateral contacts with the new prospective members. The most controversial aspect was the plan for Germany, Denmark and Poland to create a joint military force to guard the western approaches to the Baltic Sea. Criticized by Russian Defence Minister Sergeev, it was argued that the corps, which will have its headquarters in the Polish port city of Szczecin, will help extend the stabilizing influence of NATO's multilateral approach to the new democracies of Central Europe. The force – to be called the Multinational Corps North-East – will be the first mission in Central Europe to become operational.[41] In general terms, there were many indications of closer collaboration between Germany and Poland especially in the aftermath of the NATO Founding Act. At the same time the Federal Government was at pains to lend more substance to the partnership with Russia. This manifested itself in the visit to Moscow by German President Roman Herzog in September 1997, the visit by the Russian Chief of the General Staff, Anatoly Kvashnin to Bonn in November 1997, and finally Chancellor Kohl's visit to Russia at the end of November in the same year. In January 1998, Kohl's Chief Foreign Policy adviser, Joachim Bitterlich, floated the idea of offering Russia and Ukraine a 'closer association' with NATO and the European Union.[42] Thus a full-blown diplomatic effort was underway to reconcile the contradictory strands of Germany's policy towards the East and reassure Russia about its role in Europe in the aftermath of NATO enlargement.

The Berlin Republic: a dependable ally

During its time in opposition, the SPD had voiced significant dissent with respect to crucial aspects of security policy. It did not approve the government's approach to the use of German armed forces out-of-area and it opposed the enlargement of NATO. It has to be said that the reality of the first decade after unification, which was marked by the terrors of the Balkan conflicts, had a deep and lasting effect on politicians from all side of the spectrum. But also important was the fact that under Gerhard Schröder the SPD was determined to become electable again. As a result, the SPD moved closer to what was perceived to be the national consensus. The party conferences in Hanover (December 1997) and Leipzig (April

1998) laid down the new line which emphasized Germany's commitment to the European Union and the importance of NATO for German security. The critical difference to the government position appeared to be that the SPD insisted that the United Nations has the sole authority to use force in order to safeguard international peace and that therefore the participation of the Bundeswehr in peacekeeping and peace enforcement missions requires a UN Security Council mandate.[43] In the face of the Kosovo crisis the SPD leadership moved quickly to declare its support for NATO despite the absence of a more specific UN Security Council mandate.[44] Schröder made it clear that Germany could not stand aside when the general consensus among NATO governments was in favour of action.[45]

The other coalition partner, the Alliance90–Greens (Bündnis90–Die Grünen) also underwent a process of adaptation in the foreign and security policy. For a party based on pacifism and antinuclear activism and with a commitment to leave NATO, this was extraordinarily difficult, causing very deep divisions in the party. In 1995 party members and the Party Caucus rejected participation of the Bundeswehr in IFOR in Bosnia. As recent as March 1998, a party conference in Magdeburg narrowly rejected the extension of the Bosnia mission. The party members also demanded the replacement of NATO by a pan-European security system and categorically rejected peace enforcement missions according to Chapter VII of the UN Charter. The party 'realists' were able to bring about some significant changes to the official position. For one thing, it was agreed that Germany should not unilaterally leave NATO. The absolute rejection of Chapter VII missions was relaxed; the party now stated that peacekeeping missions (see Chapter 6) should be given preference.[46]

When a 'red–green' coalition of SPD–Greens formed the government as a result of the elections in September 1998, Joschka Fischer from the Green Party became Foreign Minister. The Green Party was thereby at the centre position of government with respect to foreign and security policy. Fischer soon distinguished himself not only as an able minister, but reassured both the German people and their foreign allies as to his reliability to provide continuity in German foreign and security policy. The only slight deviation from this course was Fischer's initiative to achieve a change in NATO's nuclear strategy towards a 'no first use policy'. This had not been cleared with the Chancellor or the Defence Minister and was immediately and decisively rebuffed by the US Defense Secretary William Cohen. It is a supreme irony that Germany was called upon to participate in its first military mission since the war at a time when the Green Party was in power for the first time. During the entire Kosovo crisis Fischer proved himself to be a dependable supporter of the Allied effort despite enormous pressure and even vilification from his own party. The Kosovo conflict marked a final step in the adaptation to the post-cold war international security environment not only for NATO, but especially for the Federal Republic of Germany.

Conclusion

In 1990, the future of NATO seemed uncertain. Germany, as the NATO member most involved and affected by the large-scale changes in the European system of states, was an active promoter of an alternative security architecture in Europe that would include the former Warsaw Pact and even Russia. The initial period after the cold war was characterized by uncertainty about the future of the international system. The most disconcerting feature of it was that, whereas the bipolar system had prevented the outbreak of armed conflict, there was now a zone of instability in Europe in which a number of severe conflicts erupted. It remained unclear, however, for some time, what role Western states would play in these conflicts resulting from the break-up of the Soviet Union and Yugoslavia. This was especially the case since the United States was loath to become involved directly. By shifting the burden of responsibility to the Europeans, however, the role of NATO appeared to be marginalized. Until the Partnership for Peace developed, and until NATO became more closely involved in Bosnia, NATO struggled to find a new role. It survived primarily because, in the absence of alternative European security arrangements, the members of the Alliance felt it necessary to perpetuate its existence.

At the root of the problem was the lack of a common conception of the nature of the new security environment and the political and military instruments that European states are prepared to use to deal with threats to European security. The Partnership for Peace and the concept of the Common Joint Task Forces gave NATO a new lease of life, because although they did not address the issue of NATO's role and purpose as such, they provided a plethora of worthwhile activities for NATO to engage in. NATO's involvement in the conflicts in the former Yugoslavia, first by providing the military pressure to bring about the Dayton accords and the creation of IFOR/SFOR and later by taking the lead in resolving the

Kosovo crisis seemed the final vindication of NATO as the only credible security institution in Europe. However, this vindication cannot be seen as conclusive, because while the United States finally abandoned its previous approach and became fully involved in these operations, the opposition to future direct US participation in European security operations remains. Moreover, although NATO's *Strategic Concept* (1999) supports the involvement in crisis management and response, it fundamentally remains a collective defence regime without a firm commitment to collective security.

The process of NATO enlargement once again put NATO centre stage in the European security debate. Germany was at the vanguard of the promoters of enlargement in order to stabilize the new democracies in Central Europe. This created a fundamental tension in two strands of German security policy, namely the stabilization of the former Soviet space versus the stabilization of Germany's eastern neighbours, especially Poland and the Czech Republic. This tension persists, as German leaders seek to build a partnership with Russia while at the same time pushing ahead with the integration of the three proposed new members into NATO. From the German perspective, therefore, NATO has and continues to serve a vital function in European security even in the absence of a large-scale military threat. It is the principal vector of the integration of the wider Europe prior to the widening of the European Union.

So far, contrary to the expectations of many, the policy appears to be successful. Russia has, however grudgingly, signed on to NATO enlargement. The deepening of relations with key Central European states is evident. This does not mean that there may not be problems ahead. The next phase of NATO enlargement may be a great deal more controversial than the first, especially if it involves the Baltic states. A change of political leadership in Russia could result in a rejection of the partnership with NATO and a more hostile international climate. The reliance on NATO without a *Gesamtkonzept* for European security means that the Alliance essentially continues to muddle through. The experience of the former Yugoslavia shows the potentially disastrous consequences of this approach. More importantly, it leaves the central issues about NATO's role unanswered. Despite its present success, therefore, the policy pursued so far means that the hard questions are likely to return in the future.

6
The European Union

Since the 1950s Germany's basic position in the international political and security system has been fairly well defined as a result of the *Westintegration*, whereby the Federal Republic accepted restrictions on its foreign policy in return for the security guarantee of the Alliance. Since that time Germany's political élite has been largely agreed over two major points – first Germany's firm anchorage in the Western security system and second its participation in multilateral frameworks on a co-operative basis. Bonn's commitment to *Westintegration* was not just a consequence of West Germany's security dilemmas but was also integral to its international rehabilitation. European integration was part of a vision for building a new Europe which would not be dominated by the traditional and dangerous interstate rivalries. The Federal Government's commitment to *Westintegration* was a result of the need to overcome the historic Franco-German competition for hegemony in Europe and the animosities which had resulted from two world wars.

Central to this approach was a different perception of the nature of power in international relations, and the concept of national interests and the instruments which could legitimately be employed to pursue them. This should not, however, imply that the Federal Republic's political leaders during these years had no sense of Germany's national interests. Nor were they inclined to accept a subordinate role for the FRG, internationally or within the Atlantic Alliance.[1] In this sense, the now widely quoted phrase '*Von Machtbesessenheit zur Machtvergessenheit*' is misleading.[2] Indeed, quite the opposite was the case: to achieve equality with the major European powers and to play a leading role in the Atlantic Alliance were central to West German foreign policy.

The Federal Republic differed however from France and Britain as, in view of German history, and the emerging external environment and postwar political culture, the pursuit of federal German national interests could only take place within a supranational framework. Moreover, such a framework was vital not only for Germany but for *Europe as a whole*. Politically and economically, this would be the European Community; for security, NATO. Only in such a multilateral context would it be acceptable for Germany to become a major power. Consequently West Germany was a major force for integration in Europe.

The central goal for West German foreign policy, once the Federal Republic was established, was its rehabilitation as a member of international society in general, and regaining the freedom of action in international relations which had been so heavily circumscribed after 1945 by the Western powers and the Soviet Union.[3] In view of the legacy of the Second World War, this was only acceptable if West Germany were to be firmly integrated within a Western Alliance which would serve both to contain West Germany and harness its strength to the benefit of the common security of the West. European integration was for West Germany the only way to overcome the disadvantages of the constraints imposed by the limitations of its sovereignty. European integration also provided a moral framework in which West Germany could develop its identity as a member of international society on the basis of a rejection of the militarism and nationalism that led to disaster. In particular, it was seen as a framework to overcome the Franco-German competition for hegemony in Europe and the animosities that had resulted in two world wars.

William Paterson and Simon Bulmer have argued that foreign policy and diplomacy were means whereby the West German state constructed its identity and that European policy was at the heart of this process.[4] In this view, participation in international institutions was not just an instrument of policy, but also a normative framework for policymaking that should increasingly supersede a purely national interest based approach.[5] It was also an approach that was used to contain and overcome, as far as possible, the effects of the cold war through detente (*Ostpolitik*, the CSCE) and arms control.[6]

The experience since the founding of the European community has justified many of West German expectations. The European Community has slowly but steadily, deepened and widened. Military conflict among the West European states became unthinkable, and the end of the cold war and German unification proved the success of the European model as Central European states were drawn towards membership in NATO and the European Union.

Germany and Europe after unification

The collapse of Soviet power in Europe enhanced Germany's role in every conceivable manner. To begin with, since the division of Europe manifested itself most acutely in the division of Germany, the West German government played a major role in negotiating the final settlement that enabled the peaceful withdrawal of Soviet forces from Central Europe. The fact that the territory of the Federal Republic of Germany was increased while the territory of Soviet influence was substantially reduced, until the Soviet Union itself was dissolved, was a potent symbol of the shift of power on the European continent from which Germany was the principal beneficiary. The disintegration of an empire controlled by a nuclear superpower moreover signified that a surfeit of military power was not sufficient. The Soviet collapse was not just the final defeat of a command economy; it was also a vivid demonstration that a strong modern economy was an important and necessary component of power. It appeared to demonstrate that in the international system as a whole economic power was becoming more important. West Germany was the third largest economy in the world, the largest economy in Europe and the dominant economy in the European Community. Moreover, because of its geographical position which made the united Germany effectively the bridge between Western Europe and Central and Eastern Europe, and as a result of its export oriented economy, Germany was poised to play the principal role in the economic, and maybe even the political, transformation of Central and Eastern Europe. The obvious conclusion was that in the post-cold war European system of states Germany, now free from its former constraints, would play a dominant role as a regional civilian superpower in Europe.[7]

   The reaction by the German political élite to the new international environment was not a diminution of the commitment to European integration, but rather the opposite. Moreover, the Federal Government displayed an almost unseemly sensitivity to the reaction of Germany's western and eastern neighbours to German foreign policy behaviour. This was a reaction to the perceived persistence of collective memories that make the reality of German power in Europe and any manifestation of it being exercised appear threatening.[8] Nevertheless, there is a clear perception in Germany's political élite that Germany does have to play a leadership role in Europe and exercises structural power in Europe to achieve very definite policy objectives. The consensus remains that the exercise of such power is only acceptable and feasible through the framework of the European Union.[9]

The European Union: widening and deepening

The process of European integration took a substantial step forward as a result of the Single European Act (SEA) in 1987. It entered a new phase after the end of the cold war with the Treaty on European Union (also known as the Maastricht Treaty).[10] Germany's policy towards Europe since Maastricht has consisted of the persistent effort to promote the implementation of Maastricht and push European integration yet further. The ambitious agenda that the European Union has set itself since the beginning of the 1990s is usually described as 'deepening' and 'widening'. This implies a further move towards political union, including the development of an effective Common Foreign and Security Policy, Economic and Monetary Union (EMU) and the widening of the European Union to include Central and East European countries.

The German political élite is well aware that 'deepening' and 'widening' are ambitious programmes and not necessarily compatible with each other. European Monetary Union, for example, is a enterprise fraught with risks which has the effect of harmonizing European economies as a result of the membership criteria and the harmonizing effect of a common currency. Not even all current EU members will join at first and this form of 'deepening' the union has the effect of creating a differentiation of EU membership which undoubtedly will affect the widening process. In other words, 'deepening' increases the barriers to 'widening'. Some EU members, such as the United Kingdom, are in favour of widening precisely in order to inhibit 'deepening'. Others, such as France and the Benelux countries, are more interested in 'deepening', and 'widening' could threaten their interests.[11]

The German perspective on this was more complicated. The main thrust of German policy was clearly towards deeper integration, with the Franco-German couple at the centre. At the same time widening of the European Union was considered a critical element of a strategy to ensure the political stability and democratization of Central Europe. This in turn was considered the most important element of German security policy in the post-cold war era. German views on the development of European institutions is strongly informed by the potential incompatibilities inherent in this dualism.[12]

One possible way forward that was mooted in the so-called Schäuble/Lamers paper of 1994 which referred to the possibility for Germany to fall back on a 'core Europe'. In the event that German visions for the 'deepening' and 'widening' of the European Union was not accepted by a sufficient majority of EU members the 'core group' which would include at least France and the Benelux countries could move forward to implement the objectives set by the Maastricht process.[13] Foreign Minister Klaus Kinkel and Chancellor Kohl were not supporters of the 'core Europe' notion as such and as German policy was taking shape in advance of the Intergovernmental Conference of 1996 the idea of a core group lost much of its initial significance. A more sophisticated approach that was developed by academics was that of a differentiated integration, which Josef Janning has described as

> a mix of deeper integration, greater responsibilities for committed member states and the notion of sectoral cores for high integration areas such as monetary or security integration. As a political system, it would lead to the concentration of leadership roles on those member states which are actively involved in all or most of these sectoral deepenings.[14]

Such an approach still seems inevitable given the reluctance of some members to move as far as others with European integration (for example the Schengen agreement and EMU). Moreover, this approach would actually facilitate the widening of the Union by lowering the initial requirements of membership. Indeed, a 'Europe of different speeds' may be inevitable. The principal difficulty that Janning foresees is that even this more differentiated version of the 'core Europe' concept relies to a great extent on the Franco-German relationship. This relationship remains close, but Germany and France have different priorities in their European policy. France is primarily concerned about the power of Germany, whereas Germany is preoccupied with stability in Central and Eastern Europe. The formation of integration cores may not succeed unless both countries move much closer to a common vision of the future of Europe.[15]

For the purposes of this book, we are interested especially in three aspects of European integration. The first is the development of the Common Foreign and Security Policy (CFSP) and, as a subsidiary element of that, the potential for a common European Security and Defence Identity. In other words, this will look at what role the European Union will play in international security and how German security policy may or may not be implemented through the framework of the European Union. The second is European and Monetary Union. Here we will be interested primarily in the issue of German economic power in Europe and how the process of EMU demonstrates the meaning and the implications of such power. The third is the widening of the EU to Central and Eastern Europe. What is of interest for this study are the security concerns in Germany that help to drive this process, and the implications it will have for the Union as a whole.

The common foreign and security policy

The co-ordination of foreign policies within the European Community was not part of the Rome Treaty that founded the Community, but in view of the vast network of relations with other states and the movement towards greater integration, was a logical development. For this purpose the European Political Cooperation (EPC) began in the 1970s. It remained at an informal level until the Single European Act in 1987 which institutionalized it and created a small EPC secretariat. The Treaty on European Union (TEU), created a European Union supported by three pillars – the European Community (Pillar One), the Common Foreign and Security Policy (CFSP) (Pillar Two) and co-operation in Justice and Home Affairs (JHA) (Pillar Three).

To work out a common approach to foreign and security policy has proved difficult in the past. Even if the institutional problems were resolved, the underlying difficulty is that any substantial issue brings to the fore divergences of interests. The European response to the Gulf crisis in 1990/91 is a good case in point. While the operational co-operation among those European states who sent forces to the Gulf under the WEU umbrella worked well, the co-ordination of political responses in the framework of the EC proved to be a debacle. This applies *a forteriori* to policy towards the conflicts in the former Yugoslavia.

At the root of the problem of developing a functioning CFSP are fundamental disagreements about the nature and basis of European integration. To take one end of the spectrum, the British perspective is based on a pragmatic realism, and European co-operation in foreign and security policy on intergovernmentalism. An integrated European foreign policy is not conceivable, because ultimately the national interest of the each of the member states must define their foreign and security policy. Policy initiatives at the European level are only possible and acceptable so long as they reflect these national interests. For this reason, the European Union remains incapable of taking decisive action in crisis situations, because it is extremely difficult to reconcile both the national interests of all member states and their philosophical differences to international conflict and crisis management. The debacles of the Gulf War (1991) and the Bosnian conflict are seen to support this view.

Another dimension of the British perspective is the profound scepticism regarding a grand strategy, or *Gesamtkonzept*, for European security after the cold war. At the core of West European security remains the commitment of the global superpower, the United States. This means that NATO has to remain the principal institutional framework for security. While Europe should play a strong role in NATO and contribute its fair share in terms of military commitments, it should not seek to build the mechanisms and capabilities to support an independent security policy (assuming that it could do so). As a consequence, Britain does not favour the emergence of a Common Defence Policy in the European Union as an effective rival to NATO. While Britain can see a role for the WEU, it is not in favour of the absorption of WEU by the European Union. Regional security organizations, such as the OSCE and the WEU, can play a useful role in conflict prevention and the legitimization of responses to crisis situations. For Britain, however, they are no substitute for an effective integrated military structure supported by the United States.

Although Britain and Germany agree on the fundamental need for NATO and the US commitment, there is a profound philosophical difference in their approach to the future of European security. For Germany, European integration was the cornerstone of West European security, because it removed the threat of war from Western Europe. CFSP was part of its strategy, based on an institutionalist approach, to develop a pan-European peace order whereby the large range of political actors on the European scene were to be bound into a framework of institutions designed to create and maintain political stability. The European Union was to be at the heart of these institutions, but to be effective, the development of CFSP and a Common Defence Policy seemed essential if the stabilizing policies were to be effective beyond the European Union's borders.

The move towards a European foreign and security policy was in part a response to external pressure. The United States at various times pushed its Allies, and Germany in particular, to assume greater responsibility for their own defence. The creation of a 'European pillar' of the NATO Alliance, either through the Eurogroup in the late 1960s or the revitalization of the WEU in the early 1980s had generally three purposes:

- convince the Americans that the Europeans were serious about making their own contribution;
- allow the consideration of European interests on a collective basis, in cases where they might substantially differ from those of the United States;
- enable France to be drawn into a framework of European security that was outside NATO, but not in contradiction to Alliance commitments and objectives.

Although the United States generally encouraged European defence co-operation in principle, it was nevertheless suspicious of any 'European caucus' that might affect American leadership of the Alliance or in any way appear to assume any functions of NATO. As the American military presence in Europe diminished, after the collapse of the Central Front, a strengthened European pillar of the Alliance and the formation of a stronger European defence identity was widely perceived as a logical corollary of the changed security environment. This is recognized in NATO's new strategic doctrine:

> The creation of a European identity in security and defence will underline the preparedness of the Europeans to take a greater share of responsibility for their security and will help to reinforce transatlantic solidarity.[16]

Until the late 1980s, the development of a European defence identity was hampered by the existence of a variety of competing institutional frameworks, none of which fulfilled all the perceived requirements. The German foreign ministry was very keen to develop a joint security policy in the framework of the European Political Cooperation of the EC. Thereby it would become one aspect of the process of European integration. This proved to be unacceptable to some of the smaller EC member states, one of which (Ireland) is not a member of NATO. The Western European Union was an organization more acceptable to the United States and proved itself as an effective umbrella for joint military action by some of its members during the 'tanker war' in the Persian Gulf in 1987 and the Gulf War in 1991. However, it had no direct link with the European Community. Any European defence identity emerging within the WEU would therefore have been in conflict with efforts to establish greater co-operation in security policy within the EC.

On 6 December 1990 German Chancellor Kohl and French President Mitterrand proposed that an organic link between WEU and European Political Union should be established such that a WEU with greater operational capabilities could become part and parcel of the EU. The framework of WEU would thus be used to develop a common security policy for European Political Union. Discussions among member states of the WEU indicated that there was a general consensus in favour of the establishing a link between NATO and the European Union (EU). It would serve to bind-in France and those members of NATO who are not members of the EU. Thus the Maastricht summit in December 1991 in the draft treaty for European Political Union stated the principles of a common foreign and security policy (CFSP):

> 1. The CFSP shall include all questions related to the security of the Union, including the eventual framing of a common defence policy, which might in time lead to a common defence.
> 2. The Union requests WEU, which is an integral part of the development of European Union, to elaborate and implement decisions and actions of the Union which have defence implications.[17]

This means that WEU will become the operational arm of EU in defence related matters. By way of a first step towards implementation Germany and France agreed to set up a joint 'Eurocorps'. The purpose of this initiative, which was based on conversations between Chancellor Kohl and President Mitterrand in July 1991, was to expand the Franco-German brigade to an army corps which – unlike the Franco-German brigade – would be open to other European states and could form the basis of a multinational, European corps. The details of the initiative were hammered out in four Franco-German seminars.[18] It was formally announced at the summit of La Rochelle on 21–22 May 1992.

The precise relationship of the Eurocorps to NATO, WEU or the United Nations was left ambiguous. As far as the possible use outside the NATO Treaty area was concerned, the German side insisted on legitimization by means of a UN mandate. This was rejected by the French because it would make the employment of the Eurocorps dependent on the agreement of non-Europeans. A vague compromise formula was reached which stated that the Eurocorps would act from the perspective of the European Union and in accordance with the limits imposed by national constitutions and the UN Charter. The Eurocorps could be employed for the collective defence of the Western Alliance on the basis of Article 5 of the Washington Treaty or in accordance with the Brussels Treaty. Among possible missions of the Eurocorps the following were mentioned:

- combat missions to reestablish peace;
- peacekeeping operations;
- humanitarian missions and disaster relief.

The Eurocorps is subject to a French–German security council and is administered by a WEU 'planning cell'. In the event of other European nations joining, a 'Eurocorps council' is to be formed. On 1 July 1992, a preparatory staff with 15 officers began its work in Strasbourg. It is envisaged that 35 000 troops will eventually be assigned to the Eurocorps. Initially Germany and France will each provide one division.

The reaction from the United Kingdom was sceptical, that of the United States openly negative. The overlap in mission objectives with the planned NATO Rapid Reaction Corps is evident.[19] There were fears that the Eurocorps would weaken NATO and hasten an American withdrawal before the Europeans were ready to fully assume the military burden of the security problems facing them. Brent Scowcroft, the United States National Security Advisor, wrote to Chancellor Kohl to express American misgivings. As a result, other Alliance members, such as Italy and Belgium, who had expressed interest in joining the Eurocorps, backed away from any participation.

Apart from giving concrete expression to a CFSP, the Eurocorps is designed to fulfil two important German policy objectives. One is to provide an international institutional framework in which the constitutional and political limitations of German participation in 'out-of-area' missions can be gradually overcome by becoming locked into a network of commitments. The second is to draw France closer to NATO. The Germans point to the fact that none of the troops assigned to the Eurocorps will be withdrawn from the integrated military structure of NATO, and the Eurocorps itself can be assigned to NATO command.

Both of these objectives incorporate the inherent contradictions in the initiative that may render it meaningless. Unless the domestic political opposition to 'out-of-area' missions was overcome, Germany was not able to participate in what appears in the foreseeable future the most likely contingency in which the Eurocorps would be employed. This problem may now have been resolved, but uncertainty remains and at the time it appeared to negate any useful function for the Eurocorps. Bonn's intention that France should be drawn closer to NATO has been fulfilled by the French decision to rejoin NATO Military Committee in December 1995.[20] As regards the Eurocorps, they have accepted that in a case of emergency the Eurocorps, including the French forces assigned to it, could come under NATO command.[21]

To work out a common foreign and security policy has proved difficult in the past. Even if now the institutional problems may have been resolved to some extent, the underlying difficulty is that any substantial issue brings to the fore divergences of interests. The European response to the Gulf crisis in 1990/91 is a good case in point. While the operational co-operation among those European states who sent forces to the Gulf under the WEU umbrella worked well, the co-ordination of political responses within the framework of the EC proved to be a debacle.

The Maastricht Treaty does not define the precise nature of a CDP or the future direction of CFSP. At one end of the spectrum, Germany and the Benelux countries support the absorption of WEU by the European Union. *Defence* would become the so-called *fourth pillar* of the European Union. This would mean that defence policy would be co-ordinated at the European level and decisions could be made by a qualified majority. It would also mean that the treaty obligation to use all military forces to defend any member state under attack, which is part of the modified Brussels Treaty (the WEU Treaty), would apply to the whole of the European Union. It would mean that all EU members would have to become full members of the WEU (currently five members of the EU are not full members of WEU). This is called the *communautaire* as opposed to the *intergovernmental* approach to CFSP.

Even if the 1996 Intergovernmental Conference had adopted the German vision of a CDP, this would *not* mean that the creation of a common European army or the loss of control over national armed forces. According to the *Petersberg Declaration* of 1992, any member of WEU can abstain from joint military actions. There is no prospect that this basic right will be abandoned. The Germans themselves will often have to make use of the right to opt out from joint actions because of the constitutional limitations on the use of military forces outside the NATO defence area.

A CDP would also *not* mean that WEU could create integrated military forces to replace NATO. NATO would still remain the principal military organization for the defence of Western Europe. The commitment to a collective self-defence would still be implemented through NATO in most cases. WEU however would create the planning, command and control capabilities to engage in joint military actions independent of NATO if necessary. The *Eurocorps* is not a new European army but consists of a military force normally assigned to NATO, plus French forces, which might be called upon to act if NATO decides not to get involved.

The main opposition to the German vision was likely to come from Britain. The United Kingdom has supported the principle of the CFSP and the WEU as the defence arm of the European Union. At the core of British policy was the concern that nothing should be done to undermine the role of NATO which embodies the commitment of the US to the defence of Western Europe. At the same time Britain has been keen to put all joint European actions under the umbrella of WEU. The British attitude to WEU thus remained based on the ambivalent principle that it favours the co-ordination of European activities within the Alliance or on behalf of the United Nations through WEU, but does not see much of a role for defence policy co-ordination outside the Alliance framework. The *Statement on the Defence Estimates 1995* states quite clearly:

- The role of the defence of the territory of NATO member states should remain a matter for NATO.
- WEU should be concerned with crisis management operations, peacekeeping tasks, including embargo or sanctions enforcement and humanitarian and rescue operations. The principles of the 1992 Petersberg Declaration should apply.
- Each EU member state should maintain the ability to preserve

its freedom to act in defence of its own legitimate national interests without constraint. The EU should not have a veto on actions taken by the UK, nor should the UK be forced to participate in any WEU actions.

- Britain rejects the notion of simply folding the WEU into the European Union as an intergovernmental pillar, given that the membership of EU and WEU is not the same and nine former Warsaw Pact states now have the status of associate membership. The British government has proposed a new WEU body at Head of State level (which is to include all full members, associate members and observers) to provide for joint decisionmaking on defence matters. This proposal has the following objectives:
  - To confirm the limited remit of WEU and the primacy of NATO in collective defence. Even 'European only' operations are to take place on the basis of NATO's Combined Joint Task Forces. They would permit the use of elements of NATO's command structure for European-led missions on the basis of decisions taken by WEU.
  - To prevent the emergence of a common defence policy in the EU. It is especially vital for the UK that the European Commission and the European Parliament should not be involved in defence matters.
  - To maintain the principle that defence policy remains a matter for decision at the national level and that a common approach to defence matters remains at the level of intergovernmental co-operation.[22]

The CFSP was an important item on the agenda of the Intergovernmental Conference in 1996 which is concerned with the implementation of the Maastricht Treaty. The Maastricht Treaty does not define the precise nature of a CDP or the future direction of CFSP. Germany and the Benelux countries supported the absorption of WEU by the European Union. *Defence* would become the so-called *fourth pillar* of the European Union. This would mean that defence policy would be co-ordinated at the European level and decisions could be made by a qualified majority. It would also mean that the treaty obligation to use all military forces to defend any member state under attack which is part of the modified Brussels Treaty (the WEU Treaty) would apply to the whole of the European Union. It would mean that all EU members would have to become full members of the WEU (currently five members of the

EU are not full members of WEU). This is called the *communautaire* as opposed to the *intergovernmental* approach to CFSP.

The Amsterdam Treaty states:

1. The Union shall define and implement a common foreign and security policy covering all areas of foreign and security policy, the objectives of which shall be:
• to safeguard the common values, fundamental interests, independence and integrity of the Union in conformity with the principles of the United Nations Charter;
• to strengthen the security of the Union in all ways;
• to preserve peace and strengthen international security, in accordance with the principles of the United Nations Charter, as well as the principles of the Helsinki Final Act and the objectives of the Paris Charter, including those on external borders;
• to promote international co-operation;
• to develop and consolidate democracy and the rule of law, and respect for human rights and fundamental freedoms. (J1)

Two questions arise from the German perspective:

1. Does the Amsterdam Treaty mean that the European Union has acquired a new role in foreign policy, that is, to what extent do the provisions of the Treaty extend the purview of CFSP?
2. Will a working CFSP enable the European Union to play a decisive role in the stabilization of the pan-European system of states?[23]

The Amsterdam Treaty introduced four important modifications to the operation of CFSP. The first of these was the conclusion of the debate about the personalization of the foreign and security policy of the European Union. Instead of appointing a European foreign minister or a Mr/Ms CFSP, there was a decision to appoint the Secretary-General of the Council High Representative for CFSP. The secretary-general will support the presidency in the formulation, preparation and implementation of political decisions and can conduct dialogue with third parties on behalf of the presidency.

The second important innovation was the creation of a policy planning and early warning unit in the General Secretariat of the Council. The declaration on the establishment of the unit also insists on appropriate co-operation with the Commission to make sure that its work is consistent with other aspects of the external policies of the EU. The proposed tasks of the unit are:

(a) monitoring and analyzing developments in areas relevant to the CFSP;

(b) providing assessments of the Union's foreign and security policy interests and identifying areas where the CFSP could focus in future;

(c) providing timely assessments and early warning of events or situations which may have significant repercussions for the Union's foreign and security policy, including potential political crises;

(d) producing, at the request of either the Council or the Presidency or on its own initiative, argued policy options papers to be presented under the responsibility of the Presidency as a contribution to policy formulation in the Council, and which may contain analyses, recommendations and strategies for the CFSP. (J.18)

The creation of this unit is designed to have the effect of encouraging the development of common perspectives on the assessment of the international situation and the implementation of policy. This may partly be accomplished by the continuity of a bureaucracy which institutionalizes such a process. However, it is likely that in any contentious matters the assessments and policies developed at the national level will prevail.

As regards decisionmaking, the European Council will lay down the principles and general guidelines for the CFSP. Decisions are arrived at by unanimous assent, although the Amsterdam Treaty lays down that abstention by any one party does not prevent the reaching of decisions. (J.13) The state who abstains is not bound to implement the decision, but has to recognize that it is binding for the Union as a whole.

Qualified majority voting (QMV) has been introduced when the Council adopts joint actions, common positions or any other decision on the basis of a common strategy, or their implementation (J.13). The unanimous adoption of a 'common strategy' by the European Council is the prerequisite for this extension of QMV. Qualified majority voting cannot operate if any one of the member states declares its opposition to a decision by QMV on the basis of important and stated reasons of national interest. (J.13) Qualified majority voting is weighted, based on the level of population in each member state.[24] Matters relating to defence, or military policy are explicitly excluded from QMV.

Finally, an important innovation of the Amsterdam Treaty is that CFSP should include the progressive framing of a common defence policy, which might lead to a common defence, if the European Council should so decide. (J.7). The areas of defence policy under the purview of CFSP include humanitarian tasks and rescue missions, peacekeeping missions and combat missions for crisis management including peace enforcement (so-called Petersberg missions). The operational capacity for such missions is to be provided by the WEU. It is the intention that WEU should play an integral part in the framing of EU defence policy and could become the future institutional framework for such a policy. The Amsterdam Treaty clearly envisages the possibility that WEU may be integrated into the Union eventually. The careful language of the Treaty, however, revealed the lack of consensus on this particular issue.

How can we assess the impact of the Amsterdam Treaty on CFSP? The analyses of Andrew Duff[25] and Hans-Jürgen Axt[26] are that institutional changes are beneficial and may in the long term establish greater co-ordination in foreign policy. But as Axt points out, the Amsterdam Treaty does not affect the intergovernmental nature of CFSP. Moreover, the Treaty explicitly refers to the national interest which can be invoked to prevent qualified majority decisions from being taken. Thus little has changed and in matters of foreign and security policy, the European Union will remain unable to act decisively. The nature and role of the European Union as an international actor thus remains unresolved.

The failure of a fully-fledged Common Defence Policy to emerge from the IGC was due to the following reasons:

- There was not enough support for the German approach in the European Union. Britain, Italy and other southern European states were opposed and France was also more disposed towards an intergovernmental approach.
- The *communautaire* approach to CDP assumes that all EU members are full members of WEU and that all full members of WEU are also members of NATO. This is far from being the case. France is not a member of the NATO integrated command, Ireland, Austria, Finland and Sweden are not members of NATO and have only observer status in WEU. The processes of NATO and EU extension are likely to increase these incongruities.
- Security and defence issues are not high on the agenda of the CFSP.

The outcome therefore is a compromise whereby a *communautaire* approach was adopted to create mechanisms for dealing with *political* aspects of security policy while the *military* aspects was to remain on the basis of intergovernmental co-operation through WEU and NATO.

During the time of the German presidency the issue of the Common Defence Policy did however develop a great deal more. This was partly the result of change of heart on the part of the British government, which in an endeavour to play a leading role in Europe despite its failure (so far) to join EMU. In October 1998 British Prime Minister Tony Blair had signalled that Britain would no longer oppose military co-operation within the EU provided it took place at an intergovernmental level, was militarily sound and had no negative impact on relations with the United States. The events in Kosovo gave further impetus to a British–French initiative announced at St Malo in December 1998. The new policy announced at the European Council Summit in Cologne on 3 June 1999 amounts to implementing some of the basic elements of a Common Defence Policy outlined in the Amsterdam treaty (J.7) A new decisionmaking structure is to be put in place which involves EU defence ministers meeting in the General Affairs Council, a Political and Security Committee and a Military Committee and staff. Policy is to be concerned with the so-called Petersberg tasks of peacekeeping, peace enforcement and humanitarian tasks. Military resources are to come from NATO or other European military capabilities. The mutual security guarantee which is part of the WEU treaty is not to be extended to non-WEU members. The Cologne summit also agreed to appoint the current NATO Secretary-General, Javier Solana, as Secretary-General of the Council High Representative for the CFSP.

These recent developments are certainly a significant breakthrough. One note of caution that needs to be sounded is that while the military functions of WEU have now been absorbed by the European Union, those functions have so far been very limited indeed and one cannot speak of a Common Defence Policy in any significant sense. The more ambitious objectives for a CDP will remain a long-term project.[27] The paralysis in the development of the CFSP means that the German project of a pan-European security system with the European Union at its core remains moribund. The debate over CFSP encapsulates the fundamental dilemma of European security. It is important for Germany's partners in Europe to understand that if they want Germany to take its responsibility in European security seriously, this may only happen in the context of a framework of European integration.

However, the fundamental issues at the heart of the debate over a European Security and Defence Identity remain unresolved. There is no pan-European security structure with the political and legal structure as well as the military resources to decisively deal with crisis situations on the European continent. Any response to conflicts therefore remains *ad hoc*, and, as was amply demonstrated in the case of the former Yugoslavia, ineffective until much damage had already been done. The European states maintain the illusion that the United States remains the guarantor of European security. The willingness of the United States to provide military support to deal with conflicts in Europe, however, remains in doubt. If another large-scale regional crisis were to break out in Europe, the response of West European states could well be as incoherent and ineffective as the response to the conflicts in the former Yugoslavia.

The case for an integrated and effective Common Foreign and Security Policy with a Common Defence Policy based on WEU is two-fold. The first is that it is an important step in European integration and the European Union cannot be a credible international actor without it. The second is that as long as it remains impossible to establish a pan-European security system that includes Russia, an effective West European security system that complements NATO but does not wholly rely on the United States, is essential. Without this, new crises may not meet an effective response. On the other hand, the Europeans, by and large, do not wish to contemplate a situation where they cannot rely on the United States. Unwilling to face this dilemma, it seems that in the medium term much progress on the European Security and Defence Identity seems precluded.

German economic power in Europe

The most interesting and revealing aspect of the German policy to exercise its influence and leadership role as a regional power through the European Union lies in the economic sphere. The reason is that whereas in the political and military spheres Germany is at best on a par with Britain and France (and there are problems in the military sphere), it is in the economic sphere where Germany has the capacity to play the role of a regional hegemonic power. Germany is the third largest economy in the world (after Japan and the United States) and accounts for 28.2 per cent of the GDP of the European Union as a whole. Moreover, Germany has by far the largest trade surplus, it is the only significant net contributor to the EU budget and its currency, as the most stable currency in Europe, has become the anchor of the European monetary system and the Deutsche Mark (for as long as it will exist) the second most important currency in the world. Moreover, Germany has been more effective then other European Union members in penetrating the Central and East European markets. In the context of this book, the interesting question is, how Germany has used its economic power both to promote its own economic interests, but also to pursue a larger political agenda which has resulted in the political and economic transformation of the European Union. In other words, we are looking at Germany's role in the development of Economic and Monetary Union (EMU).

Ever since the collapse of the Bretton Woods monetary system in 1971–72, there have been attempts to stabilize currencies in Western Europe, first by means of the so-called 'snake' and in 1979 by the creation of the European Monetary System. In 1988 a special committee was created by the European Council, under the chairmanship of EC Commission President Jacques Delors to develop a strategy for the creation of a full Economic and Monetary Union (EMU). The Delors Report submitted in April 1989 proposed a multi-stage move towards EMU.[28] In June 1989 the European Council agreed to initiate Stage I when members of the European Community currently outside the European Exchange Rate Mechanism of the EMS were to join. Spain joined in June 1989 and Britain in October 1990. The Intergovernmental Conference (IGC) of 1990–91 resulted in the Maastricht Treaty in 1991 which laid down January 1994 as being the starting point of Stage II for the transition to EMU. After the creation of a European Monetary Institute (EMI), the third and final stage of EMU was to begin with countries satisfying the so-called Maastricht convergence criteria by January 1997 or, at the latest, January 1999. (In the event, the later deadline was met.) The Maastricht convergence criteria stipulated by the Treaty of European Union are as follows:

- inflation rates of prospective members must be within 1.5 per cent of the average inflation rate of the three European Union countries with the lowest inflation;
- long-term interest rates must be within 2 per cent of the average rates of these three countries;
- the ratio of the governmental deficit to GDP must be less than 3 per cent;

- the ratio of public debt to GDP of prospective members must be less than 60 per cent;
- prospective member states must have participated in the ERM for at least two years before joining EMU without having initiated major realignments.

During Stage III of EMU members irrevocably locked their exchange rates. Responsibility for EU-wide monetary policy was invested in a European System of Central Banks. The European Central Bank is responsible for the management of the single European currency (called the euro). In order to maintain the stability of the system, strict rules against excessive national public deficits and their financing were put in place, alongside with sanctions in the form of very substantial fines that could be applied. Euroland, the group of countries who joined EMU in the first instance, came into existence as scheduled in January 1999.

The purpose of this section is not to debate the merits or otherwise of EMU for the economies of Western Europe, but rather to look at how German policy towards EMU can be explained and what it means about Germany's role in Europe. The unwavering support by the German political élite in favour of EMU seems paradoxical since it is unclear whether EMU is in the national interest of Germany. Moreover, public opinion in most EU member states, including Germany, is rather lukewarm towards EMU at best. EMU may therefore also not be in the interests of the German political élite.[29]

At first glance, therefore, the decisions to embark on EMU appear to contradict the neorealist approach to the study of international relations in several important ways. The first is that Stage III of EMU involves a substantial transfer of state autonomy to international institutions. This contradicts the neorealist assumption that international institutions are unimportant to states and states remain the principal actors in the international arena. Indeed, the whole Maastricht programme is such an explicitly institutionalist programme that competing theoretical approaches such as institutionalism or even idealism would more easily account for the phenomena that have been observed since the early 1980s at least.[30]

A key issue here is on what grounds it could be said that EMU is in Germany's national interest? There are a range of arguments that have been proposed:[31] the European Monetary System was unstable and only a transition to a single currency could make it stable. The European Monetary System, which was created in 1979, pegged the currencies of all the member states against a basket of other currencies. Members were obliged to maintain the value of the currency within a 2.25 per cent band above or below their parity value. There were provisions for changing the value of the parity under certain circumstances, with the consent of all other member states, but this was regarded to be very exceptional. All the member countries were to act together through the European monetary fund to provide short-term financing in order to make the preservation of parities possible. In practice, however the European monetary fund did not play a substantial role. The Deutsch Mark became the anchor currency, while the countries with weaker currencies bore the cost of keeping their currencies within the band.[32] In view of the sheer volume of international financial flows, the weaker currencies had to adjust to any decisions made by the German Central Bank (Bundesbank) to change interest rates, very quickly. Control over monetary policy was effectively transferred from the individual member states to the Bundesbank.

There are indications that such considerations played an important role in France's determination to establish EMU. Control over French monetary policy by a European Central Bank was clearly preferred over continued *de facto* Bundesbank control, and France expected, as the row over the chairmanship of the ECB revealed, to have significance influence in the ECB. Moreover, as Thomas Risse points out, the EMU convergence criteria served to legitimize domestic austerity policies and economic reform which were deemed necessary in and of themselves.[33] It is surprising that the new French Socialist Prime Minister, Lionel Jospin, abandoned his election pledge to seek renegotiation of EMU as soon as he assumed office, indicating how powerful the advantages of EMU were perceived to be by the French political élite.

It is clear however that the opposite applies to Germany. The perceived disadvantages of the EMS for other member countries all were working in Germany's favour. The EMS in effect already constituted a Deutsche Mark zone. EMU would dilute German influence and also introduce the risk that, in the Euro-zone the policies of tight money and low inflation, would not be sustained. The common currency would then be less 'hard' than the Deutsche Mark. Of course the convergence criteria were designed to forestall such a development. By persuading all potential members of EMU to accept these criteria and the strict rules constraining domestic monetary and fiscal policy, Germany in a sense imposed its monetary regime on the rest of the EMU member states. It could be argued that with EMU the whole of Europe becomes a *de jure* (and not merely a *de facto*) Deutschmark zone. It is unclear whether Germany benefits from such an arrangement. Prior to the launch of the euro, German price stability was the highest in the EU and Germany's credibility was likely to suffer, rather than, benefit from EMU, as the weakness of the currency proved during its first year of operation. It has been argued that low inflation countries have few incentives to join a monetary union with high-inflation countries, and in the case of EMU the pressure will be on the European Central Bank to adopt controls that are more lax than those adopted by the Bundesbank.[34] Moreover, the savings in transaction costs are smallest for Germany (about 0.1–0.2 per cent of GDP annually). A common currency controlled by the European Central Bank however would result in a significant transfer of autonomy to a supranational institution in an area considered to be of vital national interest. In short, this explanation fails to account for German policy and does not resolve the dilemmas of the neorealist approach. It poses very acutely the problem of 'relative gains' that Germany faces in relation to EMU.

One explanation that has at various times been proposed is that European Political and Monetary Union was the price that Germany had to pay for the support of unification.[35] The argument is that, as the perception that the end of the cold war and German unification would result in a much stronger Germany that had the capacity to play a regional hegemonic role, political élites in west European states, especially France and Britain, became concerned about the future role and behaviour of Germany in the European system of states. As a consequence European Community member states hesitated to give their support to unification unless Germany was prepared to move rapidly towards deeper European integration. The Treaty of European Union then was a bargain to achieve reunification – Germany traded monetary and political sovereignty for unification.[36]

The fundamental problem with this explanation is that the movement towards EMU was gaining momentum well before German unification was on the horizon. The German Foreign Minister Hans-Dietrich Genscher had expressed his support for EMU already in

1987 and during the German presidency of the EC in the first half of 1988 Genscher played a leading role in promoting the creation of a European currency area and a European Central Bank, and managed to obtain support from Chancellor Kohl and Jacques Delors. The result was that the European Council decided to establish the Delors Committee on EMU. This means that this explanation is at best incomplete. Moreover, France had no means at its disposal to prevent German unification which was a process that gained inevitability once the Soviet Union could no longer support the East German economy and refused to preserve the East German government in power. There is some evidence to suggest, however, that EMU did get some impetus from German unification. Scott Cooper has pointed out that whereas in June 1989 negotiations were left for an indeterminate period, in March 1990 Kohl pressed for an acceleration of EMU because of the events in Germany.[37]

There is another variant of this explanation, which states that EMU is the price that Germany was willing to pay for European Political Union.[38] There is no question that although EMU has far-reaching consequences for the economies of the European Union countries, it is primarily a political project. Indeed, it could be argued that the deepening of the EU, of which EMU is an integral part, is just one further step toward the general objective of creating an ever closer union among the European states. EMU is such a powerful step towards a closer union precisely because the power to issue money and to control the domestic currency has traditionally been seen as a symbol of sovereignty. Part of the argument against EMU in the British domestic political debate has been on these grounds, namely that EMU involves an unwarranted transfer of sovereignty to Europe. This argument derives some support from the fact that Chancellor Kohl in various statements linked the need to proceed with EMU explicitly with the future of peace and stability in Western Europe. This was partly based on the view that since, as a result of Maastricht, EMU had now become the main vector of European integration (given that CFSP and a Common Defence Policy remained moribund), success was essential in order to maintain the entire project of European integration.

If EMU were to fail, the centrifugal forces in Europe would overcome any further moves towards integration. Former chancellor Helmut Schmidt expressed this quite dramatically,

> If the Euro-currency is not realized by January 1, 1999, it will most likely never again be realized; . . . This would result in the

worst crisis of the European integration process – possibly its end! And Germany would be isolated – exactly the opposite of the binding which all chancellors from Adenauer to Kohl have pursued as the overarching strategic goal, in the vital German interest![39]

Martin Potthoff and Kai Hirschmann have elaborated in more detail on the connection between EMU and European security. They conclude that 'economic integration in Europe is a fundamental issue of modern security policy'.[40] This is based on the view that increasing European integration provides for stability, prosperity and peace, which in the authors view sums up the meaning of security in the modern world. This is especially salient in the post-cold war context, in which the greater development of international trade and economic co-operation is viewed as an important means to reduce international tension and promote peaceful relations. The European Union stands as a shining example of how this can work in practice.[41]

However, it seems to be an exaggeration to link EMU directly with the preservation of peace in Europe, as Kohl has done, since it is unlikely that the failure of EMU would raise the spectre of armed conflict in Western Europe. These statements should not be taken literally. What they point to are a range of possible scenarios that could unfold if European integration falters as a result of the failure of EMU. The failure to deepen the European Union further threatens the stability of the Franco-German relationship. This was clearly at the heart of Kohl's concern. For four decades the European Community has provided a framework to manage this relationship, which otherwise could have been unmanageable. At another level, the widening of the European Union might be put at risk if Maastricht fails. This would affect Germany's security concerns very directly, since the *Einbindung* of the Eastern neighbours in order to prevent chaos and instability beyond Germany's borders is the most vital element of Germany's national security policy.

These arguments only have acquired force since Maastricht. We are therefore dealing with a process that Germany became increasingly locked into, in part because of the initial commitments that were made. Joseph M. Grieco has demonstrated that the revitalization of the European Community with the Maastricht Treaty and EMU poses serious problems for neorealist theory.[42] It is quite clear that Germany pursued a very explicit institutionalist agenda in its European policy before and since unification. It is not surprising, therefore, that neorealist theory has difficulties in accounting for it. The decisions on Economic and Monetary Union cannot be simply described in terms of Germany's increasing hegemony as a regional power in Europe. Whether the loss of sovereignty to the German state is balanced by increasing influence over economic decision-making in Europe is at best uncertain. Moreover, it remains unclear whether EMU in and of itself is in Germany's economic interests, despite the fact that Germany gains a great deal from the single market. The determination with which Chancellor Kohl pursued this project can only be explained by the importance attached to European Political Union as a whole. This confirms that the institutionalist approach of increasing Europeanization continues to define the German foreign policy agenda even in matters vital to the interests of the state.

Widening the European Union: moving eastward

Inclusion of Central and East European states in key economic and security institutions, and especially in the enlargement of NATO, ensures that the European Union is central to the reordering of the European system of states after the cold war. For Germany in particular, the division of Europe, as manifested especially in the division of Germany, was always considered a consequence of the cold war regime imposed by the Soviet Union and no longer tenable or desirable as this regime disappeared. Germany has therefore promoted not only the unification of Germany, but also a larger European unity to encompass the former Warsaw Pact states. This general view is greatly reinforced by the perception that instability in the post-Communist states of Central Europe poses the single greatest threat to Germany security after the cold war.

In the aftermath of unification the emphasis in German policy was on promoting stability in Eastern Europe and the building of post-cold war pan-European institutions. To facilitate these objectives and a smooth transition to a new international order Germany provided generous financial support to Russia and other Central and East European countries. The deliberate deployment of financial resources in order to bring about, or at least to support political changes, or to provide political stability, has become known, somewhat pejoratively as 'chequebook diplomacy'. In 1991 Germany was the principal Western provider of industrial goods and services to the Central and East European States, accounting for about 40 per cent of Western trade to the region. Germany also was the main source of Foreign Direct Investment to the region. Since 1992 Germany's trade with the region increased and by 1995 accounted for about 50 per cent of the total volume of EU trade with the region.

However the rising net contributions to EU, the large annual transfers to East Germany, and the economic support for the CEE states soon proved to be excessively burdensome for the Federal Republic. This prompted Foreign Minister Klaus Kinkel, without much success, to call for burdensharing with aid to Eastern Europe. The success of communists in various general elections in Central Europe sent shock waves through Western capitals and considerably strengthened the belief that something needed to be done to ensure the stability of the new democracies. This manifested itself principally in support for the inclusion of Central European States in Western institutions, especially NATO and the European Union. From 1993 onwards Defence Minister Volker Rühe tirelessly pushed for NATO enlargement and during visits to Central European states declared German support for their NATO membership, thereby contributing in no small measure to the pressure that governments in Central Europe began to exert on Germany and other Western states to be admitted into NATO. Foreign Minister Klaus Kinkel and Chancellor Kohl were initially more interested in the enlargement of the EU, and from mid-1994 only was it the foreign minister who declared his support for the rapid admission of new members into the Alliance. Even then Kohl and Kinkel continued to emphasize the parallel nature of the two enlargement processes.

Indeed, since 1993 it is known that Kohl believed in the need to enlarge the EU and admit Poland, Hungary and the Czech Republic. He pressed the case again in the course of the IGC in 1996/97 and the Amsterdam European Council Summit in June 1997. It is generally recognized that the accession of CEE to the EU would require institutional and financial reform within the Union prior to enlargement. Thus Germany sought reform of the Common Agricultural Policy (CAP), EU structural funds and budgetary procedures. At the same time Germany became very concerned about the increasing size of its net contribution to the EU and sought fundamental financial reform in order to address this issue. Reform of the CAP and structural reform, while recognized as necessary by most EU member states, is politically difficult; without it neither financial reform nor EU enlargement to include new major net recipients of EU funds, are plausible.

The purpose of structural and cohesion funds is to mitigate the disparities of wealth through the Union. Structural funds are divided into six regional political objectives. Seventy per cent of the total funds are allocated to Objective 1 which goes to the regions where the GDP per capita is below 75 per cent of the EU average. Member states with a GDP per capita of up to 90 per cent of the EU average are eligible for the cohesion fund. If the ten CEE countries who are prospective new members do join, the population of the European Union would increase by 28 per cent, while its GDP would increase by a mere 9 per cent (at current levels). The GDP per head of the CEE-10 is just one third of the current EU average.[43]

It is evident that the CEE-10, whose GDP per head is lower than that of the poorest current EU members (Greece and Portugal) in every case, would require substantial structural funds. Estimates differ somewhat, but it seems likely from the various calculations that have been done that in order to cope with the accession of the CEE-10, plus Cyprus and Malta, that the structural funds would have to be doubled.[44] It would also have the effect, that since the average GDP per head in the EU would be reduced by 16 per cent, many of the current recipients of structural and cohesion funds would no longer be eligible under the current arrangements for Objective 1. Extending the Common Agricultural Policy to the CEEC would likewise have substantial financial implications. These are difficult to calculate precisely because they depend on assumptions about the potential output of agriculture in the CEE and the effect of the CAP on prices and production. Estimates range from 30 to 50 per cent of the current cost of the CAP for the EU-15.

The main political problem that enlargement presents arises from the budgetary implications of extending structural and cohesion funds and the CAP to the new members. Without major reforms these costs could reach 50 billion ECU, an untenable situation in the current fiscal context, especially given that Germany and the Netherlands are pressing to reduce their contributions. Another political issue arises from the likely reduction in transfers to existing members as a result of enlargement. A different problem would be faced by the CEE-10. The kind of transfers that would result would represent about 25 per cent of their 1994 GDP. They would be unable to absorb transfers of such magnitudes.

The political challenge that enlargement of the EU to Central and Eastern European countries represent should not be underestimated. As Heather Grabbe and Kirsty Hughes have pointed out:

There is no overarching strategy for constructing a European Union of 26 or more member states. . . . The lack of an overall strategy means that the process is likely to unfold in an uneven way that may be damaging rather than beneficial both to the applicants and to the future of the EU and its current members. The enlargement process is suffering from a lack of leadership as well as strategy.[45]

Some thought has gone into the question of designing policy options for the reform of the CAP and structural and cohesion funds. With regard to the CAP, the options are fundamentally some variant of the status quo or a shift to a market-oriented approach which would bring the EU in line with world prices for agricultural products. The extension of set aside within the current EU-15 as well as to the CEE-10, or the extension of production quotas to the CEE-10 while tightening quotas in the current EU-15, are such measures. This would only contain the costs of enlargement if the new CEE members were not paid any compensation payments (based on the 1992 McSharry reforms). Although prices in the CEE were never as high as those in the EU-15, on which compensation payments are based, this may prove politically difficult. Indeed it is hard to see how, under the status quo model, a substantial increase in the costs of the CAP can be avoided. Moreover, the appropriateness of the CAP for the CEE-10 is questionable and the effect of production and the viability of agriculture in those countries uncertain. Similar strictures apply to the second option. Moving towards a market-orientated approach would require measures to deal with the perceived agricultural income problem in the form of compensation payments unrelated to any mode of production. This again raises the problem of cost which, if such schemes are extended to the CEE-10, would be politically unrealistic.

Similar considerations apply to the question of structural and cohesion funds. It is clearly possible to design reforms that solve the problem, by moving current recipients out of structural funds and imposing limits on overall receipts. The review of structural funds in 1998, combined with the review of EU budget financing in 1999, may already have moved the EU closer to such schemes. The problem here, as Jim Rollo has put it, 'is getting the turkeys to vote for Christmas'.[46] Greece, Portugal, Spain and Ireland together almost form a blocking minority and so it may be difficult to get a qualified majority voting in favour of reform.

The reforms announced at the Berlin European Council summit on 24–25 March 1999 were predictably modest. The reform measure in the CAP was estimated to yield savings of ECU 3.7 billion by 2006, but direct income support will add another ECU 7.7 billion, with other measures costing a further ECU 2.8 billion. Spending on structural policies will remain pegged at the current limit of 0.46 per cent of GDP. New member states will receive a total of ECU 38 billion in structural funds, including their share of the cohesion fund.[47] The EU Commission puts the total cost of enlargement, spread over time, at ECU 75 billion.[48]

There is no question that EU enlargement to CEU represents an extraordinary challenge to the institutions of the EU and their procedural and financial arrangements. These, however, reflect the way in which the internal interests have formed and are represented. As any analysis of the implications of enlargement are still based on rather uncertain projections derived from hypothetical assumptions, the internal interest formation in the EU has become a slow and more complex process. This has manifested itself in the rather tentative and vague approach to enlargement. While confirming its commitment to enlargement in principle, it has avoided a complete programme and timetable for the accession of the CEE and has undertaken no legal commitments.[49] The lack of an overall strategy therefore is related to the postponement of the resolution of political conflicts of interest within the Union so long as the dimension of the adjustment required remains unclear. In other words, taking the painful medicine of structural adjustment will be put off until it is absolutely necessary and until it is known what dosage of medicine is actually going to be required for the patient to survive.

Fears have been expressed, not least by the CEE themselves, that all this means that enlargement will be postponed again and again. It is at least likely that until the CEE meet the necessary economic criteria, enlargement will suffer a series of delays. This will be exacerbated by the introduction of the euro. Although the first accession could, in principle, be as soon as 2001, the European Commission assumes that 2003 is a more likely date. It is also likely that not all of the CEE-10 will be admitted in the first phase; accession negotiations are set to start with Hungary, Poland, Estonia, the Czech Republic and Slovenia in the first instance, as these were judged to be closest to the criteria set by the European Council in Copenhagen in June 1993.

It is remarkable that Germany took a lead in promoting the deepening and widening of the EU at the same time, given that EMU and enlargement are inherently very risky endeavours. As far as enlargement is concerned German priorities have focused on the accession of Poland, the Czech Republic, Hungary and Slovakia. This indicates that the risks of including these countries in EU are outweighed, in the German view, by the risks of excluding them. The accession of other CEE has lower priority for Germany and may come at a later date.

The process of enlargement will also mean that the new member states will participate in CFSP and WEU. In other words, EU enlargement also has direct implications for European and security institutions. Currently the CEE-10 are 'associate partners' of WEU. In order to become full members of WEU after joining the European Union, they would also have to join NATO. If the debates about CFSP and WEU were to be resolved in such a manner, and such as the Germans have advocated, a 'fourth pillar' would be created in which WEU constitutes the defence arm of the EU, then all the CEE who join the EU will also have to become members of WEU and NATO. This would create a true parallel between the processes of NATO and EU enlargement.

The decisions announced at the Cologne European Council summit in 1999 however specifically separate the Common Defence Policy from WEU membership. It is nevertheless important to be aware that EU enlargement has security implications that go beyond the formal security guarantees embodied in the NATO Treaty and the WEU Treaty. It seems inconceivable that the major west European states who form the core both of the European Union and, together with the United States, of the NATO Alliance, could tolerate serious external aggression against another member of the Union, no matter what the precise status of the member in the WEU would be. Although this is never discussed at a political level, it is clear that the enlargement of the EU is also the creation of a larger common security space in Europe.

Agenda 2000 and the German EU presidency

The new German government came to power at a time when there were many dramatic developments in the international environment, not least the Kosovo crisis, and just before Germany was to assume the presidency of the European Union. During its time in opposition the SPD had flirted briefly with euroscepticism in order to capitalize on domestic unease about EMU, and Gerhard Schröder became known for his sceptical attitude toward the euro. After the SPD suffered a significant electoral defeat in Baden-Württemberg in March 1996 the party swung fully behind EMU. By the time the Red–Green coalition had formed a government all the necessary decisions had been taken for EMU Stage III to begin in 1999. The new Finance Minister, Oskar Lafontaine was manifestly unhappy about the loss of political control of the German government over monetary policy and embarked on an energetic if futile campaign to claw some of it back. His endeavour to limit the independence of the European Central Bank found no support with the Chancellor and little echo in the population.[50] He advanced the idea of internationally agreed target zones for hard currrencies including the euro, the dollar and the yen which was generally derided, from US Federal Reserve Bank Chairman Alan Greenspan to the French Finance Minister Strauss-Kahn.[51] Lafontaine conducted a public campaign in favour of social objectives, such as growth and employment, to be considered by the ECB when setting interest rates. He only just stopped short of criticizing the actual levels set by the ECB, but his comments contributed to his image as a rogue element, dangerous precisely because he was the finance minister of Germany, the largest economy in the EU. This was exacerbated considerably by his call for tax harmonization in the EU in the context of demands for the review of German transfers to the EU budget, on the basis that some member states were getting a free ride. Lafontaine's initiatives, which all failed to yield concrete results, produced considerable disquiet with Germany's partners (especially in the United Kingdom) and his sudden resignation was greeted with relief both in and outside of Germany.

An unexpected drama that occurred during the period of the German EU presidency was the sudden resignation of the entire EU Commission as investigations by the European Parliament about improprieties came to a head. While this damaged the reputation of the EU initially, the manner in which this issue was resolved might serve to improve its standing in the long term. At the same time as the EU had to respond to the Kosovo crisis and the crisis of the EU commission, it had a very ambitious programme with its *Agenda 2000*. The three challenges for Agenda 2000 were described as strengthening and reforming the Union's policies so that they can cope with enlargement and deliver sustainable growth; negotiate enlargement; finance enlargement, the advance preparations and the development of the Union's internal policies.[52] The reforms of the CAP, the Structural Fund, and the financial framework were modest but found general acceptance, while the plans for the share-out of pre-accession funding to the new members were also announced. After a difficult start, the German presidency was in the end judged a success. Most importantly, despite the change of government and the very difficult circumstances, Germany retained its European credentials.

Conclusion

The end of the cold war has not brought about a renationalization of German foreign and security policy. Although there is a much greater awareness in the German political élite that Germany can and should defend its national interests, in practice there has been an intensification of the institutionalist approach whereby inter-national institutions, and especially the European Union, became the instrument for reordering the European system of states and reconciling the national interests of the various European states. Thus Germany continues to support progressive European integration as the means to best secure the national and the common interest.

Since 1990, through the Treaty of European Union, a significant step has been taken in the direction of further integration. The new German government of Chancellor Gerhard Schröder, which took office in September 1998, is likely to continue along the path of European integration, as evidenced by the controversy over tax harmonization provoked by the former finance minister, Oskar Lafontaine, in December 1998. Indeed, the Red–Green coalition is less likely to approve of a policy based on the explicit assertion of Germany's nationalist interest and will therefore intensify an insti-tutionalist approach in which the European Union is the centrepiece.

7

The Challenge of the Future

The seismic shifts in the international system at the end of the 1980s and the unification of Germany have provoked a large spectrum of different views about the future role of the United Germany in the new Europe. Some scholars and politicians expressed the expectation that, with the restraints of the postwar settlements having been removed, Germany would now develop a foreign and security policy in keeping with its position in the international system. As the country with the largest economy in Europe, the central position between East and West and the largest population in Western Europe, playing a leading role in Europe, not least by virtue of being the largest net contributor to the budget of the European Union, it would assume a leadership role in Western Europe and Central Europe. It would overcome its *Machtvergessenheit*, in the words of Hans-Peter Schwarz, and assert its national interests. Christian Hacke thus declared the national interest as the guiding principle for Germany's future foreign policy and sought to develop some principles for the *global power against its will (Weltmacht wider Willen).*[1]

Most analysts agree that the manner in which Germany would pursue its national interest and exercise its influence would not be through a renationalization of foreign and security policy, but through multilateral institutions. The further deepening of European integration, and, paradoxically the transfer of national sovereignty to multilateral institutions, would be necessary for Germany to maximize its influence.[2] Public comments by former British prime minister Margaret Thatcher made it clear that she opposed further European integration precisely for this reason, and that a more integrated Europe would be one dominated by Germany.[3] This alleged shift in Germany's relations with the outside world is also described as 'normalization'. This is generally taken to mean that Germany would no longer eschew the explicit assertion of its national interests and the use of political, diplomatic, economic and military means at its disposal.[4]

This perspective runs completely counter to the explicit elements of institutionalism and constructivism that permeate the political discourse of German policymakers. It must be assumed therefore that the very explicit institutionalist agenda of the Federal Government must conceal deeper purposes reflecting the national interest.

Some scholars have taken quite a different view. Andrei Markovits and Simon Reich assert the essential continuity of German postwar foreign policy in their book on what they call *the German Predicament*.[5] In their analysis the burdens and trauma of collective memories result in a continuing renunciation of a responsible exercise of power. This causes considerable problems in the international system as Western Europe experiences a lack of leadership.

The evidence presented in the preceding chapters cannot finally decide between these different perspectives, and especially cannot be used to finally refute the neorealist approach, not even in terms of an explanatory framework for German foreign policy behaviour. This is a consequence of the fact that neorealist theory exists in so many different manifestations and that its concepts are capable of such a range of interpretations that it can accommodate virtually all conceivable facts. Consequently there are no agreed criteria for its falsification. Fundamentally, neorealism is a world view rather than a well-defined theory, and any facts that question its assumptions result in a modified theory (just as neorealism is a modified form of its predecessor known as realism) and the debate begins again.[6]

It is striking, for example, that the neorealist predictions for German foreign policy behaviour (if we ignore the more extreme suppositions of John Mearsheimer who predicted that Germany would strive to become a nuclear power) are almost indistinguishable from those of institutionalists. The real difference in the two perspectives on German foreign policy outlined above is the explanation for the behaviour. Lothar Gutjahr for example, predicts that Germany's foreign policy will be based on multilateral integration and what he calls *Genscherism*, in continuity with the postwar consensus, but nevertheless adopts a neorealist perspective that explains German foreign policy as a form of power politics that most suits the circumstances that Germany finds itself in.[7] Max Otte and Wille Grimes, in an attempt to devise long-term empirical tests of theoretical models of German and Japanese foreign policy behaviour, have cited a catalogue of empirical data for which they then devise explanations from each of the theoretical perspectives they consider (mainly realism, institutionalism and constructivism).[8]

Having made this point, however, it should be said that the evidence of the preceding chapters does render neorealist approaches to understanding German foreign policy highly implausible. At the root of the argument is the observation that whatever the explanation, German foreign policy is based on an explicit institutionalist (which on closer examination is better described as a form of constructivism) agenda, and the conduct of policy appears to fit this agenda.[9] Moreover, there is very substantial evidence that the norms and values embodied in this agenda are shared throughout Germany's political élite. Volker Rittberger and his research group based at Tübingen have made a systematic attempt to use the analysis of German foreign policy since unification as a test case for neorealism. The result is inconclusive, but it does show that neorealism does at least have to be substantially modified in order to avoid direct refutation.[10] Even the modified version of realism constructed by Rittberger *et al.*, which in the current context predicts influence-seeking rather than autonomy-seeking policies, is difficult to reconcile with German policy behaviour.

The key example that we have looked at in the preceding chapters is German support for EMU. All the various explanations that identify support for EMU with the German national interest fail on closer analysis. The locus of any explanation must be found in the principle that economic integration in Europe is a fundamental issue of modern security policy. This is based on the view that increasing European integration provides for stability, prosperity and peace, which in the authors view sums up the meaning of security in the modern world.

The decisions on Economic and Monetary Union cannot be simply described in terms of Germany's increasing hegemony as a regional power in Europe. Whether the loss of sovereignty to the German state is balanced by increasing influence over economic decision-making in Europe is doubtful; the development of 'Euroland' so far seems to suggest that things are not exactly going Germany's way. Indeed much of the activities of Oskar Lafontaine in his short spell as finance minister were designed to redress the loss of national political influence in monetary policy. Moreover, it remains unclear whether EMU in and of itself is in Germany's economic interests, despite the fact that Germany gains a great deal from the single market. More importantly, the transfer of decisionmaking over monetary policy to a supranational body means that Germany has now lost an important instrument whereby it could unilaterally exercise influence over other states by virtue of the sheer strength of its currency. The determination with which the German government pursued monetary union can only be explained by the importance it attached to the European Union as a whole. This could be considered evidence that the institutionalist approach of increasing Europeanization continues to define the German foreign policy agenda even in matters vital to the interests of the state.

This is not a purely academic debate. Whether the Mearsheimer prescription or an institutionalist approach is adopted, whether there is a renationalization of foreign policy in Europe or European integration continues, all this has profound consequences for European security. The research group at Trier University under the direction of Hanns Maull has advanced a third approach to the study of German foreign policy. Maull denies the basic premise of the other two approaches, namely that in an objective sense the shift in the European system of states as a result of the cold war has substantially increased Germany's weight and its potential for exercising power in the international arena. For one thing, Germany's economic resources are largely in private hands and not under the control of the state. In a globalized economy, there is little reason to believe that private resources will be influenced by the priorities of any individual state. While obviously a prosperous state has more economic and financial resources at its disposal than a poor one, the enormous debt burden created by unification and the strict rules for fiscal deficits imposed by EMU means that Berlin has very severe financial constraints. Moreover, crucial elements of economic decisionmaking have now been transferred to a supranational agency, the European Central Bank, thereby further reducing the capacity of the state to even formulate its own economic policy, never mind operationalizing it in order to conduct foreign policy and exercise influence of other states. But more importantly, is that for liberal democracies globalization European integration and other transnational relations have created an international system in which there is no well-defined locus of power.

Although Maull does not use this term, one could describe this as a form of transnationalization of bureaucratic politics. Foreign policy is not only constrained by domestic politics, but constrained by European politics and regulations, international treaties and conventions, that render the consistent pursuit of specific national priorities and policies quite problematic. In this view then, the real problem of German foreign policy is the loss of ability to influence events. Among recent examples, Maull cites the decision by the newly elected German government in 1998 to abandon civil nuclear power, which immediately resulted in Germany being in violation of international obligations. In this context Maull is scathing about the concept of the 'national interest'. Beyond very general notions, such as countering threats to the integrity of the state, and the life and well-being of the population (whatever they might be), and the well-established principles of European integration, maintaining the transatlantic relationship with the United States and co-operative security in Europe, it is impossible to define more specifically what Germany's national interests are. As a consequence, Maull describes German foreign policy being the result of 'searching and learning' rather than the consistent implementation of national priorities.[11]

In the bureaucratic politics model, states cannot be considered to be rational actors because policy is not designed to achieve specific objectives, but is the outcome of competing domestic interests and bureaucratic processes. It therefore denies the most fundamental assumptions of neorealism and institutionalism. The Trier group does not adhere to any particular model of decisionmaking, but its analysis clearly embodies elements of bureaucratic politics at the national and the transnational level. This undermines the role of the nation state as a rational actor in the international system in two different ways: on the one hand domestic bureaucratic politics constrains rational policymaking; on the other hand the state is not actually a free agent because of the constraints of international institutions. However, even at that level rational policy cannot be easily pursued because of the operation of bureaucratic politics at the supranational level and the constraints imposed by a globalized world economy. A model based on these kinds of precepts might be used to analyze specific examples; the explanation for the success of the plans for EMU might be that it was simply the outcome of bureaucratic processes resulting from the Single European Act. Once a committee was set up and proposed monetary union, the bureaucratic processes were powerful enough to overcome the national interests of the member states, the reluctance of their populations and even the interests of the political élites, all of which mitigated against EMU.

While there is much to be said for the observation that there has been much exaggeration about 'German power' after the cold war and furthermore it is important to emphasize the influence of both bureaucratic politics and institutional constraints, there is also evidence that the approach of the Trier group underestimates both German influence and the ability of the government to shape events. The most convincing example, apart from German unification, is the development of the European Union. It is fair to say that the development of the European Union in its broad strokes conforms to the German vision of the future of Europe more than that of any other of the principal member states. It is certainly the case that Germany has not achieved everything it set out to achieve, for example the inclusion of defence policy as the fourth pillar of the EU, or the congruence of EU and WEU membership and so on. It is also true that the EU in its current shape was not just created by Germany. But nevertheless its development so far is not purely accidental; it was to an appreciable extent the result of deliberate policy on the part of the government of the Federal Republic of Germany.

It is an interesting exercise to compare the grand strategy of the United Kingdom and France with that of the FRG over the last 40 years. For the United Kingdom the main objective was the stability of the geopolitical status quo in Europe and the preservation of a residual global role for the United Kingdom through its special relationship with the United States. It saw the European Community as a partnership of nations with the main emphasis on the benefits of economic co-operation and free trade. France was interested in the creation of a *Europe des nations* which would contain Germany and in which France would assume the leadership role. Although the British strategy was initially quite successful, it gradually fell victim to the shifts in the international system and became totally unsustainable after German unification. The French vision was fanciful from the start and could only be maintained for so long because it was sustained by the Franco-German relationship, but the Europe that emerged was far removed from the ambitious grand design. Germany, on the other hand, while initially preferring stability over unification, was nevertheless committed to overcome the division of Europe and thus bring about a major change in the European status quo. Its vision of Europe was one of a supranational union of states in which the divisions between the nations of Europe would be eradicated.

The first of these aims was achieved in a manner that most Germans could not have imagined. With regard to the second of these aims, the European Union is now a reality. What has been achieved so far may not go nearly as far as some of the visions that were entertained at another time. But conceptually and politically, it is closer to the German vision than to either that of Britain and France. The point to be made here is not that Germany is single-handedly responsible for creating the European system of states that exists today. It is rather that, through the deliberate and persistent pursuit of its foreign policy objectives, the Federal Republic has had a definitive influence in shaping its international environment, and it continues to do so today. For example the policies to stabilize the democracies in Central Europe and draw them into Western insitutions through NATO and EU membership have proven remarkably successful. Of course it would be incorrect to say that this success would have been possible without the contribution of other major international actors. But nevertheless Germany had very specific policies on this issues which were considered central to Germany's national security, and they were pursued successfully in the sense that German influence in NATO, the European Union and in bilateral relationships with the CEE was an important factor and the main objectives were achieved.

There are some definite conclusions that emerge from the evidence. Germany is not engaged in the practice of power politics in the traditional sense. There remains a firm commitment to multilateralism, to an institutionalist approach to international politics. Germany intends to be a 'civilian power' so that in future the world will be populated by 'civilian powers' only. Of course, Germany also has had to learn that collective security demands the use of force, and has finally come to a point where it can play a full part in the Alliance. It is true that Germany has become more aware of its national interests and of its stature in the world, but this has not displaced the values and priorities that underpin its foreign and security policy. To the contrary, it has strengthened them, since more than ever before, the political success and economic well-being of all European states is crucial to Germany. In the language of IR theory, it is the absolute gains and not the relative gains that matter. Germany has not assumed the mantle of a superpower in Europe. Its ambitions and expectations are more modest. Its vision for the future of Europe remains firm, but tempered by the experience of the last nine years which have shown the limits of the possible.

The future of European security

During the cold war period, overcoming the division of Europe through international regimes (detente and arms control) and institutions (Conference on Cooperation and Security in Europe (CSCE), NATO, the European Community) had become central to the foreign policy of the Federal Republic. The end of the cold war served to strengthen this consensus in a number of ways. In the first instance, the strategic changes in Europe and the peaceful manner in which they came about could easily be interpreted as a successful approach. If the strategic confrontation with the Soviet Union could be resolved in this way, then anything seemed possible. The successful integration of Western Europe through the European Community pointed in the same direction. There was also the perception that the end of the military confrontation in Europe marked a deeper shift in the international system, from competing ideologies to a shared sense of values, and from military force as the determinant of international relations to the international economy. The preservation of stability through collective security in Europe therefore assumed a central place in German foreign policy in relation to the post-cold war order.

Another element of the German foreign policy consensus was the commitment to democratic values, self-determination, non-violence and human rights. Again international organizations were considered as an important instrument for pursuing this commitment on a pan-European or even global scale. This approach contains elements of both institutionalist and constructivist thought to international relations. The conflicts of interests are mitigated by the institutional frameworks that states are committed to, which binds them in and reduces the capacity of domestic politics to support hostile political measures. But international co-operation not merely changes the way in which states perceive their interests, it also changes the values and norms on which their international conduct is based.

It was a high priority for Germany at the end of the cold war to develop a relationship of strategic co-operation, and the more Russia and other states from Eastern Europe could be locked into a system of collective security involving international institutions, norms and instruments of enforcement of human rights and international law could prevent the resurgence of fundamentally antagonistic relations based on a military confrontation. The danger was the resurgence of authoritarian and nationalist regimes or the descent in chaos – a political and economic partnership being the best means of preventing such developments. Thus Germany has sought to provide economic support in order to achieve a peaceful transition to a new European order and address the new security risks it has perceived. This can be described as the use of economic instruments of power in support of national and regional security. Clearly the economic stability of Eastern Europe and the former Soviet Union is of fundamental significance to German security.

The Gulf conflict in 1990–91, which proved stubbornly and dangerously insusceptible to political instruments alone, raised serious questions about the nature of the 'new world order'. Even more problematic were the conflicts in the former Yugoslavia (Croatia, Bosnia and Kosovo) and the newly independent states (Nagorno-Karabakh, Chechnya, Abkhazia) which exposed the inadequacies of European collective security arrangements. The attempt to develop a regime of collective security in Europe failed as the main players proved unwilling to invest the most obvious available institutional framework, the OSCE, with the appropriate powers. Neither Russia, nor the United States, nor the main European states were willing to take on this responsibility and subordinate their security interests to a collective security regime. This meant, however, that when the crisis came there was no prescription for a clear response, no adequate instruments to deal with it. The result was a major tragedy that Europe will have to live with.

These lessons were particularly hard for Germany, since they raised the other part of the collective security equation that could be ignored during the cold war, namely the use of force as part of a range of measures to deal with instability and armed conflicts in Europe and beyond. German policymakers had to scale back their expectations of what collective security would mean and accomplish. It turned out that the diplomatic and political instruments of collective security are based on *ad hoc* arrangements through the United Nations, the European Union, the OSCE and more informal contacts, while NATO provides the military support for peace enforcement. This is unsatisfactory for a whole range of reasons, both in terms of operational efficiency and political legitimacy, but this is the current situation.

The international system in the early post-cold war era therefore faces an enormous paradox. On the one hand the confrontation between the major powers has disappeared. This means that the West European states, including Germany, no longer face any military threat. Moreover, virtually all the states in the region either have or want to become part of international and Western institutions, and have abandoned forms of international conduct in which military force played a dominant role. At the same time there are many actual and potential conflicts in Europe, which means that a system of collective security is required, with effective military instruments, to enforce and keep the peace. This is *the central dilemma of European security*. As long as it persists, the countries of Europe, are without clear guidance and procedures as new conflicts erupt and may be unable to take the necessary steps to ensure effective conflict prevention and management. Here lies the real challenge for European security policy after the cold war.

Notes

1 Germany in the International System

1 This is a concept from game theory, based on the so-called 'prisoner's dilemma'; see Kenneth Oye (ed.), *Cooperation under Anarchy*, Princeton Princeton University Press 1986.

2 Max Otte and William Grimes, *Germany and Japan: Civilian Power, Traditional Power or Institutional Constraints*, unpublished paper 1999, p. 3.

3 Grame P. Auton and Wolfram Hanrieder, *The Foreign Policies of West Germany, France & Britain*, Englewood Cliffs: Prentice Hall 1980, chapter 9.

4 Konrad Adenauer, *Erinnerungen 1953–1955*, Stuttgart: DVA 1966, chapters IX and X.

5 Auton and Hanrieder, op. cit., chapter 9; for the formulation of West German security policy in the Adenauer era, see Josef Joffe, 'Germany and the Atlantic Alliance – The Politics of Dependence, 1961–1968' in William C. Cromwell (ed.), *Political Problems of Atlantic Partnership*, Bruge: Council of Europe 1969, pp. 321–454.

6 Valuable insights about West German thinking with regard to the Soviet Union can be gained from a secret protocol of Deutscher Bundestag, 7. Ausschuß, Bonn', 4 November 1952. (This consists of a lecture by Dr Pfleiderer on 'Vertragswerk und Sowjetpolitik' and a response by State Secretary Prof. Hallstein at the 103rd sitting of the Ausschuß für das Besatzungsstatut und auswärtige Angelegenheiten on 29 October 1952. German Military Archives, Freiburg, BW9/716.) For an assessment of the military threat, see 'Vortragsnotiz', Bonn, 12 February 1951 and Memorandum for the Federal Chancellor, Bonn, 13 June 1951, German Military Archives, Freiburg, BW9/36. This includes detailed maps indicating the various troop deployments Eastern and Western Europe (including the Western Soviet Union).

7 Adenauer, *Erinnerungen*, Vol. I, p. 349.

8 Adenauer, *Erinnerungen*, Vol. I, p. 348; Hans-Jürgen Rautenberg, 'The Federal Republic of Germany in the 1950s', in Carl-Christoph Schweitzer (ed.), *The Changing Western Analysis of the Soviet Threat*, London: Pinter Publishers 1990, pp. 221–43; p. 223.

9 For an exposition on Adenauer's concept of reunification through *Politik der Stärke* based on extensive archival research see Peter Siebenmorgen, *Gezeitenwechsel*, Bonn: Bouvier Verlag 1990, chapter III.

10 This applies *a forteriori* to the British response to the Berlin crisis of 1958, where the Germans saw the British as basically giving in to Soviet demands. A good example of the prevailing attitudes is Adenauer's negative reaction to Macmillan's visit to Moscow in February 1959 resulting in sharp Anglo-German exchanges. See Wilhelm G. Grewe, *Rückblenden*, (Frankfurt/Main: Ullstein Verlag 1979), p. 389f.

11 See for example Der Bundesminister der Verteidigung, Aufgaben und Planung der Bundeswehr, Az: 10/11, Tgb. 6/59, Bonn, 21 December 1959, p. 2 (NHP Documents, Bonn).

12 For a detailed discussion of the security policy of the SPD and its relation to the German question, see Siebenmorgen, op. cit., chapter VII.

13 See, for example, Erich Ollenhauer, Speech to the German Bundestag, 19 March 1953, *Stenographische Berichte der Verhandlungen des Deutschen Bundestages*, 1. Wp., 255. Sitzung, S.12317–12328.

14 Whereas Adenauer saw reunification as the product of global *Entspannung* and disarmament, some in the opposition considered reunification as a means of achieving detente in Europe. Some others, like Erler, had become aware of the fact that in the thinking of the Allies arms control was taking precedence over German unification and that unification could only be the product of detente in Europe. See Erler's speech in Deutscher Bundestag, DBT/II/157, 4 July 1956, pp. 8585–8.

15 Walther Stützle, *Kennedy und Adenauer in der Berlin-Krise 1961–1962*, Bonn-Bad Godesberg: Verlag Neue Gesellschaft 1973; Jack M. Schick, *The Berlin Crisis, 1958–1962*, Philadelphia: University of Pennsylvania Press; Robert M. Slusser, *The Berlin Crisis of 1961*, Baltimore: Johns Hopkins University Press 1973.

16 For an analysis of the 'Gaullist' perspective see Detlef Bischoff, *Franz Josef Strauß, die CSU und die Außenpolitik*, Meisenheim: Anton Hain 1973; see also Franz Josef Strauß, *Die Erinnerungen*, Berlin: Siedler Verlag 1989; Gerd Schmückle, *Ohne Pauken und Trompeten*, Stuttgart: dtv 1982. The author's understanding of the debate between the 'Gaullists' and the 'Atlanticists' is also based on conversations with Kai-Uwe von Hassel, Klaus Bloemer and Gerd Schmückle.

17 Siebenmorgen, op. cit., p. 377.

18 For a more detailed account, see Helga Haftendorn, *Sicherheit und Entspannung*, Baden-Baden: Nomos 1983, pp. 521–632.

19 Gerhard Schröder, 'Germany Looks to Eastern Europe', *Foreign Affairs*, Vol. 44, No. 1 (October 1965), pp. 12–25; see also Haftendorn, op. cit, pp. 282–94.

20 For more detail see Haftendorn, op. cit., p. 96; Siebenmorgen, op. cit., pp. 308–12.

21 Willy Brandt, *Begegnungen und Einsichten. Die Jahre 1960–1975*, Hamburg: Hoffmann & Campe 1976, p. 17.

22 The speech is reprinted in Boris Meißner (ed.), *Die deutsche Ostpolitik 1961–1970. Dokumentation*, Köln 1975, pp. 45–8.

23 Quoted in translation from Walter F. Hahn, *Between Westpolitik and Ostpolitik*, Beverly Hills: Sage Publications 1975, p. 26.

24 Peter Bender, *Offensive Entspannung, Möglichkeiten für Deutschland*, Köln 1964; Theodor Eschenburg, 'Die deutsche Frage 1966', *Die Zeit*, 29 April 1966; Peter Bender, *Zehn Gründe für die Anerkennung der DDR*, Frankfurt: Fischer 1968; Peter Bender, *Neue Ostpolitik: Vom Mauerbau bis zum Moskauer Vertrag*, München: dtv 1986; Eberhard Schulz, *An Ulbricht führt kein Weg mehr vorbei. Provozierende Thesen zur deutschen Frage*, Hamburg 1967.

25 Walter Scheel, 'Die deutsche Politik des Gewaltverzichts', *Frankfurter Allgemeine Zeitung*, 15 July 1970.

26 Based on Haftendorn, op. cit., p. 324; Wolfram F Hanrieder, *Germany, America, Europe*, Yale University Press, New Haven 1989, pp. 195–6.

27 Federal Chancellor Brandt, television speech from Moscow to the German people, 12 August 1970, cited from Haftendorn, op. cit., p. 335.

28 Cited from Hanrieder, op. cit., p. 203.

29 For a very detailed account, see Arnulf Baring, *Machtwechsel. Die Ära Brandt-Scheel*, München: dtv 1982.

30 'Prepared statement of the Hon. Henry A. Kissinger, Secretary of State', in *Détente*, Hearings before the Senate Committee on Foreign Relations, 93 Cong. 2 session (Washington, DC: GPO 1975), p. 247; for an exposition of American thinking on detente, see Raymond L. Garthoff, *Détente and Confrontation*, Washington, DC: Brookings 1985; Mike Bowker and Phil Williams, *Superpower Detente: A Reappraisal*, London: Sage /RIIA 1988.

31 For a more detailed discussion, see Christoph Bluth, *Soviet Strategic Arms Policy Before SALT*, Cambridge University Press 1992.

32 For the text of the Harmel report see *NATO: Facts and Figures*, Brussels: NATO Information Service 1976, Appendix 6.

33 See the replies by Foreign Minister Schröder on 23 September 1966 in Deutscher Bundestag, DBT/V59, pp. 2881–926. See also Haftendorn, op. cit., p. 424.

34 Haftendorn, op. cit., p. 436.

35 For Willy Brandt and Helmut Schmidt, MBFR was given high priority as a means of reducing the military confrontation in Central Europe and promoting the security dimension of detente, whereas Kissinger was sceptical of the prospects for MBFR. For the Nixon administration, the main value of MBFR lay in its utility to defeat the attempts in the Senate to reduce US troops in Europe. See Martin Müller, *Politik und Bürokratie: Die MBFR-Politik der Bundesrepublik Deutschland zwischen 1967 und 1973*, Baden-Baden: Nomos 1988; Phil Williams, *The Senate and U.S. Troops in Europe*, London: Macmillan 1985.

36 Although there was interparty consensus, nevertheless some notable politicians continued to oppose the *Ostpolitik* based on the Eastern treaties. For more detail see Stephen F. Szabo, *The Changing Politics of German Security*, London: Pinter 1990, chapter 5.

37 For an exposition of this argument, see Bowker and Williams, op. cit., chapter 7.

38 For an analysis of Soviet policy, see Jonathan Steele, *The Limits of Soviet Power*, Harmondsworth: Penguin 1984, pp. 226–46.

39 For a penetrating critique of the Reagan administration's approach to arms control, see Strobe Talbott, *Deadly Gambits*, London: Pan 1985.

40 For a more detailed analysis, see Fred Halliday, *The Making of the Second Cold War*, London: Verso 1983; Simon Dalby, *Creating the Second Cold War*, London: Pinter 1990.

41 For extensive analysis and documentation on this point, see Thomas Risse-Kappen, *Die Krise der Sicherheitspolitik*, München: Christian Kaiser Verlag 1988.

42 See for example Timothy Garton Ash, *The Polish Revolution: Solidarity*, London: Granta Books 1991, pp. 329–38.

43 For a more detailed analysis of Soviet military and arms control policies

under Gorbachev, see Christoph Bluth, *New Thinking in Soviet Military Policy*, London: Pinter 1990.

44 In his memoirs, former Soviet Foreign Minister Eduard Shevardnadze claims that he was aware in 1986 that the Soviet foreign policy under Gorbachev would put the issue of German unification on the agenda.

45 For a more detailed discussion of this point see Chapter 7.

46 Ash, op. cit., pp. 334–6.

47 The effect of increased travel between East and West on detente is analyzed in Norbert Ropers, *Tourismus zwischen West und Ost. Ein Beitrag zum Frieden?*, Frankfurt: Campus Verlag 1986.

48 For a critique of the neorealist approach to the cold war and a detailed discussion of the various proposed reasons for the end of the cold war, see John Lewis Gaddis, 'International Relations Theory and the End of the Cold War', *International Security*, Vol. 17, No. 3, Winter 1992/93; John Lewis Gaddis, *The United States and the End of the Cold War*, Oxford: Oxford University Press 1992; Charles W. Kegley, 'How Did the Cold War Die? Principles for an Autopsy', *Mershon International Studies Review*, Vol. 38, 1994, pp. 11–41.

49 See, for example, the substantial analysis of the domestic political and economic difficulties of the Soviet Union written in the first year of the Gorbachev period which predicted the continued pursuit of expansionist ambitions by the Soviet leadership despite internal weakness, by Seweryn Bialer, *The Soviet Paradox*, London: I.B. Tauris 1986.

50 Uwe Nerlich, 'Sicherheitsinteressen des vereinigten Deutschland', in Wolfgang Heydrich and Joachim Krause (eds), *Stabilität, Gleichgewicht und die Sicherheitsinteressen des vereinigten Deutschland*, Vol. III, Ebenhausen: SWP, 1991, pp. 104–5.

2 European Security after the Cold War

1 Hans-Dietrich Genscher, 'Eine Stabilitätsordnung für Europa', *Europäische Sicherheit*, No. 41, pp. 310–17, (June 1992); Helga Haftendorn and Otto Keck (eds), *Kooperation jenseits von Hegemonie und Bedrohung*, Baden-Baden: Nomos Verlagsgesellschaft 1997; Christoph Bluth, Emil Kirchner and James Sperling (eds), *The Future of European Security*, Aldershot: Dartmouth 1995.

2 George Bush, Address to Congress, 11 September 1990, 'Iraqi Aggression Will not Stand', in *United States Policy Information and Texts*, No. 2111, 12 September 1990, p. 17; see also *National Security Strategy of the United States*. Washington DC, White House, August 1991.

3 Charles Krauthammer, 'The Unipolar Moment', *Foreign Affairs*, Vol. 70, No. 1, 1991, pp. 23–33; Klaus-Dieter Schwarz, 'Die USA im Übergang zur postkonfrontativen Weltordnung', in W. Heydrich, J. Krause, U. Nerlich, J. Nötzold and R. Rummel (eds), *Sicherheitspolitik Deutschlands: Neue Konstellationen, Risiken, Instrumente*, Baden-Baden: Nomos 1992.

4 John J. Mearsheimer, 'Back to the Future', *International Security*, Vol. 15, No. 1, Summer 1990, pp. 5–56; Kenneth N. Waltz, *Theory of International Politics*, Reading, MA: Addison-Wesley 1979; Kenneth N. Waltz,

The Spread of Nuclear Weapons: More May Be Better, Adelphi Paper No. 171, London: IISS 1981.

5 Hans J. Morgenthau, *Politics Among Nations: The Struggle for Power and Peace*, New York: Knopf 1973; Kenneth N. Waltz (1979), ibid.

6 Mearsheimer, op. cit., p. 38.

7 The potential disputes between various Central European states (for example Hungary and Rumania) do not seem to have resulted in arms races or military confrontations and are no where near crisis point. For more detailed analysis, and support for the argument that such conflicts are likely to be of a political and economic rather than military nature, see Jan Zielonka, *Security in Central Europe*, Adelphi Paper No. 272, London: Brassey's 1992.

8 Samuel P. Huntington, *The Clash of Civilizations and the Remaking of World Order*, New York: Simon & Schuster 1996.

9 Francis Fukuyama, *The End of History and the Last Man*, New York: The Free Press 1992.

10 It is interesting how much Fukuyama is derided about how seldom his work is actually discussed in contemporary analyses of international relations and security; for a typical example see Jim George, *Discourses of Global Politics: A Critical (Re)Introduction to International Relations*, Boulder, CO: Lynne Rienner Publishers 1994, p. 8.

11 John Mueller, *Retreat from Doomsday: the Obsolescence of Modern War*, New York: Basic Books 1989.

12 Based on declassified East German Military documents; see Bundesarchiv, Militärisches Zwischenarchiv, Straußberg, AZ 32651, p. 65.

13 James Sperling and Emil Kircher, 'Economic security and the problem of co-operation in post-Cold War Europe', *Review of International Studies*, Vol. 24, No. 8, 1998, pp. 221–37.

14 Penelope Hartland-Thunberg, 'From Guns and Butter to Guns v. Butter: The Relation Between Economics and Security in the United States', *The Washington Quarterly*, Vol. 11, No. 4, Autumn 1988, pp. 47–54; Barry Buzan, Ole Wæver and Jaap de Wilde, *Security: A Framework for Analysis*, Boulder, CO: Westview 1997.

15 There is a large body of literature on this subject. Useful texts are: John Baylis and Steve Smith (eds), *The Globalization of World Politics: An Introduction to International Relations*, Oxford: Oxford University Press 1997; Ian Clark, *Globalization and Fragmentation: International Relations in the 20th Century*, Oxford: Oxford University Press 1997; Susan Strange, *The Retreat of the State. The Diffusion of Power in the World Economy*. Cambridge: Cambridge University Press 1996.

16 For more detailed discussion, see John R. Oneal and Bruce M. Russett, 'The Classical Liberals were Right: Democracy, Interdependence and Conflict, 1950–1985', *International Studies Quarterly*, Vol. 42, No. 2, June 1997, pp. 267–94; Steve Chan, 'In Search of Democratic Peace: Problems and Promise', *Mershon International Studies Review*, 41, Supp. 1, May 1997, pp. 59–91.

17 The theoretical issues arising from this statement and its empirical basis cannot be discussed here in detail. The statement that liberal democracies do not go to war against each other seems to be well-

founded empirically. For a discussion of the theoretical issues, see Robert Latham, 'Democracy and War-Making: Locating the International Liberal Context', *Millenium*, Vol. 22, No. 2, Summer 1993, pp. 139–64; Randall L. Schweller, 'Domestic Structure and Preventive War: Are Democracies More Pacific?', *World Politics*, Vol. 44, No. 2, January 1992, pp. 235–69; for an opposing view see Mearsheimer, op. cit., pp. 49–51; for an analysis of the empirical evidence, see Alex Mintz and Nehemia Geva, 'Why Don't Democracies Fight Each Other? An Experimental Study', *Journal of Conflict Resolution*, Vol. 37, No. 3, September 1993, pp. 484–503; Z. Maoz and B. Russett, 'Alliance, contiguity, wealth and political stability: Is the lack of conflict among democracies a statistical artifact?', *International Interactions*, Vol. 17, No. 3, 1992, pp. 245–67; Spencer Weart, *Never at War: Why Democracies Will Not Fight One Another*, New Haven: Yale University Press 1998; Michael Brown, Sean Lynn-Jones and Steven E. Miller (eds), *Debating the Democratic Peace*, Cambridge, MA: MIT Press 1997.

18 Northern Ireland is an example of political instability generated by a territorial status that is not accepted by a substantial portion of the population.

19 The theoretical issues arising from this statement (such as the definition of what constitutes a liberal democracy) and its empirical basis cannot be discussed within the scope of this chapter. The statement that liberal democracies do not go to war to each other seems to be well-founded empirically. For a discussion of the theoretical issues, see Robert Latham, 'Democracy and War-Making: Locating the International Liberal Context', *Millenium*, Vol. 22, No. 2, Summer 1993, pp. 139–164; Randall L. Schweller, 'Domestic Structure and Preventive War: Are Democracies More Pacific?', *World Politics*, Vol. 44, No. 2, January 1992, pp. 235–269; for an opposing view see John J. Mearsheimer, 'Back to the Future', *International Security*, Vol. 15, No. 1, Summer 1990, pp. 49–51; for an analysis of the empirical evidence, see Alex Mintz and Nehemia Geva, 'Why Don't Democracies Fight Each Other? An Experimental Study', *Journal of Conflict Resolution*, Vol. 37, No. 3, September 1993, pp. 484–503; Z. Maoz and B. Russett, 'Alliance, contiguity, wealth and political stability: Is the lack of conflict among democracies a statistical artifact?', *International Interactions*, Vol. 17, No. 3, 1992, pp. 245–267.

20 For details see Richard A. Falkenrath, *Shaping Europe's Military Order*, London: MIT Press 1995.

21 For details see Christoph Bluth, *Arms Control and Proliferation: Russia and International Security After the Cold War*, London Defence Studies No. 35, London: Brassey's 1996.

22 For more detail see Lawrence Freedman and Efraim Karsh, *The Gulf Conflict 1990–1991*, London: Faber & Faber 1993.

23 Ole Diehl, 'Eastern Europe as a Challenge for Future European Security', in Mark Curtis, Ole Diehl, Jérôme Paolini, Alexis Seydoux and Reinhard Wolf, *Challenges and Responses to Future European Security: British, French and German Perspectives*, London: European Strategy Group 1993, pp. 15–68.

24 For Russian military policy and capabilities see Roy Allison, *Military Forces in the Soviet Successor States*, IISS Adelphi Paper No. 280, London: Brassey's 1993.

25 Falk Bomsdorf, *Zwischen Destruktion und Regeneration. Zur Zukunft des postsowjetischen Raumes*, SWP S 389, Ebenhausen: Stiftung Wissenschaft und Politik 1993, pp. 11–31.

26 This does not preclude some adjustments to allow Russia to deploy forces in crisis regions, in particular the Caucasus. For an analysis of the current debate, see Jane M.O. Sharp, 'CFE Treaty Under Threat as Russia Requests Revisions', *Bulletin of Arms Control*, No. 12, November 1993, pp. 2–4.

27 For more details see Christoph Bluth, 'The post-Soviet space and Europe', in Roy Allison and Christoph Bluth (eds), *Security Dilemmas in Russia and Eurasia*, London: Royal Institute of International Affairs 1998, pp. 323–41.

28 This is exemplified in the title and argument of the study by James Gow, *Triumph of the Lack of Will*, London: Hurst & Company 1997.

29 For a detailed account see Richard Holbrooke, *To end a war*, New York: Random House 1998.

30 *Süddeutsche Zeitung*, 8 May 1992, p. 9.

31 Franz H.U. Borkenhagen, *Außenpolitische Interessen Deutschlands*, Bonn: Bouvier 1997.

32 Barbara Marshall, 'Migration from the East: Germans perceptions and policy', in Christoph Bluth, Emil Kirchner and James Sperling (eds), *The Future of European Security*, Dartmouth: Aldershot 1995, pp. 187–204.

33 Robert Reed, *The Migration Threat to German Security*, unpublished paper, Reading: Reading University 1999.

34 Adrian Hyde-Price, 'Berlin Republic Takes to Arms', *The World Today*, Vol. 55, No. 6, June 1999, pp. 13–15.

35 A series of focus studies conducted with some 34 West and East Germans by Infratest Burke Berlin in July 1991 identified some of these concerns. They were reported in a study by the RAND Corporation; see Ronald D. Asmus, *Germany in Transition: National Self-Confidence and International Reticence*, Rand Corporation: Santa Monica 1992, Rand Note N-3522-AF, p. 51.

36 For a trenchant critique of concepts of collective security by one German commentator, see Josef Joffe, 'Collective Security and the Future of Europe', *Survival*, Vol. 34, No. 1, Spring 1992, pp. 36–50; for analysis of the debate in the German political élite and among academics see Josef Janning, 'A German Europe – a European Germany? On the debate over Germany's foreign policy?', *International Affairs*, Vol. 72, No. 1, January 1996, pp. 9–32.

37 Hanns W. Maull, 'Germany in the Yugoslav Crisis', *Survival*, Vol. 37, No. 4, Winter 1995–96, pp. 99–130; this citation p. 116.

38 It should be understood that German scholars and politicians do not subscribe to the term 'New World Order as such, but it is used here because German perspectives on the post-cold war international order amount to something akin to it, if the term is not used to describe a

unipolar, US-led world. For an exception, see Ludger Kühnhardt, 'Wertgrundlagen der deutschen Außenpolitik', in Karl Kaiser and Hanns W. Maull (eds), *Deutschlands neue Außenpolitik*, München: R. Ouldenbourg 1994.

39 The core of the 'two-plus-four agreements' was of course the Soviet–German Treaty which involved substantial payments to the Soviet Union and a commitment by Germany not to produce or possess nuclear, chemical and biological weapons. There was also an agreement not to deploy non-German NATO troops in the territory of the GDR during the period of the withdrawal of Soviet troops (four years). For more details and the international context, see Karl Kaiser, 'Das Vereinigte Deutschland in der internationalen Politik', in Karl Kaiser and Hanns W. Maull (eds), *Deutschlands neue Außenpolitik: Band 1 Grundlagen*, München: R. Ouldenbourg 1994, pp. 1–14; the text of the agreements is given in Adam Daniel Rotfeld and Walther Stützle, *German and Europe in Transition*, Oxford: Oxford University Press 1991, pp. 183–6.

40 This dependency is also reflected in Germany's trade volume with the CIS countries and Central Europe. For more detail see Andrei S. Markovits and Simon Reich, *The German Predicament*, Ithaca, NJ: Cornell University Press 1997, chap. 11.

3 Defence Policy in Transition

1 Mark Almond: *National pacifism. Germany's new temptation*. London: Alliance Publishers, 1991; Hans-Eckehard Bahr (Hrsg.), *Von der Armee zur europäischen Friedenstruppe*, München: Knaur, 1990; Detlef Bald, *Militär und Gesellschaft, 1945–1990. Die Bundeswehr der Bonner Republik*, Baden-Baden: Nomos Verlag, 1994.

2 Michael Stürmer, 'Deutsche Interessen', in Karl Kaiser and Hanns W. Maull (eds), *Deutschlands neue 'Außenpolitik – Band 1: Grundlagen*, München: R. Ouldenbourg 1994, pp. 39–62; Hans-Peter Schwarz, *Die Zentralmachte Europas. Deutschlands Rückkehr auf die Weltbühne*, Berlin: Siedler 1994.

3 For a statement by Kohl, see *Europa-Archiv*, Vol. 49, No. 19, 10 October 1994, pp. 562–4; see also Roman Herzog, 'Die Globalisierung der deutschen Außenpolitik ist unvermeidlich', *Bulletin* No. 20, Bonn: Press and Information Office of the Federal Government, 15 March 1992, p. 162; Volker Rühe, *Deutschlands Verantwortung. Perspektiven für das neue Europa*, Berlin: Ullstein 1994.

4 This concept has been given wide currency by the writings of Hanns Maull. See for example Hanns W. Maull, 'Germany and Japan: The New Civilian Powers', *Foreign Affairs*, Vol. 69, No. 5, Winter 1990–91, pp. 91–106.

5 Franz-Josef Meiers, 'Germany: The Reluctant Power', *Survival*, Vol. 37, No. 3, Autumn 1995, pp. 82–103, p. 98; the author also acknowledges discussions with Hanns Maull, Franz-Josef Meiers and Karl Kaiser.

6 Joschka Fischer, *Risiko Deutschland. Krise und Zukunft der deutschen Politik*, Cologne: Kiepenheuer & Witsch 1994.

7 Michael J. Inacker, *Unter Ausschluß der Öffentlichkeit?*, Bonn: Bouvier 1991, pp. 29f.

8   Ronald D. Asmus, 'Germany and America: Partners in Leadership?', *Survival*, Vol. XXXIII, No. 6, November/December 1991, pp. 546–66.

9   Senator Richard Lugar, *German–American Relations: A Turning Point?*, Speech to the German–American Chamber of Commerce, Dresden, April 1991, published in *U.S.-German Relations*, Hearing Before the Subcommittee on Europe and the Middle East of the Committee on Foreign Affairs, House of Representatives, 9 January 1992, US Government Printing Office, Washington 1992, p. 55; Peter Philipps, *Die Welt*, 8 September 1990.

10 Rede des Bundesaußenminister vor den Vereinten Nationen, *Bulletin*, No. 115, p. 1201.

11 Knut Kirste, *Die USA und Deutschland in der Golfkrise 1990/91*, Trier: Trier University 1998.

12 *International Herald Tribune*, 17 September 1990.

13 Cited from Kirste, op. cit.

14 Klaus Becher and Karl Kaiser, *Deutschland und der Irak-Konflikt*, Bonn: DGAP 1992.

15 *International Herald Tribune*, 6 November 1990.

16 Kirste, op. cit.

17 *Frankfurter Allgemeine Zeitung*, 30 January 1991.

18 The RAND study, for example, on the basis of opinion polls taken in late 1991 found:
    - 88 per cent of the sample supported German participation in humanitarian measures
    - 52 per cent agreed with financial support for UN-sanctioned interventions
    - 58 per cent supported Bundeswehr participation in UN peacekeeping missions
    - only 23 per cent supported Bundeswehr participation in UN-sanctioned interventions like the Gulf War.

19 *Der Spiegel*, 20 July 1992, p. 27.

20 Inacker, op. cit., p. 143.

21 Thomas Kielinger, 'German foreign policy faces test of credibility', *The German Tribune*, 24 July 1992, pp. 1 and 4 (originally published in *Rheinischer Merkur*, 17 July 1992).

22 For more discussion, see *Der Spiegel*, 21 December 1992, p. 20.

23 Cited from Rotfeld and Stützle, op. cit., p. 184.

24 Jürgen Rüttgers, *Elemente einer neuen Friedenspolitik*, unpublished parliamentary paper, July 1992, p. 9.

25 *Financial Times*, 24 August 1992, p. 2.

26 For views within the FDP leadership, see *Der Spiegel*, 21 December 1992, p. 20.

27 *Süddeutsche Zeitung*, 15 May 1992, p. 1.

28 See for example, Michael Backfisch, in *Saarbrücker Zeitung*, 16 July 1992; Thomas Kielinger, *Rheinischer Merkur*, 16 July 1992; Detlef Puhl, *Stuttgarter Zeitung*, 5 May 1992; Wolf J. Bell, *Die Welt*, 2 June 1992.

29 For more detail, see *Süddeutsche Zeitung*, 23 July 1992, p. 1.

30 *Der Spiegel*, 20 July 1992, p. 29. This is despite the fact that, according to Rüttgers, several members of the SPD leadership supported the action in the Adriatic. Rüttgers, op. cit., p. 2.

31 *Rheinischer Merkur,* 4 December 1992.
32 *Süddeutsche Zeitung,* 24 August 1992, p. 4; *Der Spiegel,* 31 August 1992, p. 36; *Financial Times,* 24 August 1992, p. 2.
33 *Der Spiegel,* 24 August 1992, pp. 68–9.
34 Arthur Hoffmann, 'Germany and the role of the Bundeswehr – a New Consensus?', paper presented at the BISA Conference, Leeds, 15–17 December 1997, p. 9.
35 For analysis of this judgement and its implications, see Volker Löwe, *Peacekeping-Operationen der UN,* Hamburg: Lit Verlag 1994.
36 Cited from Hoffmann, p. 12.
37 Ronald D. Asmus, *German Strategy and Public Opinion After the Wall 1990–93,* Santa Monica: RAND Corporation 1994.
38 See Meiers (1995), op. cit., p. 85.
39 'Die NATO fragt nach deutschen Bodentruppen für Bosnien', *Frankfurter Allgemeine Zeitung,* 13 December 1994; 'Die Bundesregierung bietet der NATO Flugzeuge und Schiffe an', *Frankfurter Allgemeine Zeitung,* 21 December 1994.
40 The executive board of the SPD agreed on 12 May only to support logistical support by the Bundeswehr for UN peacekeeping missions under UN command and explicitly opposed the deployment of ground troops and combat aircraft. 'SPD-Vorstand gegen Einsatz deutscher Tornados in Bosnien', *Frankfurter Allgemeine Zeitung,* 13 June 1995.
41 The Rapid Reaction Force (involving French, British and Dutch troops) was sent to support UNPROFOR. Foreign Minister Kinkel stated explicitly that no German combat troops would be sent to Bosnia. 'Der Bundestag mit deutlicher Mehrheit für den Bosnien-Einsatz der Bundeswehr', *Frankfurter Allgemeine Zeitung,* 1 July 1995.
42 'Der Bundestag mit großer Mehrheit für die Entsendung der Bundeswehr-Soldaten nach Bosnien', *Frankfurter Allgemeine Zeitung,* 7 December 1995.
43 'Rühe: UNO-Mandat Voraussetzung für Auslandseinsätze', *Süddeutsche Zeitung,* 25 November 1994; for discussion see Meiers, op. cit., pp. 92–3.
44 David Law and Michael Rühle, 'Die NATO und das "Out-of-area"-Problem', *Europa-Archiv,* Folge 15–16, 1992, pp. 439–44.
45 'Deutschland: alte und neue Bündnistreue', *Süddeutsche Zeitung,* 17 September 1998, p. 4.
46 Joint statement by Günter Verheugen (SPD, Chief Coalition negotiator) and Ludger Volmer (Greens), *Süddeutsche Zeitung,* 17 October 1998.
47 *Stuttgarter Zeitung,* 30 October 1998, p. 1.
48 Weisser, op. cit., p. 167.
49 Sameera Dalvi, 'The Post-Cold War role of the Bundeswehr: A Product of Normative Influences', *European Security,* Vol. 7, Spring 1998, pp. 97–116.
50 Weißbuch 1994, p. 132.
51 The *Independent Commission on the future tasks of the Bundeswehr* could not agree on this issue; the report recommended that conscripts could be sent 'out-of-area', while a dissenting opinion stated that this could only take place on a voluntary basis. See Hans-Adolf Jacobsen and Hans-Jürgen Rautenberg (eds), *Bundeswehr und europäische Sicherheitsordnung,* Bonn: Bouvier 1991, p. 51.

52　For more detail, see Christoph Bluth, 'Russian military forces: ambitions, capabilities and constraints', in Roy Allison and Christoph Bluth (eds), *Security Dilemmas in Russia and Eurasia*, London: RIIA 1998, pp. 67–93.

53　Karl Feldmeyer, 'Wehrpflicht ohne Verpflichtung', *Frankfurter Allgemeine Zeitung*, 13 February 1996.

54　IISS, *Military Balance 1998/99*, Oxford, Oxford University Press 1998.

55　'Deutschland: Bundeswehr – Abstieg in die zweite Liga', *Focus*, 19 July 1999.

56　'Die Bundeswehr kann ihren Personalbedarf nicht decken', *Frankfurter Allgemeine Zeitung*, 6 March 1996.

57　Karl Feldmeyer, 'Eingriffe in die Bundeswehr', *Frankfurter Allgemeine Zeitung*, 29 May 1996.

4　The Dilemmas of Collective Security

1　Just as conservative elements in the United States saw it as a vindication of Reagan's hard-line policies towards the Soviet Union.

2　Ingo Peters, 'CSCE', in Christoph Bluth, Emil Kirchner and James Sperling (eds), *The future of European Security*, Aldershot: Dartmouth 1995, pp. 67–84.

3　Curt Gasteyger, 'Ein gesamteuropäisches Sicherheitssystem?', *Europa-Archiv*, Vol. 47, No. 17, September 1992, pp. 475–82; Michael P. Gerace, 'Transforming the Pattern of Conflict: Geopolitics and post-Cold-War Europe, *Comparative Strategy*, No. 11, 1992, pp. 373–407; Mark Lyall Grant, 'Renforcement de la CSCE: la réponse aux reves européens?', *Politique Étrangère*, Vol. 55, No. 3, Autumn 1990, pp. 589–607.

4　John Borawski and Bruce George, 'Security for All of Europe: The Role of CSCE', in Bruce George (ed.), *Jane's NATO Handbook 1991–92*, London: Jane's 1991.

5　Josef Joffe, 'Collective security and the future of Europe: failed dreams and dead ends', *Survival*, Vol. 34, No. 1, Spring 1992, pp. 36–50.

6　See Jane M.O. Sharp, 'New Roles for CSCE', *Bulletin of Arms Control*, No. 7, August 1992, pp. 14–17; Richard A. Falkenrath, *Shaping Europe's Military Order*, Cambridge, MA: MIT Press 1995.

7　Sharp, op. cit., p. 15.

8　Ingo Peters, 'Von der KSZE zur OSZE: Überleben in der Nische kooperativer Sicherheit', in Helga Haftendorn and Otto Keck (eds), *Kooperation jenseits von Hegemonie und Bedrohung*, Baden-baden: Nomos 1997, pp. 57–100.

9　Roy Allison and Christoph Bluth (eds), *Security Dilemmas in Russia and Eurasia*, London: Royal Institute of International Relations 1998.

10　For a detailed discussion of these issues, see Roy Allison, *Peacekeeping in the Soviet Successor States*, Chaillot Paper No. 18, (Paris: WEU, 1994, pp. 30–50.

11　'CSCE and the New Europe – Our Security is Indivisible', *Decisions of the Rome Council Meeeting* (Rome, 1993), p. 7.

12　For more detail on the role of the CSCE/OSCE in the FSU, see Piotr Switalski and Ingrid Tersman, 'The Organisation for Security and Co-operation in Europe (OSCE)', in Jonson and Archer, (eds) *Peacekeeping*, pp. 173–88.

13 Allison, *Peacekeeping in the Soviet Successor States*, op. cit.
14 Suzanne Crow, 'Russian Views on an Eastward Expansion of NATO', RFE/RL *Research Report*, Vol. 2, No. 41, 15 October 1993, pp. 21–54.
15 This does not preclude some adjustments to allow Russia to deploy forces in crisis regions, in particular the Caucasus. For an analysis of the current debate, see Jane M.O. Sharp, 'CFE Treaty under Threat as Russia Requests Revisions', *Bulletin of Arms Control*, No. 12, November 1993, pp. 2–4.
16 Ernst-Otto Czempiel, 'NATO erweitern oder OSZE stärken?', *HSFK-Standpunkte*, No. 4, June 1995.
17 Helmut W. Ganser, 'Die OSZE nach dem Gipfel von Budapest', *Europäische Sicherheit*, No. 44, March 1995, p. 22.
18 Adam D. Rotfeld, 'Die Zukunft des Europäischen Sicherheitssystem. Die Erweiterung der westlichen Sicherheitsstrukturen und die OSZE', *S und F*, Vol. 13. No. 4, 1995, pp. 221–6.
19 See Peters (1997) op. cit.
20 Knut Kirste, *Der Jugoslawienkonflikt*, Trier: Trier University 1998.
21 Susan L. Woodward, *Balkan Tragedy*, The Brookings Institution; Washington, DC 1995.
22 Reuters News, service, 3 July 1991.
23 Dow Jones News service, 3 July 1991.
24 *Financial Times*, 5 July 1991, p. 2.
25 Richard Murphy, 'Germany: Genscher calls for CSCE Peacekeeping Force, Security Council', Reuters News service, 4 September 1991.
26 Reuters News service, 18 September 1991.
27 James Gow, *Triumph of the Lack of Will*, London: Hurst & Company 1997, p. 64.
28 Beverly Crawford, 'Explaining Defection from International Cooperation. Germany's Unilateral Recognition of Croatia', *World Politics* Vol. 48, July 1996, pp. 482–521.
29 Gow, op. cit., p. 81.
30 David Owen, *Balkan Odyssey*, London: Victor Gollancz 1995.
31 For a detailed argument, see Peter Viggo Jakobson, *Use and Abuse of Military Threats in Bosnia-Herzegovina: Why Compellence and Deterrence Failed*, Aarhus University, Denmark 1996.
32 See the remarks of Klaus Kinkel reported in *Frankfurter Allgemeine Zeitung*, 27 May 1995.
33 Richard Holbrooke, *To End a War*, New York: Random House 1998.
34 Richard Caplan, 'Crisis in Kosovo', *International Affairs*, Vol. 74, No. 2, October 1998, pp. 745–63; for historical background see Noel Malcolm, *Kosovo: A Short History*, London: Macmillan 1998.
35 Marc Weller, 'The Rambouillet Conference', *International Affairs*, Vol. 75, No. 2, April 1999, pp. 211–52.
36 Marc Weller (ed.), *The Crisis in Kosovo 1989–1999*, Linton: Documents & Analysis Publishers 1999.
37 Maull, 'Germany in the Yugoslav Crisis', *Survival*, Vol. 37, No. 4, Winter 1995–96, p. 111.
38 Adrian Hyde-Price, 'Berlin Crisis Takes to Arms', *The World Today*, Vol. 55. No. 6, pp. 13–15.

39 Of course, the role of UNHCR and other agents played an important role with regard to the humanitarian dimension.

40 Although Russia did not resist the dissolution of the Soviet Union, the on-going Chechen crisis has been interpreted as indicating that it is prepared to use force to resist the disintegration of the Russian Federation itself. Russian actions raise serious doubts about Russia's credentials as a state committed to international norms and human rights, but the instability and anarchy in the Caucasus that partly prompted Russia's action would suggest caution about more general conclusions about the relations between Russia's government and the regions.

5   NATO: at the Heart of European Security

1 This and all subsequent quotations from the *Alliance's New Strategic Concept* are from Ulrich Wiesser, *NATO ohne Feindbild*, Bonn: Bouvier 1992, pp. 298–314.

2 For a text of the 'Washington Treaty', formally known as 'The North Atlantic Treaty', signed in Washington DC on 4 April 1949, see the *NATO Handbook*, Brussels: NATO 1972, pp. 52–5.

3 For an elaborate analysis of the origins and the nature of 'flexible response', see Christoph Bluth, *Britain, Germany and Western Nuclear Strategy*, Oxford: Oxford University Press 1995.

4 Julian Lider, *Problems of Military Policy in the Konrad Adenauer Era (1949–1966)*, Stockholm: Swedish Institute for International Affairs 1984, pp. 64–7.

5 For more detail on the creation of the ARRC, its staff, available forces and assets, role and mission see Colin McInnes, 'The Future of NATO', in Christoph Bluth, Emil Kirchner and James Sperling (eds), *The Future of European Security*, Aldershot: Dartmouth 1995, pp. 85–111.

6 Charles Barry, 'NATO's Combined Joint Task Forces in Theory and Practice', *Survival*, Vol. 38, No. 1, Spring 1996, pp. 81–97.

7 This and the following citations are from *The Alliance's Strategic Concept*, NATO Press Release NAC-S(99)65, 24 April 1999.

8 For an attempt to define the new direction for NATO, see Alyson J.K. Bailes, 'NATO: Towards a New Synthesis', *Survival*, Vol. 38, No. 3, Autumn 1996, pp. 27–40. This article describes how NATO is adapting organizationally to the new environment, but in doing so demonstrates the absence of a clear sense of purpose.

9 Based on conversations with officials in the Ministry of Foreign Affairs in Bonn.

10 Suzanne Crow, 'Russian Views on an Eastward Expansion of NATO', *RFE/RL Research Report,* Vol. 2, No. 41, 15 October 1993, pp. 2154.

11 This does not preclude some adjustments to allow Russia to deploy forces in crisis regions, in particular the Caucasus. For an analysis of the current debate, see Jane M.O. Sharp, 'CFE Treaty Under Threat as Russia Requests Revisions', *Bulletin of Arms Control,* No. 12, November 1993, pp. 2–4.

12 See for example Vaclav Havel, 'We Really Are Part of the NATO Family', *International Herald Tribune*, 20 October 1993.

13 The term 'NATO expansion' was widely used but came to be considered politically incorrect. Generally, the words 'NATO enlargement' will be used in this text instead, unless the context makes 'NATO expansion' more appropriate.

14 For a discussion of these arguments, see Ronald D. Asmus, Richard L. Kugler and F. Stephen Larrabee, 'NATO Expansion: The Next Steps', *Survival*, Vol. 37, No. 1, Spring 1995, pp. 7–33; Michael E. Brown, 'The Flawed Logic of NATO Expansion', *Survival*, Vol. 37, No. 1, Spring 1995, pp. 34–52; Philip Zelikow, 'The Masque of Institutions', *Survival*, Vol. 38, No. 1, Spring 1996, pp. 6–18.

15 Cited from John Borawski, 'Partnership for Peace and Beyond', *International Affairs*, Vol. 71, No. 2, April 1995, pp. 233–46, p. 237.

16 Cited in Brown, op. cit., p. 37.

17 John Borawski, 'Partnership for Peace and Beyond', *International Affairs*, Vol. 71, No. 2, April 1995, pp. 233–46.

18 Joseph Kruzel, Presentation to the North Atlantic Assembly Political Committe, Washington DC, 15 November 1994, cited from Borawski, op. cit., p. 234.

19 Nick Williams, 'Partnership for Peace: Permanent Fixture or Declining Asset?, *Survival*, Vol. 38, No. 1, Spring 1996, pp. 98–110.

20 Fergus Carr, 'Security Politics in the New Europe', in Fergus Carr (ed.), *Europe: The Cold Divide*, Macmillan; Basingstoke 1998, pp. 51–74.

21 'NATO–PFP Training Paves Way for Coalition Missions', United States Information Service Report (Eur 205), 30 August 1995.

22 Alyson J.K. Bailes, 'European Defence and Security. The Role of NATO, WEU and EU', *Security Dialogue*, Vol. 27, No. 1:55–64, March 1996; Alyson Bailes, Europe's Defense Challenge: 'Reinventing the Atlantic Alliance', *Foreign Affairs*, 76:1:15–20, (January/February 1997).

23 Pavel Fel'gengauer, *Segodna*, 6 October 1995.

24 Yeltsin's Press Conference, 8 September 1995.

25 Aleksandar Fomenko, 'The Contours of new Russian Geopolitics', *Review of International Affairs*, XLVIII:28–29, (15 May 1997).

26 Michael MccGwire, 'NATO expansion: a policy error of historic importance', *Review of International Studies*, Vol. 24, No. 1, January 1998, pp. 23–42.

27 This argument has been put forcefully by Zbigniew Brzezinski.

28 Christopher L. Ball, 'Nattering NATO negativism? Reasons why expansion may be a good thing', *Review of International Studies*, Vol. 24, No. 1, January 1998, pp. 43–67.

29 Michael E. Brown, 'The Flawed Logic of NATO Expansion', *Survival*, 37:1:34–52, (Spring 1995); *Comparative Strategy*, 'View from Russia: Russia and NATO: Theses of the Council on Foreign and Defense Policy', Vol. 15, No. 1, 1996, pp. 91–102; Paul Cornish, 'European security: the end of architecture and the new NATO', *International Affairs*, 72:4:751–69, (October 1996).

30 'NATO expansion wasn't ruled out', International Herald Tribune, 10 August 1995. Philip Zelikow has argued on the basis of the facts elaborated here that there was no commitment not to expand NATO eastwards, emphasizing the limited nature of the commitment in the 'two-plus-four agreement'. While technically correct, it does not encompass the

full nature of the discussions. Zelikow himself admits the Bush administration at the time did not contemplate the possibility of NATO eastward
expansion beyond East Germany.

31 *Frankfurter Allgemeine Zeitung*, 8 May 1995.
32 John Lewis Gaddis describes NATO enlargement as violating all principles of sound strategic thinking, which can only be remedied by
enlarging the enlargement process and include Russia itself. See John
Lewis Gaddis, 'History, Grand Strategy and NATO Enlargment', *Survival*,
Vol. 40, No. 1, Spring 1998, pp. 145–51.
33 John Lewis Gaddis, op. cit.
34 Based on interviews with the Head of Policy Planning in the Ministry
of Foreign Affairs, Moscow, 1997.
35 This was emphasized, for example, in official German comments on
the NATO enlargement study; 'Die deutsche Handschrift ist deutlich zu
erkennen', *Frankfurter Allgemeine*, 29 September 1995; see also George
Brock, 'Kohl cautions Nato against rush to expand eastwards', *The Times*,
4 July 1995. This article describes the policy differences between Volker
Rühe, an ardent advocate of NATO enlargement and the more cautions
tone of Chancellor Kohl. The differences are exaggerated: Kohl was stress-
ing the 'parallelism' between the NATO and EU enlargement processes.
36 'Yeltsin Foresees "Most Difficult" Talks With Clinton', Moscow Interfax
in English 11:58 GMT 14 March 1997.
37 'Yeltsin: Talk About Russia Joining NATO "Completely Unreal"', Moscow
NTV in Russian 13:00 GMT 17 March 1997, cited from FBIS-SOV-97-076,
17 March 1997.
38 Sergey Maslov, *Komsomolskaia Pravda*, 28 March–4 April 1997, p. 3.
39 Some of the elements were reported on the basis of statements by Yeltsin
in Moscow Interfax in English 08:03 GMT 8 May 1997; see also the
report on the talks between Foreign Minister Primakov and NATO Secretary General Solana by Andrei Nizamutdinov and Adrei Shtorkh Moscow
ITAR-TASS in English 14:19 GMT 10 April 1997.
40 Vasiliy Safronchuk, *Sovetskaia Rossiia*, 17 May 97.
41 Douglas Busvine, 'German defence plans spook Russia', Reuters Business Briefing, 4 February 1998.
42 William Boston 'Germany: Kohl aide suggests EU, NATO Association
for Russia', Reuters Business Briefing, 27 January 1998.
43 http://www.spd/de/archiv/events/hannover_97/aussen_1.html
44 Werner A. Perger, 'Für Gerhard Schröder ist die Kosovo-Krise einerster
außenpolitischer Test', *Die Zeit*, 18 June 1998.
45 Michael Dammann and Jörg Nadoll, 'Jugoslawienpolitik: Von der
Ausnahme zur Regel?', in Christoph Neßhöver, Hanns W. Maull and
Bernhard Stahl (eds), *Lehrgeld: Vier Monate rot-grüne Außenpolitik*, Trier:
Trier University 1999, pp. 41–56.
46 'Programme und Aussagen der Parteien zur Bundestagswahl', *Das
Parlament*, 4 September 1998; see also Dammann and Nadoll, op. cit.

6 The European Union

1 Franz-Joseph Strauß, *Die Erinnerungen*, (Berlin: Siedler Verlag, 1989); Franz Josef Strauß, *Herausforderung und Antwort*, (Stuttgart: Seewald Verlag, 1968). Although Strauß was more forthright in the propagation of such views, he was not essentially out of tune with Adenauer or even Helmut Schmidt on this. See also Richard Löwenthal (ed.), *Außenpolitische Perspektiven des westdeutschen Staates, Bd.3, Der Zwang zur Partnerschaft*, (München: R. Ouldenbourg, 1972).

2 Hans-Peter Schwarz, *Die gezähmten Deutschen: Von der Machtbesessenheit zur Machtvergessenheit*, (Stuttgart: Deutsche Verlagsanstalt, 1986).

3 Konrad Adenauer, *Erinnerungen 1953–1955*, Stuttgart: DVA 1966, chapters IX and X.

4 Simon Bulmer and William E. Paterson, 'Germany in the European union: gentle giant or emergent leader?', *International Affairs*, Vol. 72, No. 1, 1996, pp. 9–32.

5 J. Anderson and J. Goodman, 'Mars or Minerva; a united Germany in a post-Cold War Europe', in R. Keohane, J. Nye and S. Hoffmann (eds), *After the Cold War: international institutions and state strategies in Europe, 1989–1991*, Cambridge MA: Harvard University Press, 1993, pp. 23–4.

6 Christoph Bluth, 'A West German View', in Richard Davy (ed.), *European Detente: A Reappraisal*, Sage, 1992, London, pp. 31–53.

7 On the concept of Germany as a civilian power, see Hanns W. Maull, 'Germany and Japan: The New Civilian Powers', *Foreign Affairs*, Vol. 69, No. 2, Winter 1990–91, pp. 91–106.

8 For a deeper analysis of collective memories and their effect on the perception of Germany, see Andrei S. Markovits and Simon Reich, *The German Predicament*, Cornell University Press: Ithaca 1997.

9 Volker Rühe, *Deutschlands Verantwortung. Perspektiven für das neue Europa*. Berlin: Ullstein 1994; Wolfgang Schäuble, *Und der Zukunft zugewandt*, Berlin: Siedler 1994; Joschka Fischer, *Risiko Deutschland. Krise und Zukunft der deutschen Politik*, Cologne: Kiepenheur & Wietsch 1994; Karl Kaiser and Hans W. Maull (eds), *Die Zukunft der europäischen Integration: Folgerung für die deutsche Politik*, Bonn: DGAP 1993.

10 For German perspectives on the Maastrich Treaty, see Karl Kaiser and Hanns W. Maull (eds), *Die Zukunft der europäischen Integration: Folgerungen für die deutsche Politik*, DGAP, Bonn 1993.

11 Josef Janning, 'Europa braucht verschiedene Geschwindigkeiten', *Europa-Archiv*, Vol. 18, 1994, pp. 527–36.

12 Josef Janning, 'Germany's foreign policy', *International Affairs*, Vol. 72, No. 1, January 1996, pp. 9–32.

13 CDU/CSU-Fraktion des deutschen Bundestages, 'Überlegungen zur Europapolitik', Bonn, 1 September 1994; for more discussion of the concept of a 'core Europe', see Christian Deubner, *Deutsche Europapolitik. Von Maastricht nach Kerneuropa?*, Baden-Baden: Nomos 1995.

14 See Janning, 'Germany's foreign policy', op. cit., p. 41.

15 Ibid.

16 UlrichWeisser, *NATO ohne Feindbild*, Bonn: Bouvier 1992, p. 303.

17 *Draft Treaty on European Union*, Article D.

18 Interestingly, the German ministry of defence was not involved; the German side was entirely represented by the Chancellor's office. See Karl-Heinz-Kamp, 'Ein Spaltpilz für das Atlantische Bündnis', *Europa-Archiv*, Folge 15–16, 1992, pp. 445–452.

19 See Peter Schmidt, 'Partner or Rivals: NATO, WEU, EC and the Reorganization of European Security Policy – Taking Stock', in Peter Schmidt (ed.), *In the Midst of Change: On the Development of West European Security and Defence Cooperation*, Baden-Baden: Nomos 1992, pp. 187–228; p. 219.

20 Robert P. Grant, 'France's New Relationship with NATO', *Survival*, Vol. 38, No. 1, Spring 1996, pp. 58–80.

21 The *Economist*, 3 October 1992, p. 52.

22 Alyson J.K. Bailes, 'European Defence and Security. The Role of NATO, WEU and EU', *Security Dialogue*, Vol. 27, No. 1 March 1996, pp. 55–64.

23 Heinz-Jürgen Axt, 'Die EU nach Amsterdam: Kompetenzzuwachs für Außen- und Sicherheitspolitik?', *Europäische Rundschau*, No. 4, 1997, pp. 3–7.

24 This creates 87 votes, and at least 62 have to agree to the proposition being voted, which can be adopted only if at least 10 member states agree. The Council adopts decisions by a simple majority. For more detail see Axt, op. cit., p. 10.

25 Andrew Duff (ed.), *The Treaty of Amsterdam (Text and Commentary)*, The Federal Trust, London 1997.

26 Axt, op. cit., p. 11–12.

27 *The Irish Times*, 5 June 1999.

28 *Report on Economic and Monetary Union in the European Community*, Brussels, April 1990.

29 Michele Chang, *The Electoral Connection; Crisis and Credibility in the European monetary System*, paper presented at the American Political Science Association Annual Conference Chicago 1995.

30 See Joseph M. Grieco, 'The Masstricht Treaty, Economic and Monetary Union and the neo-realist research programme', *Review of International Studies*, Vol. 21, No. 1, January 1995, pp. 21–40.

31 Scott Cooper, *Governments Against Independent Central banks: Explaining German Acceptance of EMU*, paper presented at the American Political Science Association Annual Conference Washington 1997; Thomas Risse, *To Euro or Not to Euro? The EMU and Identity Politics in the European Union*, European University Institute, Working Paper RSC No. 98/9, Florence 1998.

32 Tomaso Padoa-Schioppa with Michael Emerson, Mervyn King, Jean-Claude Milleron, Jean Paelinck, Lucas Papademos, Alfred Pastor and Fritz Scharpf, *Efficiency, stability, and equity: a strategy for the evolution of the economic system of the European Community*, Oxford: Oxford University Presss 1987.

33 Risse, op. cit.; however, as a consequence, EMU became less popular among the French population.

34 Paul de Grauwe, *The economics of monetary integration*, Oxford; Oxford University Press 1994, pp. 186–7.

35 Cooper, op. cit., for an outline of this argument (p. 2).

36 Max Otte and William Grimes, 'Germany and Japan: Civilian Power, Traditional Power or Institutional Constraints?', unpublished paper 1999.

37 Cooper, op. cit., p. 4; David Buchan, *Financial Times*, 24 March 1990, p. 2.
38 Kenneth Dyson and Kevin Featherstone, 'EMU and Economic Governance in Germany', *German Politics*, Vol. 5, No. 3, December 1996, pp. 325–55.
39 Cited from Risse, op. cit.
40 Martin Potthoff and Kai Hirschmann, 'Ein integrationsprojekt in der Diskussion: Ökonomische Mechanismen und politische Absichten', *Die Europäische Währungsunion – Ein Testfall für die europäische Integration?*, Berlin: Arno Spitz Verlag 1997, pp. 9–31, p. 10.
41 Mordechai E. Kreinin, 'Regional and Global Economic Integration', in Potthof and Hirschmann, op. cit. pp. 35–46.
42 Grieco, op. cit., p. 39. This author is not convinced by the extension to neo-realist theory whereby Grieco attempts to provide a framework in which neo-realist theory might account for EMU since it conspicuously fails to account for German policy on EMU.
43 Heather Grabbe and Kirsty Hughes, *Eastward Enlargement of the European Union*, London: Royal Institute of International Affairs RIIA 1997, pp. 38–56; Jim Rollo, 'Economic Aspects of EU Enlargement to the East', in Marc Maresceau, *Enlarging the European Union*, Harlow: Addison Wesley Longman 1997, pp. 252–75.
44 Grabbe and Hughes, op. cit., pp. 100–3.
45 Grabbe and Hughes (1998), op. cit., pp. 119–20.
46 Rollo, op. cit., p. 269.
47 For more detail, see Presidency Conclusions, Berlin European Council 24–25 March 1999, http://www.eu.int.
48 *Agenda 2000 – For a stronger and wider Union*, http://europe.eu.int/comm/agenda2000/overview/en/agenda.htm.
49 Péter Balázs, 'Globalization: Symptoms and Consequences', in Maresceau, op. cit., pp. 358–75.
50 *Die Welt*, 3 November 1998.
51 *Capital*, 1 January 1999.
52 *Agenda 2000 – For a stronger and wider Union*, http://europe.eu.int/comm/agenda2000/overview/en/agenda.htm.

7 The Challenge of the Future

1 Christian Hacke, *Weltmacht wider Willen. Die Außenpolitik der Bundesrepublik Deutschland*, Berlin: Ullstein TB Verlag 1997; Christan Hacke, 'Die Bedeutung des Nationalen Interesses für die Außenpolitik der Bundesrepublik', in Gottfried Niedhart, Detlef Junker and Michael W. Richter, *Deutschland in Europa*, Mannheim: Palatium Verlag 1997, pp. 18–35.
2 Lothar Gutjahr, *German Foreign and Defence Policy after Unification*, London: Pinter 1994; Peter Katzenstein (ed.), *Tamed Power, Germany in Europe*, Ithaca, NJ: Cornell University Press 1997.
3 Margaret Thatcher, *The Downing Street Years*, London: Harper Collins 1993, p. 791.

4 Florian Gerster and Rupert Scholz, Deutschland auf dem Weg zur internationalen Normalität, *Der Mittler-Brief,* Vol. 9, No. 1, (1. Quartal 1994); Karl-Heinz-Kamp, 'German Armed Forces and International Military Action: Step by Step toward Normalization', *Enjeux Atlantiques,* No. 7, July 1993, pp. 28–31; Jacques le Rider, Un an après l'unification: retour à la normalité de la nation allemande, *Politique Étrangère,* Vol. 56, Winter 1991, pp. 913–27.

5 Andrei S. Markovits and Simon Reich, *The German Predicament. Memory and Power in the New Europe,* Ithaca, NJ; Cornell University Press 1997.

6 For a discussion of Karl Popper's idea on falsification in IR theory, see Martin Hollis and Steve Smith, *Explaining and Understanding International Relations,* Oxford; Clarendon Press 1991, Chapter 3.

7 Gutjahr, op. cit.

8 Max Otte and William Grimes, 'Germany and Japan: Civilian Power, Traditional Power or Institutional Constraints?', unpublished paper 1999.

9 This is of course an interpretation of the German foreign policy agenda in theoretical terms. Some authors have used the term 'sociological institutionalism' to describe a range of approaches. Constructivism is quite a broad movement and is used here in a more specific sense. See David Dessler, 'Constructivism within a positivist social science', *Review of International Studies,* Vol. 25, No. 1, January 1999, pp. 123–37.

10 Rainer Baumann, Volker Rittberger and Wolfgang Wagner, *Power and Politics: Neorealist Foreign Policy Theory and Expectations about German Foreign Policy since Unification,* unpublished paper 1998.

11 Hanns W. Maull, 'Rot-grüne Außenpolitik – Von den Höhen guter Absichten in die Nidererungen globalisierter Politik', in Hanns W. Maull, Christoph Neßhöver/Bernhard Stahl (eds), *Lehrgeld: Vier Monate rot-grüne Außenpolitik,* Trierer Arbeitsparpier zur Internationalen Politik, No. 1, March 1999, pp. 1–12.

Select Bibliography

Adenauer, Konrad, *Erinnerungen 1953–1955*, Stuttgart: DVA 1966

Algieri, Franco and Anand Menon (eds), *Managing Security in Europe. The European Union and the Challenge of Enlargement*, Gütersloh: Bertelsmann Foundation Publishers, 1996

Allison, Roy, *Military Forces in the Soviet Successor States*, IISS Adelphi Paper No. 280, London: Brassey's 1993

Allison, Roy, *Peacekeeping in the Soviet Successor States*, Chaillot Paper No. 18, Paris: WEU, 1994

Allison, Roy and Christoph Bluth (eds), *Security Dilemmas in Russia and Eurasia*, London: Royal Institute of International Affairs 1998

Almond, Mark, *National pacifism. Germany's new temptation*, London: Alliance Publishers, 1991

Altenhof, Ralf and Eckhard Jesse (Hrsg.), *Das Wiedervereinigte Deutschland. Zwischenbilanz und Perspektiven*, Düsseldorf: Droste, 1995

Asmus, Ronald D., 'Germany and America: Partners in Leadership?', *Survival*, Vol. XXXIII, No. 6, November/December 1991, pp. 546–66

Asmus, Ronald D., *Germany after the Gulf*, Santa Monica, CA: Rand, 1992 (Rand Note N-3391-AF)

Asmus, Ronald D., *Germany in Transition: National Self-Confidence and International Reticence*, Rand Corporation: Santa Monica 1992, Rand Note N-3522-AF

Asmus, Ronald D., *German Strategy and Public Opinion After the Wall 1990–93*, Santa Monica: RAND Corporation 1994

Asmus, Ronald D., Richard L. Kugler and F. Stephen Larrabee, 'NATO Expansion: The Next Steps', *Survival*, Vol. 37, No. 1, Spring 1995, pp. 7–33

Auswärtiges Amt, Deutsche Außenpolitik nach der Einheit 1990–1993. Eine Dokumentation. Bonn: DCM-Verl., 1993

Auswärtiges Amt, Deutschlands Außenpolitik. Schwerpunkte und Perspektiven. Fachausschuß Außenpolitik der CSU, (Grünwald: Atwerb Verl., 1994)

Axt, Heinz-Jürgen, 'Die EU nach Amsterdam: Kompetenzzuwachs für Außen- und Sicherheitspolitik?', *Europäische Rundschau*, No. 4, 1997, pp. 3–7

Bahr, Egon, *Sicherheit für und vor Deutschland. Vom Wandel durch Annäherung zur Europäischen Sicherheitsgemeinschaft*, München: Hanser, 1991

Bahr, Hans-Eckehard, (Hrsg.), *Von der Armee zur europäischen Friedenstruppe*, München: Knaur, 1990

Bailes, Alyson J.K., 'European Defence and Security. The Role of NATO, WEU and EU', *Security Dialogue*, Vol. 27, No. 1:55–64, March 1996

Bailes, Alyson J.K., 'European Defence and Security. The Role of NATO, WEU and EU', *Security Dialogue*, Vol. 27, No. 1 March 1996, pp. 55–64

Bailes, Alyson J.K., 'NATO: Towards a New Synthesis', *Survival*, Vol. 38, No. 3, Autumn 1996, pp. 27–40

Bailes, Alyson, 'Europe's Defense Challenge: Reinventing the Atlantic Alliance', *Foreign Affairs*, Vol. 76, No. 1, January/February 1997, pp. 15–20

Bald, Detlef, *Militär und Gesellschaft, 1945–1990. Die Bundeswehr der Bonner Republik*, Baden-Baden: Nomos Verlag, 1994

Ball, Christopher L., 'Nattering NATO negativism? reasons why expansion may be a good thing', *Review of International Studies*, Vol. 24, No. 1, January 1998, pp. 43–67

Baring, Arnulf (ed.), *Germany's New Position in Europe: Problems and Perspectives*, Oxford: Berg, 1994

Barry, Charles, 'NATO's Combined Joint Task Forces in Theory and Practice', *Survival*, Vol. 38, No. 1, Spring 1996, pp. 81–97

Bartke, Matthias, Verteidigungsauftrag der Bundeswehr. Eine verfassungsrechtliche Analyse Baden-Baden: Nomos Verlag, 1991

Baylis, John and Steve Smith (eds), *The Globalization of World Politics: An Introduction to International Relations*, Oxford: Oxford University Press, 1997

Becher, Klaus and Karl Kaiser, *Deutschland und der Irak-Konflikt*, Bonn: DGAP 1992

Becker, Johannes M., Militär und Legitimation. Eine vergleichende Studie zur Sicherheitspolitik Frankreichs und der Bundesrepublik Deutschland; Mit einem Exkurs über Großbritannien von Gert Gohde: Marburg: IAFA, 1997

Bergner, Jeffrey T., *The New Superpowers. Germany, Japan, the U.S. and the New World Order*, New York: St. Martin's Press, 1991

Bluth, Christoph, *Britain, Germany and Western Nuclear Strategy*, Oxford: Oxford University Press 1995

Bluth, Christoph, *Arms Control and Proliferation: Russia and International Security After the Cold War*, London Defence Studies No. 35, London: Brassey's 1996

Bluth, Christoph, Emil Kirchner and James Sperling (eds), *The Future of European Security*, Aldershot: Dartmouth 1995

Bomsdorf, Falk, *Zwischen Destruktion und Regeneration. Zur Zukunft des postsowjetischen Raumes*, SWP S 389, Ebenhausen: Stiftung Wissenschaft und Politik 1993

Borawski, John, 'Partnership for Peace and beyond', *International Affairs*, Vol. 71, No. 2, April 1995, pp. 233–46

Borkenhagen, Franz H.U., *Außenpolitische Interessen Deutschlands*, Bonn: Bouvier 1997

von Bredow, Wilfried, *Der KSZE-Prozess. Von der Zähmung zur Auflösung des Ost-West-Konflikts*, Darmstadt: Wiss. Buch, 1992

Brown, Michael, Sean Lynn-Jones and Steven E. Miller (eds), *Debating the Democratic Peace*, Cambridge, MA: MIT Press 1997

Brown, Michael E., 'The Flawed Logic of NATO Expansion', *Survival*, Vol. 37, No. 1, Spring 1995, pp. 34–52

Bruck, Elke and Peter M. Wagner (Hrsg.), *Wege zum '2+4'-Vertrag. Die äußeren Aspekte der deutschen Einheit*, (Schriftreihe der Forschungsgruppe Deutschland, Band 6), München: Forschungsgruppe Deutschland, 1996

Brunner, Stefan, *Deutsche Soldaten im Ausland. Fortsetzung der Außenpolitik mit militärischen Mitteln?*, München: Beck, 1993

Bulmer, Simon and William E. Paterson, 'Germany in the European union: gentle giant or emergent leader?', *International Affairs*, Vol. 72, No. 1, 1996, pp. 9–32

Bundesminister der Verteidigung, *Einsatz der Bundeswehr im Zusammenhang mit dem Golfkonflikt.* Dokumentation der Berichte beteiligter Soldaten, Informations- und Pressestab, Referat Öffentlichkeitsarbeit, Bonn, 1992

Buzan, Barry, Ole Wæver and Jaap de Wilde, *Security: A Framework for Analysis,* Boulder, CO: Westview 1997

Caplan, Richard, 'Crisis in Kosovo', *International Affairs,* Vol. 74, No. 2, October 1998, pp. 745–63

Carr, Fergus, (ed.), *Europe: The Cold Divide,* Macmillan; Basingstoke 1998

Chan, Steve, 'In Search of Democratic Peace: Problems and Promise', *Mershon International Studies Review,* 41, supp. 1, May 1997, pp. 59–91

Chernoff, Fred, *After Bipolarity: The Vanishing Threat, Theories of Cooperation, and the Future of the Atlantic Alliance,* Ann Arbor: University of Michigan Press, 1995

Clark, Ian, *Globalization and Fragmentation: International Relations in the 20th Century,* Oxford: Oxford University Press 1997

Collinson, Sarah, *Beyond Borders: West European Migration Policy Towards the 21st Century,* Royal Institute of International Affairs with Wyndham Place Trust, 1993

Collinson, Sarah, *Europe and International Migration,* London: Pinter for Royal Institute of International Affairs, 1994

Comparative Strategy, 'View from Russia: Russia and NATO: Theses of the Council on Foreign and Defense Policy', Vol. 15, No. 1, 1996, pp. 91–102

Cornish, Paul, 'European security: the end of architecture and the new NATO', *International Affairs,* Vol. 72, No. 4, October 1996, pp. 751–69

Cornish, Paul, *Partnership in Crisis: The US, Europe and the Fall and Rise of NATO,* London: Pinter for Royal Institute of International Affairs, 1997

Crawford, Beverly, 'Explaining Defection from International Cooperation. Germany's Unilateral Recognition of Croatia', *World Politics* Vol. 48, July 1996, pp. 482–521

Crow, Suzanne, 'Russian Views on an Eastward Expansion of NATO', RFE/ RL *Research Report,* Vol. 2, No. 41, 15 October 1993, pp. 21–54.

Curtis, Mark, Ole Diehl, Jérôme Paolini, Alexis Seydoux and Reinhard Wolf, *Challenges and Responses to Future European Security: British, French and German Perspectives,* London: European Strategy Group 1993

Czempiel, Ernst-Otto, 'NATO erweitern oder OSZE stärken?', *HSFK-Standpunkte,* No. 4, June 1995

Dalvi, Sameera, 'The Post-Cold War role of the Bundeswehr: A Product of Normative Influences', *European Security,* Vol. 7, Spring 1998, pp. 97–116

Danchev Alex and Thomas Halverson (eds), *International Perspectives on the Yugoslav Conflict,* London: Macmillan Press, 1996

Davy, Richard (ed.), *European Detente: A Reappraisal,* London: Sage, 1992

Deighton, Anne, (ed.), *Western European Union 1954–1997: Defence, Security, Integration,* Oxford: European Interdependence Research Unit, St Antony's College, University of Oxford, 1997

Dessler, David, 'Constructivism within a positivist social science', *Review of International Studies,* Vol. 25, No. 1, January 1999, pp. 123–37

Deubner, Christian, *Deutsche Europapolitik. Von Maastricht nach Kerneuropa?,* Baden-Baden: Nomos 1995

Downs, George W. (ed.), *Collective Security beyond the Cold War,* Ann Arbor, MI: University of Michigan Press, 1994

Duff, Andrew (ed.), *The Treaty of Amsterdam (Text and Commentary)*, The Federal Trust, London 1997

Dyson, Kenneth and Kevin Featherstone, 'EMU and Economic Governance in Germany', *German Politics*, Vol. 5, No. 3, December 1996, pp. 325–55

Eberwein, Wolf-Dieter and Karl Kaiser (eds), *Deutschlands neue Außenpolitik: Band 4 Institutionen und Ressourcen*, München: R. Ouldenbourg 1998

Falkenrath Richard A., *Shaping Europe's Military Order*, London: MIT Press 1995

Fischer, Joschka, *Risiko Deutschland. Krise und Zukunft der deutschen Politik*, Cologne: Kiepenheuer & Witsch 1994

Fomenko, Aleksandar, 'The Contours of new Russian Geopolitics', *Review of International Affairs*, XLVIII: 28–29, (15 May 1997)

Freedman, Lawrence (ed.), *Military Intervention in European Conflicts*, Oxford: Blackwells, 1994

Freedman, Lawrence and Efraim Karsh, *The Gulf Conflict 1990–1991*, London: Faber & Faber 1993

Fukuyama, Francis, *The End of History and the Last Man*, New York: The Free Press 1992

Gaddis, John Lewis, 'History, Grand Strategy and NATO Enlargment', *Survival*, Vol. 40, No. 1, Spring 1998, pp. 145–51

Ganser, Helmut W. Die OSZE nach dem Gipfel von Budapest, *Europäische Sicherheit*, No. 44, March 1995, p. 22.

Garton Ash, Timothy, *In Europe's Name: Germany and the Divided Continent*, London: Cape, 1993

Gasteyger, Curt, 'Ein gesamteuropäisches Sicherheitssystem?', *Europa-Archiv*, Vol. 47, No. 17, September 1992

Genscher, Hans-Dietrich, 'Eine Stabilitätsordnung für Europa', *Europäische Sicherheit*, No. 41, pp. 310–17, June 1992

George, Bruce (ed.), *Jane's NATO Handbook 1991–92*, London: Jane's 1991

George, Jim, *Discourses of Global Politics: A Critical (Re)Introduction to International Relations*, Boulder, CO: Lynne Rienner Publishers 1994

Gerace, Michael P., 'Transforming the Pattern of Conflict: Geopolitics and Post-Cold-War Europe, *Comparative Strategy*, No. 11, 1992, pp. 373–407

Gerster, Florian and Rupert Scholz, 'Deutschland auf dem Weg zur internationalen Normalität', *Der Mittler-Brief*, Vol. 9, No. 1, 1. Quartal 1994

Gordon, Philip H., *France, Germany and the Western Alliance*, Boulder, CO; Oxford: Westview, 1995

Gow, James, *Triumph of the Lack of Will*, London: Hurst & Company 1997

Grabbe, Heather and Kirsty Hughes, *Eastward Enlargement of the European Union*, London RIIA 1997

Grabbe, Heather and Kirsty Hughes, *Enlarging of the EU Eastwards*, London RIIA 1998

Graf, William D. (ed.), *The internationalization of the German political economy: evolution of a hegemonic project*, London: Macmillan, 1992)

Grant, Mark Lyall, Renforcement de la CSCE: la réponse aux reves européens?, *Politique Étrangère*, Vol. 55, No. 3, Autumn 1990, pp. 589–607

Grant, Robert P., 'France's New Relationship with NATO', *Survival*, Vol. 38, No. 1, Spring 1996, pp. 58–80

de Grauwe, Paul, *The economics of monetary integration*, Oxford, Oxford University Press 1994, pp. 186–7

Grieco, Joseph M., 'The Maastricht Treaty, Economic and Monetary Union and the neo-realist research programme', *Review of International Studies*, Vol. 21, No. 1, January 1995, pp. 21–40

Grimes, William and Max Otte, 'Germany and Japan: Civilian Power, Traditional Power or Institutional Constraints?', Conference Paper, Trier University 1999

Gutjahr, Lothar, *German Foreign and Defence Policy after Unification*, London: Pinter 1994

Habermas, Jürgen, *Die Normalität einer Berliner Republik. Kleine Politische Schriften VIII*, Frankfurt/Main: Suhrkamp, 1995

Hacke, Christian, *Weltmacht wider Willen. Die Außenpolitik der Bndesrepublik Deutschland*, Berlin: Ullstein TB Verlag 1997

Haftendorn, Helga and Christian Tuschhoff (eds), *America and Europe in an era of change*, Boulder, CO: Westview, 1993.

Haftendorn, Helga and Otto Keck (eds), *Kooperation jenseits von Hegemonie und Bedrohung*, Baden-Baden: Nomos Verlagsgesellschaft 1997

Haglund, David G. (ed.), *Will NATO Go East? The Debate Over Enlarging the Atlantic Alliance*, Kingston, Ontario: Queen's University Centre for International Relations, 1996

van Ham, Peter, *The EC, Eastern Europe and European Unity: Discord, Collaboration and Integration*, London: Pinter, 1993

Hartland-Thunberg, Penelope, 'From Guns and Butter to Guns v. Butter: The Relation Between Economics and Security in the United States', *The Washington Quarterly*, Vol. 11, No. 4, Autumn 1988, pp. 47–54

Herzog, Roman, 'Die Globalisierung der deutschen Außenpolitik ist unvermeidlich', *Bulletin* No. 20, Bonn: Press and Information Office of the Federal Government, 15 March 1992

Heydrich, W., J. Krause, U. Nerlich, J. Nötzold and R. Rummel (eds), *Sicherheitspolitik Deutschlands: Neue Konstellationen, Risiken, Instrumente*, Baden-Baden: Nomos 1992

Hoffman, Oskar, *Bundeswehr und UN-Friedenssicherung. Die friedenssichernden Maßnahmen der Vereinten Nationen und die Frage einer Beteiligung deutscher Streitkräfte – völkerrechtliche, verfassungsrechtliche und politische Probleme*, Frankfurt a.M.: Lang, 1991

Hoffmann, Oskar, *Deutsche Blauhelme bei UN-Missionen. Politische Hintergründe und rechtliche Aspekte*, München: Verlag Bonn Aktuell, 1993

Hoffmann, Stanley, *The European Sisyphus: Essays on Europe 1964–1994*, Boulder, CO; Oxford: Westview, 1995

Hogan, Michael J. (ed.), *The End of the Cold War: Its Meanings and Implications*, Cambridge: Cambridge University Press, 1992

Holbrooke, Richard, *To End a War*, New York: Random House 1998

Holland, Martin, *European Community Integration*, London: Pinter, 1992

Holland, Martin, *European Union Common Foreign Policy: From EPC to CFSP Joint Action and South Africa*, London: Macmillan 1995

Hollis, Martin and Steve Smith, *Explaining and Understanding International Relations*, Oxford: Clarendon Press, 1991

Holst, Christian Sicherheitsorientierung und status quo. Einstellungen zur Bundeswehr in der Bevölkerung in Ost- und Westdeutschland 1992 bis 1993; DFG Projekt 'Struktur und Determinanten außen- und sicherheitspolitischer Einstellungen in der Bundesrepublik Deutschland', Forschungsbericht Nr. 6., Bamberg: Universität Bamberg, 1993, (Bamberger Politikwissenschaftliche Beiträge)

Hubel, Helmut, *Ein 'normales' Deutschland? die souveräne Bundesrepublik in der ausländischen Wahrnehmung*, Bonn: Europa-Union-Verlag, 1995

Huntington, Samuel P., *The Clash of Civilizations and the remaking of World Order*, New York; Simon & Schuster, 1996

Hyde-Price, Adrian, 'Berlin Republic Takes to Arms', *The World Today*, Vol. 55, No. 6, June 1999

Hyde-Price, Adrian, *The International Politics of East Central Europe*, Manchester: Manchester University Press, 1996

IISS, *Military Balance 1998/99*, Oxford: Oxford University Press 1998

Inacker, Michael J., *Unter Ausschluß der Öffentlichkeit?*, Bonn: Bouvier 1991

Jacobsen, Hans-Adolf and Hans-Jürgen Rautenberg (eds), *Bundeswehr und europäische Sicherheitsordnung. Abschlußbericht der Unabhängigen Kommission für die Künftigen Aufgaben der Bundeswehr*, Bonn: Bouvier, 1991

Jakobson, Peter Viggo, *Use and Abuse of Military Threats in Bosnia-Herzegovina: Why Compellence and Deterrence Failed*, Aarhus University: Denmark, 1996

Janning, Josef, 'Europa braucht verschiedene Geschwindigkeiten', *Europa-Archiv'*, Vol. 18, 1994, pp. 527–36

Janning, Josef, 'A German Europe – a European Germany? On the debate over Germany's foreign policy?', *International Affairs*, Vol. 72, No. 1, January 1996, pp. 9–32

Janning, Josef, 'Germany's foreign policy', *International Affairs*, Vol. 72, No. 1, January 1996, pp. 9–32

Joffe, Josef, 'Collective Security and the Future of Europe', *Survival*, Vol. 34, No. 1, Spring 1992, pp. 36–50

Kaiser, Karl and Joachim Krause (eds), *Deutschlands neue Außenpolitik. Band 3. Interessen und Strategien*, München: R. Ouldenbourg Verlag, 1996

Kaiser, Karl and Hans W. Maulll (eds), *Die Zukunft der europäischen Integration: Folgerung für die deutsche Politik*, Bonn: DGAP 1993

Kaiser, Karl and Hanns W. Maull (eds), *Deutschlands neue Außenpolitik: Band 1 Grundlagen*, München: R. Ouldenbourg 1994

Kaiser, Karl and Hanns W. Maull (Hrsg.), *Deutschlands neue Außenpolitik. Band 2. Herausforderungen*, München: Ouldenbourg, 1995

Kamp, Karl-Heinz, 'Ein Spaltpilz für das Atlantische Bündnis', *Europa-Archiv*, Folge 15–16, 1992

Kamp, Karl-Heinz, 'German Armed Forces and International Military Action: Step by Step toward Normalization', *Enjeux Atlantiques*, No. 7, July 1993, pp. 28–31

Katzenstein, Peter (ed.), *Tamed Power, Germany in Europe*, Ithaca, NJ : Cornell University Press 1997

Keohane, R., J. Nye and S. Hoffmann (eds), *After the Cold War: international institutions and state strategies in Europe, 1989–1991*, Cambridge MA: Harvard University Press, 1993

Kirchner, Emil and James Sperling, 'Economic security and the problem of co-operation in post-Cold War Europe', *Review of International Studies'*, Vol. 24, No. 8, 1998, pp. 221–37

Kirste, Knut, *Der Jugoslawienkonflikt*, Trier: Trier University 1998

Kirste, Knut, *Die USA und Deutschland in der Golfkrise 1990/91*, Trier: Trier University 1998

Krause, Christian, Wehrpflicht in alle Zukunft?, (Bonn: Friedrich-Ebert-Stiftung, 1992), (Studie der Abteilung Außenpolitikforschung: Studiengruppe Sicherheit und Abrüstung (Forschungsinstitut der Friedrich-Ebert-Stiftung; Nr. 51)

Krause, Christian, Die Entwicklung der Bundeswehr unter mittel- und langfristigen Aspekten, Bonn: Friedrich-Ebert-Stiftung, 1994, (Studie zur Außenpolitik; Nr. 60)

Krauthammer, Charles, 'The Unipolar Moment', *Foreign Affairs*, Vol. 70, No. 1, 1991, pp. 23–33

Kugler, Richard L., *US-West European Cooperation in Out-of-Area Military Operations: Problems and Prospects*, Santa Monica, CA: National Defense Research Institute, RAND, 1994

Kugler, Richard L. *Enlarging NATO: The Russia Factor*, Santa Monica: RAND, 1996

Latham, Robert, 'Democracy and War-Making : Locating the International Liberal Context', *Millenium*, Vol. 22, No. 2, Summer 1993, pp. 139–64

Law, David and Michael Rühle, 'Die NATO und das "Out-of-area"-Problem', *Europa-Archiv*, Folge 15–16, 1992, pp. 439–44

Lider, Julian, *Problems of Military Policy in the Konrad Adenauer Era (1949–1966)*, Stockholm: Swedish Institute for International Affairs 1984

Löwenthal, Richard (ed.), *Außenpolitische Perspektiven des westdeutschen Staates, Bd.3, Der Zwang zur Partnerschaft*, München: R. Ouldenbourg, 1972.

Maoz, Z. and B. Russett, 'Alliance, contiguity, wealth and political stability: Is the lack of conflict among democracies a statistical artifact ?', *International Interactions*, Vol. 17, No. 3, 1992, pp. 245–67

Malcolm, Noel, *Kosovo: A Short History*, London: Macmillan 1998

Maresceau, Marc (ed.), *Enlarging the European Union*, Harlow: Addison Wesley Longman 1997

Markovits, Andrei S. and Simon Reich, *The German Predicament*, Ithaca, NJ: Cornell University Press 1997

März, Wolfgang, *Bundeswehr in Somalia. Verfassungsrechtliche und verfassungspolitische Überlegungen zur Verwendung deutscher Streitkräfte in VN-Operationen*, (Berlin: Duncker & Humblot, 1993)

Maull, Hanns W., 'Germany and Japan: The New Civilian Powers', *Foreign Affairs*, Vol. 69, No. 5, Winter 1990–91, pp. 91–106

Maull, Hanns W., 'Germany in the Yugoslav Crisis', *Survival*, Vol. 37, No. 4, Winter 1995–96, pp. 99–130

Maull, Hanns W. Christoph Neßhöver and Bernhard Stahl (eds), *Lehrgeld: Vier Monate rot-grüne Außenpolitik*, Trierer Arbeitsparpier zur Internationalen Politik, No. 1, March 1999

McGwire, Michael, '"NATO expansion": a policy error of historic importance', *Review of International Studies*, Vol. 24, No. 1, January 1998, pp. 23–42

Mearsheimer, John J., 'Back to the Future', *International Security*, Vol. 15, No. 1, Summer 1990, pp. 5–56

Meiers, Franz-Josef, 'Präsident Bush und die neue nukleare Ordnung', *Europa-Archiv*, 22:654–662, (25 November 1991)

Meiers, Franz-Josef, 'Germany: The Reluctant Power', *Survival*, Vol. 37, No. 3, Autumn 1995 pp. 82–103

Meiers, Franz-Josef, 'Von IFOR zu FOFOR. Ein 'unmöglicher' Auftrag für die NATO?', *Internationale Politik*, 11:59–60, (November 1996)

Mintz, Alex and Nehemia Geva, 'Why Don't Democracies Fight Each Other? An Experimental Study', *Journal of Conflict Resolution*, Vol. 37, No. 3, September 1993, pp. 484–503

Morgenthau, Hans J., *Politics Among Nations: The Struggle for Power and Peace*, New York: Knopf 1973

Naumann, Klaus, *Die Bundeswehr in einer Welt im Umbruch*, Berlin: Siedler, 1994

Neßhöver, Christoph, Hanns W. Maull and Bernhard Stahl (eds), *Lehrgeld: Vier Monate rot-grüne Außenpolitik*, Trier: Trier University 1999

Niedhart, Gottfried, Detlef Junker and Michael W. Richter, *Deutschland in Europa*, Mannheim: Palatium Verlag 1997

Oldenburg, Fred, Germany's interest in Russian stability, Köln: BIOST, 1993, (Berichte des Bundesinstituts für ostwissenschaftliche und internationale Studien; 33–1993)

Oneal John R. and Bruce M. Russett, 'The Classical Liberals were Right: Democracy, Interdependence and Conflict, 1950–1985', *International Studies Quarterly*, Vol. 42, No. 2, June 1997, pp. 267–94

Owen, David, *Balkan Odyssey*, London: Victor Gollancz 1995

Padoa-Schioppa, Tomaso (with Michael Emerson, Mervyn King, Jean-Claude Milleron, Jean Paelinck, Lucas Papademos, Alfred Pastor and Fritz Scharpf), *Efficiency, stability, and equity: A strategy for the evolution of the economic system of the European Community*, Oxford: Oxford University Presss 1987

Philippi, Nina, *Bundeswehr-Auslandseinsätze als außen- und sicherheitspolitisches Problem des geeinten Deutschland*, Frankfurt: Peter Lang, 1997

Potthoff, Martin and Kai Hirschmann, *Die Europäische Währungsunion – Ein Testfall für die europäische Integration?*, Berlin: Arno Spitz Verlag 1997

le Rider, Jacques, Un an après l'unification: retour à la normalité de la nation allemande, *Politique Étrangère*, Vol. 56, Winter 1991, pp. 913–27

Risse, Thomas, *To Euro or Not to Euro? The EMU and Identity Politics in the European Union*, European University Institute, Working Paper RSC No. 98/9, Florence 1998

Risse-Kappen, Thomas, *Cooperation Among Democracies: The European Influence on US Foreign Policy*, Princeton, NJ: Princeton University Press, 1995

Rotfeld, Adam D., 'Die Zukunft des Europäischen Sicherheitssystem. Die Erweiterung der westlichen Sicherheitsstrukturen und die OSZE', *S und F*, Vol. 13. No. 4, 1995, pp. 221–6

Rotfeld, Adam Daniel and Walther Stützle, *German and Europe in Transition*, Oxford: Oxford University Press 1991

Rühe, Volker, *Deutschlands Verantwortung. Perspektiven für das neue Europa*, Berlin: Ullstein 1994

Rühl, Lothar, *Deutschland als europäische Macht. Nationale Interessen und internationale Verantwortung*, Bonn: Bouvier Verlag, 1996

Rummel, Reinhardt (ed.), *Toward Political Union: Planning a Common Foreign and Security Policy in the European Community*, Boulder, CO; Oxford: Westview; Baden-Baden: Nomos Verlag, 1992

Sauder, Axel, *Souveränität und Integration. Französische und deutsche Konzeptionen europäischer Sicherheit nach dem Ende des Kalten Krieges (1990–1993)*, Baden-

Baden: Nomos Verlagsgesellschaft, 1995, (Nomos Universitätsschriften: Politik; Bd. 59)

Schäuble, Wolfgang, *Und der Zukunft zugewandt*, Berlin: Siedler 1994

Schlotter, Peter, Norbert Ropers and Berthold Meyer, *Die neue KSZE. Zukunftsperspektiven einer regionalen Friedenstrategie*, Opladen: Leske/Budrich, 1994

Schmidt, Peter (ed.), *In the Midst of Change: On the Development of West European Security and Defence Cooperation*, Baden-Baden: Nomos 1992, pp. 187–228

Schmähling, Elmar, *Der unmögliche Krieg. Sicherheit und Verteidigung vor der Jahrtausendwende*, Düsseldorf: Econ Verlag, 1990

Schmähling, Elmar, *Kein Feind, kein Ehr. Wozu brauchen wir noch die Bundeswehr?*, Köln: Kiepenheuer & Witsch, 1994

Schönbohm, Jörg, *Zwei Armeen und ein Vaterland. Das Ende der Nationalen Volksarmee*, Berlin: Siedler, 1992

Schönbohm, Jörg, 'Zukunftsaufgaben deutscher Sicherheitspolitik. Vortrag anläßlich der "Freiberger Gespräche"', Atlantik-Brücke/Bergakademie Freiberg, Sachsen, 14 May 1993, Bonn: Atlantik-Brücke, 1993, (Rundschreiben/ Atlantik-Brücke; 4/1993)

Scholz, Rupert, *Weltpolitische und europäische Faktoren der europäischen Sicherheit – NATO und WEU nach der Auflösung des Warschauer Paktes*, Bonn: Bouvier, 1993

Schwarz, Hans-Peter, *Die gezähmten Deutschen: Von der Machtbesessenheit zur Machtvergessenheit*, Stuttgart: Deutsche Verlagsanstalt, 1986.

Schwarz, Hans-Peter, *Die Zentralmacht Europas. Deutschlands Rückkehr auf die Weltbühne*, Berlin: Siedler 1994

Schweller, Randall L., 'Domestic Structure and Preventive War: Are Democracies More Pacific?', *World Politics*, Vol. 44, No. 2, January 1992, pp. 235–69

Sharp, Jane M.O., 'New Roles for CSCE', *Bulletin of Arms Control*, No. 7, August 1992, pp. 14–17

Sharp, Jane M.O., 'CFE Treaty Under Threat as Russia Requests Revisions', *Bulletin of Arms Control*, No. 12, November 1993, pp. 2–4

Stares, Paul B. (ed.), *The New Germany and the New Europe*, Washington DC: The Brookings Institution, 1992

Strange, Susan, *The Retreat of the State. The Diffusion of Power in the World Economy*. Cambridge: Cambridge University Press, 1996

Strauß, Franz Josef, *Herausforderung und Antwort*, (Stuttgart: Seewald Verlag, 1968)

Strauß, Franz-Joseph, *Die Erinnerungen*, (Berlin: Siedler Verlag, 1989)

Thatcher, Margaret, *The Downing Street Years*, London: HarperCollins 1993

Waltz, Kenneth N., *The Spread of Nuclear Weapons: More May Be Better*, Adelphi Paper No. 171, London: IISS 1981

Waltz, Kenneth N., *Theory of International Politics*, Reading, MA: Addison-Wesley 1979

Weart, Spencer, *Never at War: Why Democracies Will Not Fight One Another*, New Haven: Yale University Press 1998

Weller, Marc (ed.), *The Crisis in Kosovo 1989–1999*, Linton: Documents & Analysis Publishers 1999

Weller, Marc, 'The Rambouillet Conference', *International Affairs*, Vol. 75, No. 2, April 1999, pp. 211–52

Weisser, Ulrich, *NATO ohne Feindbild*, Bonn: Bouvier 1992

Williams, Nick, 'Partnership for Peace: Permanent Fixture or Declining Asset?', *Survival*, Vol. 38. No. 1, Spring 1996, pp. 98–110

Woodward, Susan L., *Balkan Tragedy*, The Brookings Institution: Washington, DC, 1995

Zelikow, Philip, 'The Masque of Institutions', *Survival*, Vol. 38, No. 1, Spring 1996, pp. 6–18

Zelikow, Philip and Condoleeza Rice, *Germany Unified and Europe Transformed. A Study in Statecraft*, Cambridge, MA; London: Harvard University Press, 1995

Zielonka, Jan, *Security in Central Europe*, Adelphi Paper No. 272, London: Brassey's 1992

Index